Train Your Mind for Athletic Success

Train Your Mind for Athletic Success

Mental Preparation to Achieve Your Sports Goals

JIM TAYLOR, PH.D.

ROWMAN & LITTLEFIELD
Lanham • Boulder • New York • London

Published by Rowman & Littlefield
A wholly owned subsidary of The Rowman & Littlefield Publishing Group, Inc.
4501 Forbes Boulevard, Suite 200, Lanham, Maryland 20706
www.rowman.com

Unit A, Whitacre Mews, 26-34 Stannary Street, London SE11 4AB

British Library Cataloguing in Publication Information Available

Library of Congress Cataloging-in-Publication Data

Names: Taylor, Jim, 1958– author.
Title: Train your mind for athletic success : mental preparation to achieve
    your sports goals / Jim Taylor.
Description: Lanham : Rowman & Littlefield Publishing Group, Inc., [2017] |
    Includes bibliographical references.
Identifiers: LCCN 2017002827 (print) | LCCN 2017028193 (ebook) | ISBN
    9781442277090 (electronic) | ISBN 9781442277083 (hardback : alk. paper)
Subjects: LCSH: Sports—Psychological aspects. | Athletes—Psychology.
Classification: LCC GV706.4 (ebook) | LCC GV706.4 .T39 2017 (print) | DDC
    796.01/9—dc23
LC record available at https://lccn.loc.gov/2017002827

Printed in the United States of America

Contents

Introduction

Athletic Success Begins and Ends with the Mind

It's become almost a cliché. Everyone seems to agree with legendary New York Yankee Yogi Berra, who said, "Baseball is 90 percent mental and the other half is physical." Although certainly lacking in logic and math acumen, this statement seems to encompass what most athletes believe, that the mind plays a vital role in sports success. But how important is it really to athletes and coaches? Let's find out by asking several essential questions.

HOW IMPORTANT IS THE MIND TO ATHLETIC SUCCESS?

When I speak to athletes or coaches, I ask them how important the mind is to athletic success compared to the physical and technical aspects of sport—less important, as important, or more important? There are always a few in the audience who have the chutzpah to challenge me by saying that the mind isn't that important. What matters, they say, is natural talent, physical fitness, and practiced skills. Gratifyingly, most members of the audience say the mind is as important as fitness and technique. And a surprisingly large number believe that the mind is actually more important. While I appreciate this last sentiment given that my life's passion is sport psychology, I don't believe that the mind is more important. Why? Because you may have all the mental strength in the world, but if you don't have the physical and technical capabilities to execute in your sport, you have no chance of success. You have to be able to hit the tennis or golf ball; throw the baseball or football; sink the basket; or run, ride, or swim at a certain pace to be successful. The reality is that the physical, technical, and mental are all important. But the mind is undoubtedly an essential piece of the sport performance puzzle that is often undervalued and neglected.

Consider the best athletes, male or female, in any sport. Are they all physically gifted? Absolutely. You don't get to such a high level without a remarkable set of genes. In fact, I would argue, to get to the highest levels of sport, they have to be genetic freaks of nature. Are they in exceptional physical condition? For sure. Would Lionel Messi be considered the best soccer player in the world if he wasn't in peak physical condition in terms of strength and stamina? It's quite simple. Athletes couldn't perform at the highest level of sport unless they had the requisite fitness to meet the grueling demands of their sport. Are the best athletes in every sport technically exceptional? Undoubtedly. Would Serena Williams be one of the greatest tennis players in history if she had major technical flaws in her serve, forehand, or backhand? Any sport that involves skills—which means just about all of them, whether golf, tennis, baseball, hockey, track and field, or soccer—makes development of those skills mandatory for success. Do they have the best equipment? Undeniably. Could the 2015 Formula One driving champion, Lewis Hamilton, have emerged victorious in a 1972 Chevrolet Impala? Of course not. Without the best equipment, extraordinary performance in a sport is simply impossible. In fact, at the highest level of sport, everyone has it all. And, at any level of sport, whether collegiate, youth, or even rec league, everyone has generally similar fitness, skills, and equipment. So, on the day of a competition, what separates the winners from the also-rans? These other factors being equal, it must be what goes on between their ears.

I will also add that, in the greater scheme of life, I could argue that the mental side of sport is vastly more important than physical fitness and technical prowess, at least for young athletes. Why? Because, realistically speaking, relatively few athletes will make it to the top of their sport. But, the attitudes, mental tools, and life lessons that athletes learn from their sport, for example, motivation, confidence, focus, perseverance, resilience, the ability to handle pressure, the list goes on, will serve them well in all aspects of their lives when they enter adulthood.

The thing about the game at this level [MLB] is that there is very little difference in physical skills between players; the real difference between them is upstairs. It is what is "in your head" that makes the difference.

—Clete Boyer, two-time World Series champion[1]

HOW COMMITTED ARE ATHLETES TO MENTAL TRAINING?

Having established that the mental side of sport is at least as important as other contributors to athletic success, I then ask these same athletes how many hours a day they spend on their conditioning or technical training. If they are at all serious, they will answer with anywhere from two to six hours a day. I then ask, If the mind is so important, are they also spending that amount of time on their mental training? In every case, a silence falls over the group as they are confronted with this obvious contradiction. To ease their discomfort, I tell them that they do mental training all the time without even realizing it, for example, they motivate themselves, think positively, and attempt to focus. But they have to admit that their efforts at mental preparation pale in comparison to the time and energy they devote to other aspects of their sport. And this imbalance can hold them back from performing their best and achieving their sports goals.

WHY ISN'T MENTAL TRAINING TREATED THE SAME AS PHYSICAL AND TECHNICAL TRAINING?

This question has been a source of frustration for me and others who work in sport psychology for years. If everyone in sport says that the mind is so important, why does it receive so little attention?

To be sure, sport psychology does have a presence in most sports. Sport psychologists and mental trainers work with many professional athletes and teams, as well as Olympic and collegiate teams. And many others work with youth programs in many sports throughout the United States and the world.

Yet, when compared to its physical and technical counterparts, sport psychology clearly has second-class status. While serious sports programs and teams at every level of competition have full-time technical and conditioning coaches, few have full-time sport psychologists or mental trainers. Moreover, when sport psychology is offered to athletes, its presence is usually vastly different from the rigorous physical conditioning regimens and sophisticated technical regimens that athletes at every level of sport routinely benefit from.

Let's consider what makes physical conditioning and technical development effective and then compare it to the use of mental training in most sports settings today. Three key elements come to mind.

First, physical and technical training programs don't just touch on a few areas that impact sports performance. Rather, they are *comprehensive* in design, aimed at ensuring that every contributor to sports success is addressed and developed maximally. For example, conditioning programs include strength, agility, stamina, and flexibility. Technical progressions include, depending on the sport, stance, balance, upper-body position, footwork, and much more.

Second, when athletes work out, they don't just walk into the gym and do random strength or agility exercises. Instead, they engage in organized workouts based on a *structured* program that coaches believe will result in optimal physical preparedness for their sport. Similarly, when athletes go onto the field, court, course, hill, or whatever their performance venue, they don't just play around and hope to improve. Rather, they follow a technical progression based on their stage of development. In sum, both the physical and technical components of athletic development have an organized program comprised of a framework and process that guides athletes systematically toward their goals.

Third, athletes wouldn't get more fit if they worked out every few weeks. And their sport skills wouldn't improve if they only practiced once a month. What enables athletes to get stronger and more technically skilled is that they engage in physical and technical training *consistently.* Day in and day out, week in and week out, and month in and month out, athletes regularly put time and energy into their conditioning and technical efforts.

Using these three criteria—a comprehensive, structured, and consistent program—it's pretty obvious that the mental side of sport isn't getting the attention it is due. Yes, many athletes get some exposure to sport psychology either through contact with sport psychologists or from their coaches. But, based on my own experience and feedback I have gotten from thousands of athletes, coaches, and parents throughout the world, this exposure lacks the comprehensiveness, structure, and consistency that is essential for maximizing its value to athletic development.

So, is there a clear answer to my original question: Why isn't mental training treated the same as physical and technical training in sports? I don't think so, but I do have a few theories.

First, although sport psychology has been a field of study for more than 100 years, it has not been a traditional part of training for most sports. Old attitudes, habits, and methods die hard, and new approaches to improving athletic performance are not easily accepted and adopted. Perhaps it will take a new generation of coaches who have been exposed to sport psychology as competitors and then in their coaches' education for the tide to turn toward wider acceptance and consistent use of mental training with athletes.

Second, the reality is that the best athletes in the world have done pretty darned well without formal mental training. They simply developed mental skills through their training and competitive experiences. In contrast, I don't think there has ever been a successful athlete who didn't have a rigorous conditioning or technical program (at least not in the last 40 years). As a result, the need for structured mental training may not seem great. I would suggest, however, that for every successful athlete who develops mental toughness on their own, there are one or more who are equally talented and motivated to become successful but need help in developing their mental capabilities.

Additionally, more and more athletes from every corner of the earth are entering sport and pursuing the highest levels of success. The competition for the coveted spots at the top of the pyramid has become far more competitive than in previous generations. Due to this increased competitiveness, training has become more scientific and sophisticated, and athletes are looking for every competitive advantage they can find. Mental training is one powerful way for athletes to get a leg up on their competitors.

Third, psychology lacks the concreteness of conditioning and technical training. You can readily see the areas in need of improvement physically and technically, for example, amount of weight lifted in the gym or technical problems revealed on video. The mental side of sport is not so easily seen, quantified, or measured. As a result, it's harder to gauge where athletes are in different aspects of their mental preparation, what areas they need to work on, and any improvement that is made mentally. This lack of clarity makes it more difficult for athletes to appreciate, commit to, and see the benefits of mental training.

Fourth, sport psychology can suffer from "guilt by association" with the broader field of psychology, which still carries the stigma that only screwed-up people seek professional help. This perception, however inaccurate, can prevent athletes, coaches, and parents from seeing mental preparation for what it is, namely, an essential contributor to sports performance that must be developed proactively. This fear can also scare them away from getting sport psychology help when it is needed.

I predict that it will take some time before our athletic culture pays the same attention to mental preparation as it does its physical and technical counterparts. But, as the stakes get higher and the competition gets tougher, from the development level to the world stage, athletes and coaches will look for every opportunity to gain the competitive edge that separates success from failure. As the limits of physical conditioning and technique are reached, it will be both natural and necessary to leverage all that sport psychology has to offer athletes. Only then will sport psychology, at long last, stand as equal partner with physical conditioning and technical training as athletes pursue their sports goals.

But, if you want to gain an advantage over your competitors now, you shouldn't wait until there is a shift in how your sport approaches mental preparation. You should start now to make it simply a part of what you do to strive toward your athletic goals. And, in doing so, you will have that competitive advantage that every athlete looks for.

You can hit the gym every day for the rest of your life, but unless you work out your mind, you won't go far.

—Unknown[2]

SHOULD PEAK PERFORMANCE BE YOUR GOAL?

One of the most popular phrases in sport is "peak performance." It has become part of not only our sports vocabulary, but also the gold standard for what athletes should achieve. Peak performance has also extended its reach into other performance areas, including business and the military. Peak performance is typically thought of as athletes performing their very best, as being at the top of their game. That sounds good, doesn't it? Who wouldn't want to achieve peak performance? And when I came out of graduate school, peak performance was what I wanted athletes to achieve.

But as I became more experienced as a consultant and a writer, I came to appreciate the power of words and how important it is that the words I use are highly descriptive of what I want to communicate. I decided that peak performance was not descriptive of what I wanted my athletes to achieve. I saw several problems with peak performance:

- A peak is very small, so you can't stay there long. Would you be satisfied if you had one good competition and several poor ones?
- Once the peak is reached, there's only one way to go—down!—and, as with most peaks, the drop is usually precipitous. Have you experienced those big swings in competitive performance where one week you're totally "in the zone" and the next you're completely out of it?
- You may arrive at the peak too early or too late, missing a chance for success. Have you felt the frustration of lost opportunity because you weren't mentally "on" for your big event?

So I needed a phrase that accurately described what I wanted athletes to achieve. I struggled for several years, unable to find such a phrase that really worked for me. Then, one day I had one of those rare meetings of timing and readiness. Walking through the meat section of a supermarket, I saw a piece of beef with a sticker that read, "Prime Cut." A light bulb went off in my head; I had an "aha" experience. I returned to my office and looked up "prime" in the dictionary. It was defined as, "of the highest quality or value." I had finally found the phrase "Prime Performance," in this case, Prime Sport, which I believed was highly descriptive of what I wanted athletes to achieve.

I define Prime Sport as, "performing at a consistently high level in the most challenging conditions." There are two essential words in this definition. First, "consistently." I'm not interested if you can have only one or two great performances and then some poor ones; that is not enough for you to be truly successful. What makes the great athletes great is that they are able to train and compete at a high level day in and day out, week in and week out, month in and month out, all season long for years on end. Being consistent doesn't mean never having some variation in the quality of your training and competitive performance. The reality of being a human being, as well as an athlete, is that you're going to have swings in your performance. There are going to be highs in which you are completely healthy and rested, motivated, confident, and focused, resulting in outstanding performances. And, inevitably, there are going to be lows in which you are tired, sick, stressed, distracted, unmotivated, and lacking confidence, which will result in a decline in performance. Being consistent does mean training and competing with minimal ups and downs instead of the large swings in performance that are so common among athletes.

Second, there is the word "challenging." I'm not impressed if you can perform well under ideal competitive conditions against an easy field of opponents in an unimportant competition. Anyone can do that. What makes the great athletes great is their ability to perform their best in the worst possible conditions (e.g., bad weather, terrible field conditions, hostile crowd) against the toughest field imaginable in the biggest competition of their lives. What also makes them great is their ability to transcend fatigue, illness, injury, pressure, and other challenges; rise to the occasion of a big event; and perform at their highest level.

A question you may ask is, Where does Prime Sport come from? Although I'll be focusing on its mental contributors, the mind is only one necessary piece of the Prime Sport puzzle. You must also be at a high level of physical health, including being well-conditioned and well-rested, eating a balanced diet, and being free from injury and illness. Prime Sport also isn't possible if you're not technically and tactically sound. If you're physically, technically, tactically, and mentally prepared, you will have the ability to achieve Prime Sport.

Now here's a question for you: Have you ever experienced Prime Sport? Let me describe what it's like:

- *Effortless:* It's comfortable, easy, and natural.
- *Automatic:* Your body does what it knows how to do, and there's no mental interference.
- *Sharpened senses:* You are seeing, hearing, and feeling everything more acutely than normal.
- *Time shift:* Everything slows down, enabling you to react more quickly.

- *Total focus:* You're totally absorbed in the experience without external distractions or mental clutter.
- *Boundless energy:* All of your energy is directed entirely toward your efforts without any energy wasted on negativity or obstacles.
- *Prime integration:* The physical, technical, tactical, and mental are working together, enabling you to perform your best.

If you can achieve Prime Sport and, in doing so, experience consistently high performance in the most challenging conditions, you will fully express your passion for and ability in your sport, and take a giant step toward your athletic goals and dreams.

WHAT "GAME" ARE YOU COMPETING IN?

When you enter the athletic arena on any given day, you will, in fact, be trying to win three competitions (whether games, races, meets, or events). The obvious competition is the one that occurs against the rest of the field, the goal of which is to beat your opponents and get the best result possible. But before you can perform your best in that competition, there is another you must win, namely, that against the elements (e.g., weather, course, court, or field conditions). These conditions, whether heat or cold, rain or snow, dry or muddy, smooth or rough, seem to conspire against you to prevent you from achieving your goals on that day. But to win against the elements, the most important competition you must prevail in is the mental one in which you compete against yourself. Here is a simple reality: If you don't win the mental competition, you can't win against the conditions or against your competitors.

So, how do you win the mental game, you may ask. Well, that is what *Train Your Mind for Athletic Success* is all about. It explores the depth and breadth of the psychology of sport and provides you with the insights, information, and practical tools you need to win the mental game.

WHAT ARE YOU PREPARING FOR?

As my definition of Prime Sport indicates, I want you to be consistently prepared for every training session and competition in which you perform. This unwavering level of preparation ensures that you get the most out of your practice efforts and maximize your competitive performance.

At the same time, the chances are that you also have a big competitive goal for the season that you are aiming for. Perhaps it's the state finals, national championships, or maybe even winning a world title or a Super Bowl ring. I call this competition "Prime Time," which involves your toughest competitors, the most challenging conditions, and the most at stake for this season or perhaps even in your athletic career. Although you will have many competitions during the year that are important to you, this one means the most to you. All of your efforts leading up to Prime Time are devoted to ensuring not that you peak for the event, but rather that you are totally prepared to perform your best when it matters most. *Train Your Mind* is committed to helping you prepare your mind for Prime Time.

WHAT DOES IT TAKE TO ACHIEVE ATHLETIC SUCCESS?

A fundamental question I have been exploring in the 30 years that I have been helping athletes achieve their goals is, What does it take to succeed? My life's work has been devoted to answering this question so that anyone who is willing to pursue their dreams can find success.

Yet, in recent years, I have come to the conclusion that this question is not the question that should be asked. Athletic success is, of course, the highly desired destination, but, in most people's minds, it lies at the end of a journey, whether earning a college athletic scholarship, winning an Olympic gold medal, or attaining some other sought-after athletic achievement. Furthermore, athletic success can have as many meanings as the people who pursue it. For a few, success means the tangible results of victory, for instance, a long career as a professional athlete. For some, it means competing for a NCAA Division I school. For others, it's playing for their high school varsity team. And for still others, success may be a bit more ethereal, for example, developing a love of a lifetime sport, gaining a certain level of competency in a sport, enjoying the camaraderie of being part of a team, or persevering in the face of the normal physical and mental challenges of sports participation. As a result, while pursuit of athletic success is the ultimate goal, it should not be the focus of your efforts.

Here's another simple reality: If you can learn how to systematically pursue your athletic goals and perform your best, some degree of success is inevitable. How much success depends on factors both within and outside your control, including genes, time commitment, opportunity, and support. But I go under the assumption that if you continue to perform at your highest level possible and strive for success, good things will happen.

So, instead of focusing on success, the challenge is to figure out the process by which success will result and how you can master that process. In other words, your fundamental goal should be to maximize your performance. Certainly, there are many contributors to athletic success, including physical fitness, nutrition, technique and tactics, equipment, and, of course, the mind. Although all of these areas must be maximized to perform your best, *Train Your Mind* focuses on the mental aspects of athletic performance.

Throughout the years, I and others have identified mental factors that we believe are necessary to perform at your highest level and achieve success in sports, for example, motivation, confidence, resilience, emotions, habits, focus, practice, and many others. Yet, I have always felt that these explanations were, standing alone, too simplistic to adequately explain such a complex phenomenon as athletic performance. What is lacking is a means of pulling together the many and disparate influences into a comprehensive and cohesive framework. The culmination of this thinking has led to the development of my Prime Sport System, which provides a comprehensive and deep understanding of the mental aspects of athletic success. My Prime Sport System is comprised of five broad areas that are essential for athletic success. Within each of these five areas lies five specific sport-related factors that provide the framework for *Train Your Mind*.

MAKE MENTAL TRAINING A PRIORITY IN YOUR SPORT

Train Your Mind is a challenge for you to take an essential, yet often neglected, piece of the sports success puzzle and make it a priority in your athletic efforts. Let me elaborate in several ways. I work with a number of athletes each year, from juniors with big dreams to pros and Olympians who are realizing their dreams. What has become abundantly clear to me is that, once the foundation of fitness, technique, tactics, and equipment is established, it is the mind that separates athletes who achieve their goals from those who don't. This occurs at two levels. Having the right mentality and preparation enables you to get the most out of your training by being able to stay focused and avoid frustration. And, on the day of a competition, being able to stay positive, calm, and withstand the pressure—self-imposed and external—will enable you to perform your best when it really counts.

Additionally, of the athletes who come to me, the number-one reason is because they perform well in training, but they can't seem to translate that into successful competitive performance and results. And they don't understand why they can't. So, what makes competitions different from training? Objectively, there is often little difference. A pitcher throwing to a hitter in practice is no different than pitching in a game—same height mound, same distance to home plate, same strike zone. A 100-meter swim in practice is the same distance and conditions as in a race. Yet, there is one very dramatic difference: Results matter in competitions. And that difference occurs entirely in your mind. Your challenge is to either ignore the difference or embrace the difference.

Let me say that you actually do quite a bit of mental training without realizing it. I'm sure that you attempt to motivate yourself, think positively, fire yourself up, and focus in training and competitions. Well, that is mental training. Here's the problem: Do you approach mental training in the same way you approach physical and technical training? As I discussed earlier, do you have a comprehensive, structured, and consistent mental training program? Probably not. For you to maximize your ability and achieve your athletic goals, you must give the mental aspects of your sport the attention they deserve.

Have I convinced you yet that you should make mental training a priority in your sports preparations? If so, here's what you can do as you read *Train Your Mind*:

- Complete the assessments at the beginning of each chapter to help you better understand yourself as an athlete and identify what mental areas you need to work on (see the following for more details).
- Get feedback from your coaches on where they think you need to improve mentally.
- Read *Train Your Mind* carefully and make note of the strategies you can use to train the mental areas you identified in the assessment.
- Make a real commitment to developing and implementing consistently a comprehensive and structured mental training program.

Certainly, you should continue to work on your fitness and technique. But if you commit to an equally rigorous mental training program, I can say with confidence that you will be even more prepared to find success and achieve your sports goals.

PHYSICAL TESTING FOR THE MIND

A difficulty with dealing with the mental aspects of sport is that they're not tangible or easily measured. If you want to learn about your physical strengths and weaknesses, you can go through a physical testing program that gives you objective data about your physical condition. If you want to assess your technical capabilities in your sport, you can do video analyses or even biomechanical testing. By engaging in what I call "physical testing for the mind," you can also make your sport-related mental capabilities as concrete and objective as possible.

An assessment method known as performance profiling (in this case, Prime Sport profiling) is a simple and scientifically proven way to gauge your mental strengths and areas in need of improvement related to your sports participation. Prime Sport profiling offers several important benefits. It will help you better understand the areas that I deem essential for athletic success and that act as the superstructure for *Train Your Mind*. Prime Sport profiling also helps you understand where you fit into these crucial areas. Finally, it provides you with direction as you incorporate mental training into your overall athletic development regimen.

In developing greater self-understanding, you must recognize your strengths and your weaknesses. Most athletes love to focus on their strengths but don't like to admit that they have weaknesses. This attitude will limit your development because most athletes think that they're as good as their greatest strengths. For instance, a tennis player believes that his power and height advantage will enable him to win and that his lack of quickness and consistency won't hurt him. The truth is, however, that you are only as good as your biggest weakness. Returning to that example, if the player's opponent is fast and a good counterpuncher, his power and height can be neutralized, and his lack of speed and consistency may determine the outcome of the match.

Think of athletic strengths and weaknesses as a mathematical equation. On a scale of 1 to 10, where a 1 is very poor and 10 is the best, if a basketball player is a good shooter (8) but a poor defender (2), her overall performance would be moderate (8 + 2 = 10). If she focused on and improved her shooting (from 8 to 9), she wouldn't improve that much overall because, already a capable shooter, there isn't much room for improvement (9 + 2 = 11). But if she improved her defense (from 2 to 7), her overall performance would rise significantly (8 + 7 = 15). Of course, you want to continue to build your strengths, but the more you improve your weaknesses, the higher your overall performance and the more successful you will be.

It's important for you to have an open mind with Prime Sport profiling. Rather than being uncomfortable with facing your weaknesses, you should be willing to consider the information in a positive and constructive way. When weaknesses are identified, it doesn't mean that you're incapable of performing well. It may be that you haven't had to use these skills at your current level or you've been able to hide them with the strengths you have. But the information you gain from Prime Sport profiling will enable you to improve, and you'll have a better chance of achieving your goals.

Completing the Prime Sport Profiles

You will find Prime Sport Profiles at the beginning of the first five chapters of *Train Your Mind*. You will read the description of each mental area discussed in the chapter and be asked to rate yourself on a scale of 1 to 10.

Using Your Prime Sport Profiles

Having completed the Prime Sport Profile, you will have a clear picture of what you believe to be the mental strengths and weaknesses in your sport. Typically, a score of less than 8 indicates an area on which you need to work. Place a question mark next to each factor you scored as less than an 8. These are the factors that you'll want to focus on as you read *Train Your Mind* and what you should work on when you create your Prime Sport mental training program that I will describe in more detail at the end of chapter 7.

You can also use Prime Sport profiles to measure progress in your mental training. Periodically, perhaps every few months, complete the profile and compare it with your past profiles. You should see improvement in the areas on which you've worked. Also, ask your coaches about positive changes they've seen in those areas. When your ratings move to an 8 or higher, select other factors to work on and follow the same procedure.

THE VOCABULARY OF SPORT

It's challenging to write about the psychology of sport for all athletes in all sports because there isn't a common vocabulary of sport. Some athletes play a sport, for example, baseball, basketball, football, hockey, lacrosse, tennis, or golf (mostly ball sports), and you are a player of these sports. These sports are played on fields, courts, courses, and rinks. But there are other sports, for instance, swimming, track and field, ski racing, race car driving, equestrian, cycling, and mountain biking that you don't play but rather participate in, perform, or compete in. And you are not a player, but instead either an athlete or, specific to a sport, a swimmer, runner, ski racer, skater, driver, rider, or cyclist. Plus, these sports occur in pools and on tracks, hills, roads, and trails.

Despite these linguistic differences, all athletes in all sports do basically the same thing, namely, compete with the goal of maximizing performance and achieving certain results and goals. So, for the purpose of *Train Your Mind*, we need a common vocabulary that reflects all sports and describes what all athletes do without alienating others who don't fit into one category of sport's particular language. To that end, I will most often use "athlete" instead of "player," "perform" or "compete" rather than "play," and "competition" in place of "game" (apologies in advance if I slip a few times). Because there doesn't seem to be a generic term for field, course, court, rink, pool, track, and so forth, I will, when necessary, simply list some of the more common settings in which athletes train and compete.

NOT JUST ABOUT SPORTS

A final point I want to make before we move forward is that *Train Your Mind*, while focusing on the psychology of sport, isn't just about achieving athletic success. The reality is that relatively few athletes reach great heights in their sport, for example, becoming a professional or an Olympic athlete.

Yet, you, like every other athlete pursuing their sports dreams, can find your own personal greatness regardless of how far you go in your sport by giving your fullest effort and fully realizing whatever ability you have. And, perhaps more importantly, you can continue to use the many lessons you learn from sport and apply them to your education and career to help you find success in another performance setting and attain your longer-term life goals.

As you read *Train Your Mind*, apply what you learn to your sport. But at the same time, keep in mind that this book isn't about sport skills, sport psychology skills, or even performance skills. Rather, everything I talk about is aimed at giving you the insights, information, and tools you need to find your own personal greatness in the game called life.

WHAT LIES AHEAD?

The purpose of *Train Your Mind* is to act as your guide on your journey in developing the mental capabilities you need to achieve athletic success. This process will take you through the five steps of my Prime Sport System, where you will learn about the attitudes you need to maintain, the obstacles you must remove, the preparation you must do, the mental muscles you must strengthen, and the tools you need to put in your mental toolbox. Along the way, you will learn about not only why and how these areas are so important to athletic success, but also where you are in relation to them with the Prime Sport profiling. And, most importantly, *Train Your Mind* will show you many practical strategies and tools you can use to alleviate any weaknesses you may have and fully develop yourself mentally as an athlete.

Train Your Mind will also provide you with several important resources that will support your efforts. First, each chapter offers you "Tips from the Top," essential lessons about athletic success from some of the finest professional and Olympic athletes. Second, if you're a young athlete, this book includes a section for parents devoted to helping them best support you as you pursue your athletic goals. Finally, there is a section your coaches should read that will help them be the best coaches they can be.

What's the goal of *Train Your Mind*? As someone who has been a researcher of and consultant on what it takes to maximize athletic performance for more than 30 years, as well as an elite athlete who has practiced what he preaches in pursuing his own sports goals, my goal is to offer you the deep insights, practical information, and useful mental tools necessary to bring high performance and athletic success within your reach as you pursue your sports dreams.

1

PrimePsyche: Five Attitudes

PRIME SPORT PROFILE: ATTITUDES

Instructions: Rate yourself on a scale of 1 to 10 using the five PrimePsyche attitudes described here.

Ownership: Taking full responsibility for everything that impacts your sports performance; doing everything you can to develop every contributor to athletic performance; avoiding the urge to make excuses or blame others. (1: no ownership; 10: complete ownership)

Process: Focusing on what will enable you to perform your best and accomplish your athletic goals rather than the outcome you want to achieve. (1: total outcome focus; 10: total process focus)

Challenge: Seeing training and competitions as challenges to pursue rather than threats to avoid. (1: total threat; 10: total challenge)

Long-Term: Focusing on your future goals and what you will need to achieve them rather than short-term results. (1: short-term focus; 10: long-term focus)

Risk: Taking appropriate risks to succeed while performing in your sport rather than performing cautiously. (1: always cautious; 10: always willing to take a risk to succeed)

Attitudes are important to athletic success because they act as the filter through which you look at, understand, interpret, and evaluate yourself, other people, and situations in which you find yourself and experiences you have in your sport. Your attitude will have a wide-ranging impact on what you think, how you feel emotionally, how you behave, and, ultimately, how you perform. For example, let's say you arrive at a competitive venue in which you are competing against a tough opponent in bad weather. Your attitude toward these challenges of competitor and conditions will largely determine how you perform. If your attitude is one of intimidation by your capable opponent and doubts about the weather, you will likely lack confidence, experience anxiety, and perform poorly. Conversely, if you see your skilled competitor as a challenge to overcome and the bad weather as conditions you've trained in, you will probably feel confident and energized, and, as a result, you will perform well.

Your attitudes can be either tools that boost your efforts or weapons that hinder them. Attitudes as tools are positive, supportive, calming, and focusing. Attitudes as weapons are negative, critical, stress inducing, and distracting. As you will learn in the next two chapters, a challenge with attitudes is that they can be either conscious or unconscious. By conscious, I mean that you know where they came from, they are readily available to think about, and they are relatively easy to change. In contrast, unconscious attitudes are rather murky. You may not know how they developed, and they aren't easy to access. As a result, they are more difficult to change. Your goal is to ensure that you have attitudes about your sport—whether about your goals, training, competitors, competing, or success or failure—that will support your efforts in pursuit of your goals. You can accomplish this objective with several steps. First, from *Train Your Mind*, gain an understanding of the most important attitudes that impact your sport. Second, become aware of your attitudes in these specific areas (by completing the aforementioned Prime Sport Profile) and whether they help or hurt you. Finally, if you have attitudes that interfere with your athletic efforts, understand how they developed, identify healthier attitudes, and gradually shift those attitudes in a more productive direction.

Chapter 1 focuses on five attitudes you can use as tools to support your athletic efforts. They provide the foundation for how you think, feel, and react to every situation in which you find yourself in your sport. These five attitudes set the stage for either success or failure as you pursue your athletic goals.

Nothing can stop the man with the right mental attitude from achieving his goal; nothing on earth can help the man with the wrong mental attitude.

—Thomas Jefferson, founding father[1]

OWNERSHIP

There's a metaphor I use to help people understand why ownership lies at the heart of how you approach your sport. Here's a question: Which would you treat better, a car that you own or a car that you rent? Clearly, you would take better care of a car that you own. Why? Because it's yours. You've invested in it financially and emotionally. You want to take care of it by having regular check-ups and tune-ups. You want it to look good, so you get it washed, vacuumed, and polished. You want the car you own to perform its best and last a long time. There's an expression that relates here: "Pride of ownership." You're proud of owning your car, so you put time and effort into its care and maintenance.

Just as the engine of your car propels you toward your destination, ownership of your sport is the engine that drives you toward your athletic goals. There is a big difference in how you approach your sport based on whether you feel you have full ownership, you only have partial ownership, or someone else owns it. Truly successful athletes own their sport. Ownership means that you believe that your participation is truly your own—your determination, your efforts, your successes and failures, and your rewards. In contrast, a lack of ownership shows itself in low commitment, poor effort, excuses, and little resilience in the face of challenges.

To find success as an athlete, you must care deeply about your involvement in your sport. Athletes who have ownership of their sport have a great passion for it and participate for no reason other than the value they place on it for themselves. As a result of this ownership, successful athletes take responsibility for all aspects of their efforts because they are internally motivated and believe they have control over their efforts and outcomes.

He [my father] laid out all the necessary steps for me. It was up to me what I did with them.

—Kyrie Irving, member of the NBA champion Golden State Warriors and Olympic basketball gold medalist[2]

Speaking of pride of ownership, a few years ago, I attended a staff meeting at Burke Mountain Academy, an accredited boarding school in Vermont, of which I am an alum, established to help ski racers pursue their goals. During the meeting, the teachers and coaches reviewed each student-athlete's progress to that point of the school year. They described the strengths and areas in need of improvement for each student-athlete and discussed what each young person needed to work on in the near future. In talking about one boy, a coach said, "He takes pride in everything he does." This simple statement struck me as profound, and I concluded that *taking pride in everything you do* is the greatest compliment a young athlete can receive and the ultimate goal of having ownership of your sport.

What does this statement mean? When you take pride in everything you do, you are expressing your own self-respect because you care enough about yourself to care deeply about your participation in your sport. You are thoroughly engaged in every aspect of your sport, leaving no stone unturned and no detail unimportant. You value your efforts enough to attempt to imbue all of those efforts with the greatest quality you can. Doing the best you can in everything you do is a fundamental value that directs your life. If you have this pride, you understand that your involvement in your sport is a privilege to be grateful for and an opportunity to be fully embraced. You take the challenge of this opportunity seriously and appreciate and respect the gift by giving your best effort in your pursuits. You recognize that one of the true joys of life is experiencing the process of achieving, not just the fruits of those efforts. If you own your sport in this way, you revel in the rewards of success and make no excuses for failure because you understand that, ultimately, there are no excuses, only your efforts and the results they produce. Taking pride in everything you do in your sport is both a goal toward which you should strive and the result of your considerable efforts.

Do you own your sport? Here are a few questions to ask yourself:

- Do you take responsibility for everything that impacts your athletic performance?
- Do you give your best effort consistently?
- Do you make excuses or blame others when you don't perform well?
- Do you give up quickly when things get difficult?

If you answered "yes" to these questions, your parents probably have more ownership of your sport than you do. And that lack of ownership on your part will not serve you well as you pursue your athletic goals. If your goals are at all high and you want to have any chance of achieving them, you must take ownership of your sport. This ownership means having your own reasons for participating. You have to give your best effort in every aspect of your sport. You need to accept responsibility for everything that happens to you, whether great successes (that's easy to do) or disappointing failures (that's really hard to do).

The best motivation always comes from within.

—Michael Johnson, four-time Olympic gold medal sprinter[3]

Own Your Sport

I hope I've convinced you that ownership is essential for your athletic success. It certainly sounds good in theory, doesn't it? But it's one thing to think about ownership and an entirely different thing to actually gain and maintain ownership in your sport. So, at a practical level, what does it mean to own your sport?

If you don't own every aspect of your sport and aren't doing everything you can to maximize those areas, the simple reality is, if your goals are at all high, you will have little chance of achieving them. Additionally, and perhaps this will provide you with a bit more incentive to own your sport, it is likely that many of your competitors are owning their sport and doing everything they can to achieve their athletic goals. If you combine your lack of ownership with their full ownership, your chances of accomplishing your goals get even smaller.

Own Your Mind

As I discuss in the introduction, athletic success begins with the mind. So, that's where you want to begin to own your sport. If you can own all of the areas of the mind that impact your sport performance, you will more readily be able to own your sport.

Owning your mind involves several important steps. First, you must understand how the mind in general influences sports performance. You will learn all you need to know about this relationship by reading *Train Your Mind*. Second, you need to understand how your mind, in particular, impacts your own sports performance. Third, you must develop, implement, and commit to a comprehensive, structured, and consistent mental training program that prepares your mind to perform its best, in the same way that a physical conditioning program prepares your body to perform its best.

Tip from the Top: Own the Little Things

As you improve as an athlete and climb higher up the competitive ladder, you can assume that just about everyone you compete against will have the basics of your sport down pretty well. Most of your competitors will be in great physical condition, be solid technically and tactically, and be fairly mentally prepared. The basics are certainly necessary, but not sufficient, to get to the top. So, none of those areas will ultimately determine who is successful and who isn't. The higher you get in your sport, the more important the little things become because it is the small details that will end up separating the winners from the also-rans. Because small differences can make a huge difference in who succeeds and who doesn't, you should pay careful attention to the details that subtly impact your practice and competitive efforts.

This realization requires that you *own the little things*, meaning you should identify the details in your athletic and general life that can make those small differences in performance and make sure you address them as completely as you can. At its broadest level, the idea of owning the little things involves making sure that your sport is a priority in your life and that you are making choices that ensure they best serve your athletic goals. These

DO YOU OWN YOUR SPORT?

1. Ask yourself whether you have ownership of your sport. If so, how? If not, why not and who does own it?
2. Identify the different areas that impact your sports efforts.

    a. technique

    b. tactical

    c. equipment

    d. mental

    e. sleep

    f. diet

    g. conditioning

    h. school

    i. relationships

    j. life

3. Ask yourself the following questions about your ownership of your sport:

    a. In what ways are you or are you not owning these important areas?

    b. Are you doing everything in these areas to achieve your goals?

    c. Are you making your sport a priority in your life?

    d. Are you making decisions that will help you reach your goals?

4. Set specific goals for each area you need to gain more ownership of.

    a. What you need to do to own the area.

    b. When, where, and how you will own the area.

decisions aren't always easy because other aspects of your life may pull you away from making good choices. There are several areas of your broader life that cause you to take several steps back from your goals even as you are taking steps forward in your sport. For example, your social needs (e.g., being with friends) can cause you to choose your social life over your athletic life. Other areas in which your interests may conflict with your sports goals are sleep (e.g., staying up late to be on your social media) and your diet (e.g., eating junk food that tastes good but isn't healthy).

There are also little things directly related to your sport that can mean the difference between achieving your goals and falling short. The fact is, a lot of what you do as you pursue your athletic goals is boring, tedious, tiring, and painful. Examples include maintaining your physical conditioning, warming up before and cooling down after practices, taking care of your equipment, and doing your mental training. It can be easy to convince yourself that these things don't matter that much and that it won't hurt you to do them halfheartedly or not at all every once in a while. Well, let me tell you, they do matter, and if you do them half-baked or skip them altogether, you are hurting your chances of achieving your athletic goals.

PROCESS

There are a lot of misconceptions about the role of results in achieving your athletic goals. Of course, you need good results to be successful, but the question is how to go about getting those results, and, ironically, the answer is not what many athletes, coaches, and parents think.

First, I want to define the words *outcome* and *process*. An outcome attitude involves focusing on results, rankings, and beating others. Notice that this attitude is focused on things outside of you and not always within your control. In contrast, a process attitude involves focusing on what you need to do to perform your best, for example, fitness, technique, and tactics. Unlike an outcome attitude, focusing on the process is on you and entirely within your control.

I often ask athletes, coaches, and parents which attitude is best to have before a competition, an outcome attitude or a process attitude. Much to my surprise, many say an outcome attitude is better because it keeps their "eye on the prize" and pushes them toward the result they want. I would suggest, however, that this outcome attitude actually hurts more than it helps. With that said, let me explain what I see as the paradox of an outcome attitude. As I just noted, many people think that, to get the results you want, you need to focus on those results. But, and here's the paradox, having an outcome attitude actually reduces the chances of achieving the results you want. Here's why. First, when does the outcome of a competition occur? At the end, of course. If you're focused on the outcome, you aren't focused on the process, namely, what you need to do to perform your best from start to finish of the competition. Second, what makes you nervous before a competition, the process or the outcome? Chances are it's the outcome—more specifically, a bad outcome, for instance, not winning or not achieving your goals. The bottom line is, when you focus on the outcome, you are far less likely to get the outcome you want.

In contrast, with a process attitude, you increase your chances of getting the results you want. If you focus on the process, that is, what you need to do to perform your best, how are you likely to perform? Pretty well, you can assume. And if you perform well, you're more likely to achieve the result you wanted in the first place.

Once you start thinking about results, and with the Olympics, once you start thinking about the Olympic Games, you're screwed, because you're thinking about the big things that you can't control. . . . For me in rowing, it would be the little details of my hands going around the finish or the blade being clear off the water.

—Marnie McBean, three-time Olympic rowing gold medalist[4]

Here is my wish for you: Never think about results. In an ideal world, I would like you to have an entirely process attitude and basically never have results cross your mind. Here's another wish: In that ideal world I mentioned earlier, I would have parents and coaches never talk about results either. The fact is there is no point. You know when you've had a good competition, and you definitely know when you've had a bad one. If you're like most athletes, when your parents and coaches talk about results, you hear their chatter as expectations, pressure, or disappointment.

Parents, if you're reading *Train Your Mind*, after any competition, good or bad, give your children a hug, tell them you love them, and ask them if they're hungry. If you're too excited about a good performance or too disappointed about a bad one, stay the heck away from your children, particularly if they had a bad performance, because they will sense your negative emotions no matter how hard you try to mask them.

Coaches, if your athletes had a good day, don't say "good job." Instead, help them understand why they performed well so they can do it again in the next competition. If they had a bad day, pat them on the back, tell them you still believe in them, identify what held them back, and help them figure out how to perform better in the next competition.

Results Matter

Here's where the real world collides with the ideal world that I wish existed. We don't live in that ideal world, and until someone invents a "process pill," it's not likely that you will be able to expunge results from your mind. In the real world, results do matter. As an athlete, you are a competitive person with big goals participating in a competitive sport within a culture that worships at the altar of competition.

I can't expect you to not think about results. In fact, I'm going to assume that you are going to think about results a lot. An outcome attitude isn't always a bad thing. It can be useful to motivate you and keep reminding you why you're doing the hard work. At the same time, thinking too much about results, especially at particular times, for example, on the day of a competition, actually hurts your chances of success, so your challenge is what to do when your mind does fixate on results.

There are several reasons why your mind fixates on results. First, you may have been obsessing about results for years, so an outcome attitude has become a deeply ingrained habit of your mind. Moreover, this way of thinking has become hardwired into your brain's physiology. Second, your world, that is, your coaches, parents, family, friends, supporters, and fans, may continue to communicate messages about results. For instance, how often do you hear such statements as, "You gonna win today?" or "I just know you're going to get a medal!" from well-meaning people. It's difficult to think differently when you're constantly being bombarded by messages about results.

From Outcome to Process

This change from outcome to focus requires a fundamental change in your relationship with results and the role it plays in your athletic life. In doing so, you alter your attitude toward results and, as a consequence, change the way results impact how you think, feel, and perform in your sport. In a way, making this shift from outcome to process is just like retraining a bad technical habit you've developed. It involves commitment, effort, persistence, and patience. The following is a process you can go through to help you move from an outcome attitude to a process attitude.

Understand Outcome and Process Attitudes

You must first understand why you are making this shift. As I hope I have convinced you by now, an outcome attitude hurts your sports efforts in many ways, including the ways you think about, the emotions you experience during, how you react to, and how you perform in competitions. In contrast, a process attitude will help you perform your best and achieve your athletic goals by producing thinking, emotions, and reactions that encourage quality performances. If you really believe it is possible to achieve these differences, a process attitude will provide you with a clear rationale and a strong incentive to make this shift.

Recognize Outcome Attitude Moments

Your outcome attitude probably arises and influences you in common situations, like before competitions. These are the forks in the road discussed in the introduction. You can't take a different road if you don't see the fork. You should have your mental "radar" on when you are approaching those situations in which your outcome attitude is most likely to be activated. With this recognition, you'll be in a position to make the positive shift from outcome attitude to process attitude.

Pink Elephants and Blue Hippos

It would be great if I could just tell you to not think about results and it would stop your outcome attitude. But that just wouldn't work. In fact, the more I tell you to avoid thinking about results, the more you are going to think about them. Here's another way to think about it: I don't want you to think about a pink elephant. What did you just think about? The pink elephant, of course. If I keep repeating, "Don't think about a pink elephant," you will continue to think about that pink elephant, and, in fact, that thought will gain a hold in your mind and it will be difficult to let go of it. So, it's basically impossible to not think about something that's important to you. Instead, the solution is to think about something else because as humans, we are incapable of thinking about two things at once.

Let's try a variation of the pink elephant scenario. I want you to think about a blue hippo. What did you just think about? The blue hippo, obviously. What did you not think about? Gee, the pink elephant. Now wasn't that easy. Of course, it's easier to make the shift from pink elephant to blue hippo than outcome attitude to process attitude, but the basic path is the same. When your outcome attitude begins to take control of your thinking, you must first recognize it and then consciously make the change to a process attitude.

Additionally, as I discussed earlier, part of the challenge of letting go of an outcome attitude and embracing a process attitude involves resisting the forces that exist in your world that keep you preoccupied with results. You should identify the people (e.g., parents, coaches), groups (e.g., team, school), and cultural forces (e.g., social media) that keep pulling you toward an outcome attitude. Your goal is to remove or ignore these messages. This is challenging because you can't change your parents, readily find another team or school, or stop following social media altogether.

There are, however, a few things you can do. First, ask your parents and coaches to stop talking about results, while explaining why it will help you get the results they want. Second, realize that everyone associated with your team who is focusing on results is making a well-intentioned, although misguided, effort to support you. Thus, instead of paying attention to the obvious messages about results being sent by the people around you, it's better to focus on the underlying messages, most notably, how much the people around you want you to be successful. Third, do your best to stay away from social media that emphasizes results, for example, websites that provide results, ranking, and statistics. The bottom line is that the more you can reduce the messages that reinforce your outcome attitude, the easier it will be to change to a process attitude.

Like any sort of change, making this shift requires commitment, effort, time, perseverance, and patience. At first, it will be a real struggle because you are pushing against years of approaching your sport in a certain way and hearing particular messages about your sport from others. These approaches have become deeply entrenched in your psyche to the point that they are ingrained habits and knee-jerk reactions when you enter the competitive arena. But, just like retraining a bad technical habit, the more you make this shift and see its benefits, the easier it will become. In time, you will transform your old and unproductive outcome attitude into a new and helpful process attitude that will serve you well before and during competitions.

I love wrestling and the process behind it. I love getting better every day, making myself the best wrestler—and person—I can possibly become. To me, it wasn't about the medals or the glory or the accolades. It was just about my love for the sport and everything surrounding it. Whether I won or lost didn't matter—all that mattered was whether I gave it my best effort.

—Brandon Slay, Olympic wrestling gold medalist[5]

Tip from the Top: Stay in the Now

When you love your sport, it's easy to go down the dark roads of time. You can easily get stuck on the road from the past. There's an old saying, "You can't change the past, but you can ruin a perfectly good present by worrying about it." If you had some poor results recently, you can dwell on those past performances, focusing on your mistakes and failures. You will feel a wide range of unpleasant emotions, including disappointment, frustration, and regret. These emotions make you feel bad and can hurt your motivation, confidence, intensity, and focus. Carrying the past around on your shoulders, whether after a poor performance or a good one, interferes with your psychology and physiology, making it impossible for you to perform your best in the present.

The future is no better place to dwell than the past. You think about what might happen. The future brings the weight of expectation. An outcome attitude may take hold of you, and you begin to focus on the results you want, worry about whether you can achieve them, and feel fear about the consequences of your failures. The future not only distracts you from doing your best in the present, but also, like the past, creates a psychology and physiology that make a successful future less likely.

An attitude that focuses on the present sets the stage for you to be totally prepared to perform your best. A simple question to ask yourself if you start to go down the roads of the past or the future is, What do I need to do now? This question is powerful for several reasons. First, it pulls your mind away from the past and future, and directs it into the present. Second, it encourages you to focus on the actions you can take in the present to prepare to perform. Third, this "action orientation" will give you confidence and energize you because you are not carrying the weight of the past or future, and you are taking steps you can control that will prepare you to perform your best in the present.

EXERCISE

CHANGE FROM OUTCOME ATTITUDE TO PROCESS ATTITUDE

1. Using your Prime Sport Profile score from the beginning of the chapter, determine the degree to which you have an outcome attitude that is interfering with your performance.

2. If you have an outcome attitude, examine your relationship with it.

   a. Where and how did you develop an outcome attitude (e.g., your parents, coaches, or others)?

   b. How has an outcome attitude made an impact on the way you think, your emotions, and your performance?

   c. What are the benefits of a process attitude?

3. Make the shift from an outcome attitude to a process attitude.

   a. Identify the situations in which an outcome attitude arises and interferes with performance (e.g., before a competition).

   b. Create a narrative about a process attitude (write down what you will say to yourself about the downside of having an outcome attitude and the benefits of a having process attitude).

   c. Recognize an outcome attitude when it arises.

   d. Implement your process attitude plan (i.e., say your narrative to yourself or someone else).

   e. Focus on your process-oriented preparations.

CHALLENGE

I have found that a simple distinction often lies at the heart of whether athletes are able to perform their best or collapse, particularly in difficult conditions or in a competition: Do they view the situation as a threat or a challenge? Whether you see a situation as a threat or challenge produces in you diametrically opposed reactions that include your thoughts, emotions, physiology, and goals, and this, in turn, determines the quality of your performance.

Let's consider what happens when you have a threat attitude toward a situation. First, an important question to ask is, Where does threat come from in sports? Although the threat of injury is ever-present in many sports, I have found that the most common and most powerful threat comes from a fear of failure as you pursue your athletic goals (see more on fear of failure in chapter 2). What will happen if you fail? The threat attitude arises when you believe that there will be dire consequences for not achieving your goals, for example, you will embarrass yourself, let down your family and friends, feel that your sports participation has been a waste of time, or be devastated because you didn't fulfill your sport dreams. The irony is that by responding with a threat attitude, you actually cause the very thing that is most threatening to you, namely, failure, to happen.

Second, the cause of this threat attitude is an overinvestment of yourself in your sport (see more on overinvestment in chapter 2). Your sports participation is too large a segment of your self-identity, that is, who you see yourself as (i.e., an athlete). Your self-esteem, that is, how you value and feel about yourself as a person, is excessively dependent on your athletic achievements. And the attainment of your goals is your all-encompassing priority. As a result, when you compete, you are putting your self-identity, self-esteem, and goals on the line. Aside from a threat of injury, there is nothing more threatening to an athlete than the loss of those very personal attributes.

Third, how do you react to the threat? Physiologically, your muscles tighten up, your heart rate increases, you hold your breath, your balance falls back, and your center of gravity rises. None of these physical reactions are conducive to optimal athletic performance. Psychologically, your motivation is to flee from the threat. Your confidence plummets because you don't feel capable of confronting the situation (that's one reason it's a threat to you). You are focused only on the enormity of the threat. And you experience fear, helplessness, and despair because you believe that the threat will be realized. Your primary goal is to protect yourself from the threat by putting as much space between you and the threat as possible. In sum, everything, both physically and mentally, goes against you, making it virtually impossible for you to overcome the threat, perform to the best of your ability, and achieve your goals.

Where, then, does challenge attitude come from? It starts with a perception of the situation as an opportunity to push yourself, get out of your comfort zone, seek out your limits, achieve your goals, and reach a new level of excellence. With this perception, you are focused on pursuing your athletic goals with complete confidence, courage, and commitment, and without doubt, worry, or fear. Challenge is associated with your embracing the process of your sport rather than fearing the results of your efforts. The emphasis is on having fun and seeing competitions as exciting and enriching. Your sport, when seen through the lens of a challenge attitude, is an experience that is relished and sought out at every opportunity. Thus, challenge is highly motivating, to the point where you love being in pressure situations. When you develop a challenge attitude, you put yourself in the best possible position to perform your best and succeed because everything that impacts your performance is on your side.

Not surprisingly, a challenge attitude produces an entirely different set of physical and mental reactions. Physiologically, you feel energized, but not too fired up, with just the right amount of adrenaline to make you feel ready to perform your best. Your muscles are loose, your breathing is deep and controlled, your balance is forward, and your center of gravity is low. Psychologically, your singular motivation is to go at that thing that is challenging you and overcome it. You are confident that you have the capabilities to surmount the challenging situation. Your focus is like a laser beam on the challenge in front of you and what you need to do to succeed. As for emotions, you feel excitement, inspiration, pride, and courage. Your fundamental goal is to face and conquer the challenge. In sum, your entire physical and psychological being is directed toward triumphing against the challenge, and your chances of finding success are high.

The interesting thing about threat versus challenge is that it's all in your mind; it's rarely about the reality of a situation, but rather how you perceive it. Think about it this way: Let's say you're a tennis player in a match being contested in some difficult weather conditions, for example, on a hot and windy day. During the match, you're not the only one playing in the high temperatures and having the wind mess with your service toss and ground strokes. Your opponent is facing the same difficulties. My point is that everyone has, more or less, the same conditions in a competition. What determines whether you see those conditions as a threat or a challenge boils down to your attitude toward them.

Let's take the tennis example a step further. Upon arrival at your match against your opponent, who is of equal ability and as equally well prepared as you are, you see the conditions and think, "These are tough conditions, but I've been practicing in these conditions and, anyhow, my opponent has to deal with the heat and wind too. I'm going to crush it!" In contrast, your opponent is thinking, "This is awful. I hate these conditions. How am I going to play well today?" You see the match as a challenge, while your opponent sees it as a threat. Who do you think will have a better match? Who do you think is more likely to win? You, obviously.

So, next time you're faced with a really tough training or competitive situation, whether bad weather, difficult conditions, unfriendly spectators, a tough field of competitors, or the biggest competition of your life, ask yourself whether you see it as a threat or a challenge. Then, embrace the challenge and tell yourself, "Bring it on!"

Be bold. If you're going to make an error, make it a doozy, and don't be afraid to hit the ball!

—Billie Jean King, tennis legend[6]

Tip from the Top: Shift from "What If" to "When"

When you have a threat attitude, you are consumed by negativity in so many ways. You focus on the worst-case scenario, the "what ifs," which only turn up the volume on your experience of threat. Examples include "What if I don't perform my best?" "What if I lose badly?" "What if I disappoint my parents?" "What if I embarrass myself?" "What if this is as far as I can go?" What makes a "what if" statement so harmful is that they are followed by some unspoken, although truly terrifying, consequences, for instance, "I will be a total loser," "My parents won't love me," or "I will never achieve my athletic goals." This threat attitude leads to a psychology and physiology that almost certainly dooms you to the failure that you most want to avoid.

These "what ifs" cause you to have doubts because you don't believe you can overcome the threat. You feel pressure because you absolutely must succeed or those bad consequences will be realized. You experience fear because you believe that your life (not your physical life) is in danger. The result is a self-fulfilling prophecy of the very thing that is causing the threat attitude in the first place: poor performance and disappointing results.

When you feel yourself moving toward a threat attitude, a direct way to help you shift toward a challenge attitude is to actively change the way you

EXERCISE

SHIFT FROM THREAT TO CHALLENGE

1. Describe how a threat attitude hurts your performance in and enjoyment of your sport.

   a. Detail the thoughts, emotions, and actions that a threat attitude triggers in you.

2. Identify the cause of your threat attitude (see chapter 2 for the most likely causes).

3. Debunk what you believe will be the dire consequences of failure (they are probably not going to happen).

4. Describe how a challenge attitude will help your performance in and increase enjoyment of your sport.

5. Detail the thoughts, emotions, and actions you associate with a challenge attitude.

6. When you experience a threat attitude:

   a. Shift from "what if" to "when."

   b. Shift from outcome focus to process focus (see chapter 4).

   c. Shift from negative self-talk to positive self-talk (see chapter 4).

   d. Breathe and relax your body (see chapter 4).

   e. Choose to fight not flee.

think about the upcoming performance and adopt "when" statements rather than "what if" statements. Examples include "When I give my best effort . . .," "When I have fun . . .," and "When I stay my own best ally . . ." The tone of "when" statements catalyzes a challenge attitude in several ways. They remove the threat by removing the bad consequence that a "what if" statement leads to. "When" statements reorient you in a positive direction where, following a "when," good things are bound to happen. For example, "When I give my best effort . . . I usually perform well," "When I have fun . . . I am relaxed and energized," and "When I am my best ally . . . I give myself a chance to succeed."

"When" statements fill your mind with the good things that can happen, which boosts your motivation and confidence to pursue your goal for the day. You also feel excited and inspired to compete. This shift creates a self-fulfilling upward spiral in which your psychology and physiology ignite one another and prepare you to perform your best, thus increasing your chances of success.

LONG-TERM

One of the greatest lessons you can learn in your life that applies to your sport, education, career, or relationships is that nothing of value comes quickly or without hard work. There are no quick fixes, instant results, or short cuts to success. For every great athlete, there has been a long, hard, and winding road from where they started to where they stand at or near the top of their sport. The pursuit of big goals takes time, effort, patience, and persistence. And this journey requires a long-term attitude in which you fully embrace just how long and difficult it will be. This attitude enables you to absorb and respond positively to the many bumps in the road as you pursue your athletic goals.

So at 22, I look at that and think that I've got so many years before I peak, before I get to my best, so much more to learn. What's the point in risking an injury now that could take me out for my whole career?

—Holly Bleasdale, Olympic pole vaulter[7]

Avoid Short-Term

Unfortunately, we live in a culture that communicates the message, "I want it now and I want it without any effort." You can see this adage realized with the microwave (i.e., food when you want it without having to cook it), the

Internet (i.e., information at your fingertips), and reality TV (i.e., instant fame without any observable talent or effort). Athletes these days feel tremendous pressure to produce immediate results or they are led to believe that their goals will never be realized. These persistent messages are difficult to resist and can lead you to experience frustration, disappointment, a decline in motivation and confidence, and even despair. This short-term attitude will not only hinder your development as an athlete, but also it may cause a "give-up" reaction in which you simply stop trying because you're not progressing toward your goals or getting the short-term results as quickly as you would like. Obviously and unfortunately, this short-term attitude ensures that you don't even give yourself a chance to see what you're capable of.

Think Long-Term

An important part of adopting a long-term attitude is remembering that immediate or short-term success doesn't matter. If you're a young athlete, you, your parents, and your coaches want you to experience success now because you and they believe that early success is highly predictive of later success in your sport. Our athletic culture is obsessed with the "phenom" and the "can't-miss kid," who show earlier dominance in a sport. Yet, although there have been phenoms who went on to great success later in their careers, this perception is as much fantasy as reality. For example, out of the thousands of young baseball players who have competed in the Little League World Series throughout the years, fewer than 50 went on to major-league careers. In fact, phenoms are a statistical rarity, and those can't-miss kids often do miss later in their athletic careers. More often than not, it is the athletes who keep at it through setbacks, plateaus, and failures who ultimately "make it." Your efforts early on as you strive for your sports goals should be devoted to preparing yourself for success in the future, when it matters most, not achieving quick and immediate success.

Four Ps of a Long-Term Attitude

A long-term attitude has a direct and important influence on your entire psychological approach to your athletic development. It starts with seeing the inevitable difficulties you will face as you pursue your goals as normal bumps in the road—bumps that jostle you but don't serve as concrete barriers that stop you in your tracks and prevent you from continuing down the road.

Perspective

A long-term attitude enables you to keep your sports experiences in *perspective*, which means having a realistic and balanced view of them. A long-term attitude makes it possible for you to continue to feel passionate about and find enjoyment in your sport when you experience setbacks and difficulties. Perspective involves keeping competition, success, and failure in their rightful and reasonable place within the broader context of your sport and your life. In the big picture, a long-term attitude enables you to keep your sport in perspective, serving as a reminder to you that your sport is a big part of your life but not life itself.

Patience

Patience is a powerful tool that a long-term attitude provides you with as you strive toward your athletic goals. The dictionary defines patience as the "capacity to accept or tolerate delay, trouble, or suffering without getting angry or upset," "even tempered," and "diligent." Sounds like an important attitude to have as an athlete, doesn't it? Patience is essential for long-term success. It allows you to stay positive and motivated during down periods when you are struggling in training or confronted with a series of poor competitive performances. It enables you to stay focused on the process and the present when you could easily be pulled toward an outcome attitude and thoughts of past disappointments or future worries. Because you aren't looking for unrealistic progress or quick results, patience keeps you focused on the small steps that are necessary to continue toward your athletic goals. It also allows you to recognize and accept the long road ahead and the need to do the work and put in the time to achieve your goals.

Patience is not passive waiting. Patience is active acceptance of the process required to attain your goals and dreams.

—Ray A. Davis, author[8]

Persistence

Success doesn't always go to the most talented. As you climb the competitive ladder in your sport, the level of talent rises as well, so talent often doesn't make the difference in who ultimately makes it and who doesn't.

Oftentimes, it is the athletes who are the most persistent, meaning they just keep steadily plugging away at the things they need to do to achieve their goals. They go to the gym for conditioning, the field, the court, the course, the hill, the track, or what have you to develop themselves physically, technically, and tactically. They do the mental training they need to do. They take care of their equipment to the best of their ability. And persistent athletes continue to do what it takes day in and day out, week in and week out, month in and month out, and year in and year out simply because they know they must. Moreover, they persist in the face of monotony, boredom, and the desire to do other things. This persistence ensures that they develop their abilities fully and are as prepared as they can be to perform their best when they enter the competitive arena.

Perseverance

Perseverance is a variation of persistence that emphasizes your continuing to plug along in the face of the ups and downs that are an inevitable part of the road to your sports goals. Whether pain, fatigue, illness, injury, plateaus, difficulties in the mastery of new skills, or competitive setbacks, perseverance allows you to keep taking steps forward every time you are forced to take steps back as you pursue your goals. With every pothole you hit, metaphorically speaking, in the road to your goals, it's easy to get discouraged, lose confidence, and question whether you are on the right road and, if so, how you can handle jostling without breaking down. The first three Ps of a long-term attitude provide you with tools necessary to maximize your perseverance during difficult periods in your sports participation.

Tip from the Top: Sports Are Like the Stock Market

Even the best athletes in the world have ups and downs physically and mentally, so you should expect the same. You have really great days where you feel rested, strong, and ready to go. On these days, you are at the top of your game, performing your best and having a lot of fun too. Then there are those other days when you feel terrible, tired, weak, and not psyched at all. On these days, you perform poorly, and there is no fun to be had. Sometimes the causes are obvious, for example, you are overtrained, tired, or stressed out. Other times, the causes are less clear; it seems like you just woke up on the wrong side of the bed. Perhaps you are just a little off physically or you're distracted by things happening in other parts of your life, for instance, school, work, or relationships. These down days should be accepted as a normal part of the training and competitive cycle.

Unfortunately, what starts out as a small drop in performance can turn into a plunge when a short-term attitude infects your thinking. The decline in performance can cause you to lose motivation and confidence, have doubt and worry, and shift into a threat attitude, further exacerbating the down period. What began as a natural—and usually short-lived—drop in performance can turn into an enduring slump.

It is during these tough periods that you should think of sports as being like the stock market. If you look at one bad day on the stock market, for example, a drop of 300 points on the Dow Jones Industrial Average, you would think that investing in the stock market is a really bad idea. If you have money in the stock market, you may want to pull your money out right away. Similarly, if you have a bad day competing, you may think that continuing to invest your time and energy in your sport isn't a good decision either. Both rely on a short-term attitude that limits your perspective and provides you with a skewed and unrealistic view of your investments of money, and time and effort, respectively.

If you look at the stock market during the last 50 years, yes, you see a jagged line with many ups and downs (some with long and dramatic declines, as in the Great Recession of 2007); however, more importantly, you see that the jagged line progresses steadily upward. From this long-term perspective, putting your money in the stock market—and keeping it there during downswings—is a good investment. Looking at your sports involvement with the same long-term view would show a similar upward trend throughout time and an equally good commitment of your time and energy. As with the stock market, you shouldn't panic on those bad days and let them change your overall investment in your sport.

This long-term attitude involves not being too focused on immediate results and having a long-term plan, like a financial plan, that guides you steadily toward your future athletic goals. Another important lesson is not to judge your performances based on your most recent practice session or competitive result. That's like looking at the stock market on a bad day. Instead, look at the general direction of your efforts during a period of weeks and months. Like the stock market, you will see some down periods, but you

SHIFT FROM SHORT-TERM ATTITUDE TO LONG-TERM ATTITUDE

1. Describe how a short-term attitude impacts your thinking, emotions, and performance.
2. Describe the benefits of a long-term attitude to your athletic efforts.
3. Shift from short-term attitude to long-term attitude.

   a. Identify those situations that trigger your short-term attitude (e.g., setbacks, disappointments, experiences of frustration).

   b. Create an alternative set of thoughts grounded in a long-term attitude.

   c. Recognize your thoughts and emotions in reaction to your short-term attitude when they occur.

   d. Shift to the long-term set of thoughts you have developed.

   e. Shift your focus to immediate process goals and direct your effort toward those goals.

will also see an overall trend of progress toward your goals. This long-term attitude—and seeing your sports participation as akin to the stock market—will keep you motivated, positive, and calm, even on your worst days.

RISK

Let me preface this discussion of risk-taking by saying that, when I talk about taking risks, I don't mean taking stupid risks, like texting while driving, jumping off the roof of your house, or taking drugs. I also don't mean taking sport-related risks for which you are unprepared, that involve little chance of success, or where the consequences of failure are dire. That's not taking risks, that's being stupid. Instead, risk-taking in sports involves weighing the rewards and costs of a particular course of action, evaluating the chances of success and failure, determining your preparedness to take the risk, and deciding on your willingness to accept the consequences of failure. At a practical level, risk-taking means getting out of your comfort zone, pushing your limits, and doing things on the field of play that may lead to greater success but also greater failure.

Yes, risk-taking is inherently failure-prone. Otherwise, it would be called "sure-thing-taking."

—Jim McMahon, Super Bowl–winning quarterback[9]

What Is Risk?

The dictionary defines risk as a "situation in which you expose yourself to danger." Although physical risk is an inevitable part of many sports, the risks I'm talking about are more psychological and emotional in nature. Clearly, risk is essential for success, not only in sports, but also in every aspect of life, whether winning an Olympic gold medal, starting a tech company, or telling someone "I love you." If you don't take risks, you won't improve, grow, or achieve your athletic goals. And, importantly, you will never find out what you are truly capable of or how far you can go.

This kind of risk comes when you face a test of your ability, effort, and preparation. You are putting your self-identity, self-esteem, goals, hopes, and dreams on the line. After the competition, you will learn whether you succeed. The risk then becomes clear: failure!

Given the risks of taking risks, there are obvious upsides to not taking risks. You stay safe. You never get uncomfortable. And you minimize the risk of failure (to be discussed further in chapter 2). Of course, there are far more significant downsides to not taking risks. You will be perpetually stuck where you are. You will never be truly successful. You will feel frustrated. And you will never be completely satisfied with your efforts.

He who is not courageous enough to take risks will accomplish nothing in life.

—Muhammad Ali, boxing legend[10]

To Risk or Not to Risk, That Is the Question

Hopefully, I have convinced you of the necessity of risk in your sport. But taking risks in sports is a simple but not an easy choice. It's a simple choice, because would you rather take risks and give yourself a strong chance of real success or play it safe and guarantee failure? The answer is obvious. At the same time, it's not an easy choice because no one likes to fail, and when you take risks, failure is a distinct possibility (that's the nature of risks). Also, there are a variety of powerful psychological and emotional forces that hold you back from taking risks. They are as follows:

- Fear of failure (no way you'll take a risk if you're afraid to fail)
- Perfectionism (the bar is set so high anything less than perfection is failure)
- Need for control (taking a risk requires that you give up control)
- Lack of confidence in your abilities or preparation (you're not going to take a risk if you don't think you can succeed)

At the heart of risk-taking is the willingness to accept that, when you take risks, you might fail, and if you do fail you may feel bad, but in the end you'll be okay. By their very nature, you are more likely to fail when you take risks. But, paradoxically, when you take risks, your chances of success also increase. If you can truly accept failure, it is no longer a danger, and without that danger of failure, there's no reason not to take risks because all you see are the upsides.

I'm not saying that you should take risks indiscriminately; that's a recipe for disaster. Your goal should be to increase your willingness to take appropriate risks when the time and situation are right and the chances of the risk paying off are higher than not.

Risk-Taking Is a Lifestyle Choice

Risk-taking is not so much a skill as a lifestyle choice. Chances are if you're not a risk-taker in your broader life, you're probably not one in your sport either. So, to become a risk-taker on the field, course, court, track, hill, or what-have-you, you should embrace risk in all aspects of your life. If you can make taking risks a part of who you are, risk-taking in your sport will simply be what you do.

Two great places where I challenge athletes I work with to take risks are socially and academically. For example, if you can ask someone you like out on a date (but haven't been willing to take the risk of rejection), you'll find it's a lot less scary to take a risk in your sport. And if you can speak up in class when your teacher or professor asks a question, taking a risk on the field of play will seem like a piece of cake.

Regardless of the setting, every time you consider taking a risk you are, without realizing it, doing a risk–reward analysis in which you weigh the benefits and costs of taking a risk, whether, for example, it is going for an ace in tennis, hitting over a water hazard in golf, or throwing long in football. Of course, you don't want to take risks every time; there is a place for risk and a place to perform more judiciously. You have to determine your chances of succeeding when you take a risk and whether the risk will be rewarded.

Moreover, risk-taking isn't just something that you do; rather, it is something that must be planned for and worked on. Like making a technical or tactical change without careful thought and planning, a spontaneous approach to risk-taking will most likely result in failure for most athletes. Sure, the world's best athletes can sometimes get away with throwing caution to the wind because they are talented, experienced, and confident. But for everyone else, it's not an approach to risk-taking I would recommend.

No Time Like the Present to Take Risks

It never feels like the right time to take risks because, well, there are risks to taking risks. First, when you start taking risks as you learn to push your limits, those risks won't be rewarded right away. In other words, you'll likely make mistakes and experience failure more than usual because you're performing at a level that you are not accustomed to.

Risk-taking is, in a sense, a skill that takes time, commitment, and persistence to develop. Just like any skill, however, when you first start taking risks in your sport, your mind and body aren't going to be used to it, so your performance may take a step or two backward in your practices and competitions. Because you haven't ingrained the skills fully, it won't immediately translate into improved performance.

I once worked with a world-class athlete who experienced this initial inconsistency. He had a history of performing conservatively. In the first competitions of the season, he had some periods of great performance but also made mistakes that cost him. But after about a half-dozen events, his risk-taking stared to click, and he had a series of outstanding performances in big competitions that resulted in a big leap in his world ranking.

Second, because you will struggle at first, your confidence may also suffer, and you may question whether risk-taking is the right path to be on. You might say to yourself, "Gosh, my past, safer approach worked pretty well, certainly much better than the way this is going now, so maybe I should just stick with what has worked." But what may have worked in the past and has gotten you to where you currently are won't work in the future or get you where you want to go. As an old Texas saying goes, "If all you ever do is all you've ever done, then all you'll ever get is all you've ever got." Your efforts shouldn't be devoted to where you are now but where you want to be next month, next year, or in five years in your sport. You need to prepare yourself for performing at the next level. And performing safe just won't cut it.

In an ideal world, the offseason is the best time to start taking risks because you have no concern about results, and you have the time to practice the skill of risk-taking. But I would argue that there is no time like the present to start taking risks, regardless of the time of year. If you're going to make a real commitment to risk-taking to get your performances to the next level, you might as well start now, because the sooner you start, the sooner you'll reap the benefits.

You'll always miss 100 percent of the shots you don't take.

—Wayne Gretzky, hockey legend[11]

Threat versus Challenge with Risk

As I've discussed, the real risk of taking risks is that you might fail. And if you are overly focused on the costs of risk-taking, usually driven by fear of failure or feeling pressure to get results, chances are you will shift into a threat attitude in which you're driven to protect yourself from that threat. As a result, you become risk averse (because risk that leads to failure is a threat to your self-identity, self-esteem, and goals), and you're not likely to take the risks necessary to perform your best. Moreover, even if you do get yourself to take a risk, it will probably not pay off because, in threat mode, as mentioned earlier in the section on challenge and threat, changes in your physiology and psychology will likely cause the risk to go unrewarded.

You want to see risk-taking as a challenge to pursue, not a threat to avoid. With this challenge attitude, physiology and psychology will shift in a way that will increase the chances of the risk being rewarded. You will feel energized, committed, confident, and focused, which will help you make those risks pay off in the form of great competitive performances.

Finally, you may think that taking risks is, well, risky for your sport. But the reality is that not taking risks is far more risky to your athletic goals because performing safe will not get you where you want to go. If you take risks, you will certainly have some setbacks in the short run. But, in the long run, you give yourself a lot better chance of performing your best and achieving your sports goals when you take risks. So, when you look at it that way, taking risks in your sport isn't risky at all.

Tip from the Top: Take a Leap of Faith

Taking risks is an uncertain endeavor. You don't know whether you can actually take the risks you need to take or whether those risks will pay off, even with the best of intentions and significant effort. No one, not your coaches, family, friends, or, well, sport psychologist, can foresee what will happen to you if you take a risk. There is going to be that fear of the unknown: Can you take the risk, and will it pay off?

Ultimately, if you want to become the best athlete you can be, you must take a *leap of faith*. A great philosopher once said, "You do or you do not. There is no try." No, it wasn't Aristotle or Socrates who spoke those simple, yet profound, words; the great thinker was . . . Yoda, the Jedi Master of *Star Wars* fame.

I often use an analogy from the film *Indiana Jones and the Last Crusade*, in which Indiana Jones is in search of the Holy Grail. He is following a map that leads him on a treacherous journey. Near the end of the film, Jones comes to a seemingly bottomless chasm, across from which is the doorway to the room where the Holy Grail is kept. There is no apparent bridge across the abyss, yet the map shows a picture of a man stepping into the void and speaks of taking a leap of faith that will enable Jones to traverse the gap. Additionally, his father has been injured, and the only way to save him is to pour water from the Holy Grail on the wound. Clearly, the consequences of failure in taking this leap of faith are dire, namely, plummeting to his death. Yet, mustering

MAKE A RISK-TAKING PLAN

1. Do a risk analysis.

    a. Do you have the technical, tactical, and performance capabilities to succeed?

    b. Are you as prepared as you can be to succeed?

    c. Is the situation conducive to risk-taking and succeeding?

    d. Is the risk worth it if you succeed, and are the consequences manageable enough if you don't?

2. Put risk-taking into action.

    a. Discuss with your coaches how to incorporate risk-taking into your sport training.

    b. Accept the short-term risks and acknowledge how low the risks are, because it is training.

    c. Highlight the long-term benefits.

    d. Before the training performances, make a conscious commitment to and be totally focused on taking the risk.

    e. Make sure you are as prepared as you can be to succeed.

his courage, Jones takes that leap of faith and finds that there is an invisible bridge that he can walk across to seize the Holy Grail. Against the most severe consequences if the risk didn't pay off, Jones had the faith to choose the path that led him to the Holy Grail. Similarly, you must also have the strength of your conviction to take that initial leap of faith to discover your Holy Grail, that is, achievement of your athletic goals (especially realizing that your worst-case scenario is nothing like that faced by Indiana Jones).

The leap of faith begins with the conviction that only by getting out of your comfort zone and taking risks do you have any chance of achieving your sports goals. The leap of faith continues with, well, faith—faith that the risks you take will, in fact, result in improved performance and results. The leap of faith involves having a basic belief in yourself and a fundamental trust in what you want to accomplish as an athlete. The leap of faith involves the belief that good things will happen when you choose to take risks. You must also recognize that some misgivings are a normal part of the process. You can never be 100 percent certain that things will work out the way you want; if you didn't have doubts, it wouldn't require a leap of faith. Lastly, you must also understand that this leap of faith is not complete blind faith. Rather, you have committed many hours of effort to developing yourself as an athlete in your sport, and this time has prepared you to succeed when you take the leap of faith. Thus, the leap of faith may seem immense to you, just as it did to Indiana Jones, but, in reality, the risks are not so great, and your chances of success are very high and those of failure surprisingly low.

If things seem under control, you are just not going fast enough.

—Mario Andretti, Indianapolis 500 winner[12]

PrimeHeart: Five Obstacles

Do you ever feel as if something is holding you back from making progress in achieving your athletic goals? Like while a big part of you wants to get where you want to go, there seems to be another part of you that doesn't want to get there? Do you sometimes feel like there is an internal battle being waged between your inner ally and inner enemy, and your inner enemy is winning? Do you feel confused and frustrated when you do things that are clearly not in your best interests, but you can't seem to stop yourself from going down the bad road? If so, you're not alone. Athletes often come to me because they aren't performing well and don't know why. After we explore what is going on with them, the vast majority learn that there is something holding them back. They just don't know what that something is.

Make sure your worst enemy doesn't live between your own two ears.

—Laird Hamilton, world champion surfer[1]

THE POWER OF THE UNCONSCIOUS

Many athletes feel as if something is holding them back but can't figure out what it is because of what I call the "power of the unconscious." So much of what drives us is outside of our awareness. This experience is frustrating because we, as humans, like to know why we do what we do. Yet, there are forces in our unconscious that impact what we think, how we feel, and how we act on and react to the world around us. And these same forces have an immense influence on your sports performance. Some of these forces—what I call the "light side"—have a positive impact on you, for example, unconscious values, attitudes, and beliefs that motivate you, give you confidence, and fire you up before a competition. You experience them as a challenge attitude, fun, excitement, pride, and inspiration.

Unfortunately, many of the forces—the "dark side," if you are a *Star Wars* fan—have the opposite effect; they have an unpleasant, unproductive, or unhealthy influence on you. You may experience this side of you as doubt, worry, stress, fear, frustration, and many other thoughts and emotions that hurt your efforts, performance, and enjoyment in your sport. In all likelihood, this unhealthy part of you is driven by one, some, or all of the five obstacles described in this chapter.

Until you make the unconscious conscious, it will control your life.

—Carl Jung, renowned Swiss psychiatrist[2]

WHAT WAS ONCE FUNCTIONAL IS NOW DYSFUNCTIONAL

To help you better understand the impact of these obstacles on your sports performance, its important to understand where they come from and how they arise. Most basically, the obstacles develop from the experiences you have in your social world, primarily experiences with your parents and significant others in your life—coaches, teachers, siblings, extended family, and, more recently, our culture as communicated through technology and social media. The purpose of these obstacles was once to protect you from people with whom and situations in which you felt uncomfortable. These forces sent you messages about how to live comfortably in your world. If you grew up in an environment that you perceived as threatening, you developed strategies to help you cope with the difficult situation. The obstacles caused you to think, feel, and behave in ways that helped you function and feel safe.

For example, imagine you grew up with a perfectionistic and controlling father who not only role modeled these qualities in his own behavior, but also sent you messages of conditional love (if you got straight As and won in your sport, he lavished you with love and praise; if you got a B+ or had a poor sports performance, he expressed anger toward you). To deal with this uncomfortable situation, you adopted the same qualities, driving yourself unmercifully to success and needing to feel in control. At the time, these qualities were highly functional because they enabled you to avoid your father's wrath. Moreover, because these thoughts, feelings, and behaviors were functional, you continued to use them. They became ingrained habits, and you became a perfectionistic and controlling person.

As you transitioned from childhood to adolescence to adulthood, you continued these practices out of habit, even though, with the natural maturation process, you gained experience, improved your coping skills, and had more resources that could provide other, healthier ways of dealing with your father. Your perfectionistic and controlling tendencies caused you to be severely self-critical, fear failure, avoid reasonable risk-taking, and feel miserable. As a consequence, these qualities shifted from being functional to dysfunctional. In other words, they went from helping you in your life by making you feel safe around your father to interfering with your life as you pursued your athletic and life goals.

As you explore this chapter and identify obstacles that are getting in your way and holding you back, you should have two goals. First, more generally, you must let go of those now-dysfunctional habits and think, feel, and act in ways that are based on who you are now (not who you once were) and support, rather than interfere with, the pursuit of your goals. Second, at a more practical level, you need to make the unconscious obstacles conscious by doing the following:

- Understand how the obstacles affect you.
- Become aware of when they get in your way.
- Gain insight into where they came from.
- Remove them so you have a clear path to your goals that you can pursue without doubt, worry, or hesitation, and with confidence, courage, and abandon.

Whatever we plant in our unconscious mind and nourish with repetition and emotion will one day become a reality.

—Earl Nightingale, human development expert[3]

REMOVING THE OBSTACLES

In approaching how to remove the obstacles, you can first take a short-term strategy to mitigate the obstacles temporarily and then employ a long-term strategy to hopefully remove them permanently.

Short-Term

When you let these obstacles take you to a place where you are your own worst enemy, they exert a significant and negative influence on your thoughts, emotions, behavior, and athletic performance. They can cause you to become fixated on all that is negative and wrong in your efforts and performance. It will require considerable determination and persistent effort to diminish the negative impact of the obstacles on your performance. Your main goal in the short-term is to take your mind off of these obstacles so they have less of an effect on you. The basic strategy involves distracting yourself so the negative thoughts don't consume you and affect you as much.

There are two general approaches you can use. First, you can immerse yourself in your preparations. If you are focused on what you need to do to get ready to perform, whether in training or competition, you're less likely to pay attention to the negative thoughts. Specific strategies related to your preparations can include getting your equipment ready, getting physically warmed up, and doing mental imagery of your upcoming performance. These strategies not only take your mind off of the messages that the obstacles are sending you, but also inspire you, build your confidence, and generate positive emotions that can further help you resist the negativity.

The second approach involves taking your mind completely off of your performance efforts. One way to do that is to socialize with friends. If you're chatting it up or goofing around with your friends, you're having fun, which is a great short-term tool for taking your mind off of the negativity that the obstacles may be trying to impose on you. Music is another powerful tool for reducing the impact of the obstacles. As I will discuss in more detail later, music has a profound psychological, emotional, and physiological influence on us. If you're listening to music that gets you fired up or calmed down, inspires you, and gives you confidence, you are marshalling formidable forces against your negativity. Anything you enjoy doing before a competition (when you are most likely to experience negativity), whether reading, playing games, dancing, checking your social media, or anything else that makes you feel good, can be useful in reducing the impact of the obstacles on your performance.

Long-Term

The aforementioned strategies can help you keep your negativity at bay temporarily, but your goal is to remove the obstacles altogether so they lose their influence on your athletic efforts. This objective, admittedly, is not easy because the obstacles have become habits of mind and body, and are deeply ingrained and resistant to change. At the same time, my experience in working with thousands of athletes throughout the years has shown me that it is possible to let go of the obstacles and liberate yourself to perform freely and fully.

The first step is to identify which obstacles are affecting you most. The Prime Sport Profile in the next section and your reading of chapter 2 will help you accomplish this step. It involves thinking about the five obstacles described in this chapter and seeing how each, if any, interferes in giving your best effort and pursuing your goals.

Second, once you have identified the obstacles, you need to understand how in your upbringing and past experiences the obstacles developed. For example, if you have a fear of failure, what messages did you get from your parents and others when you were young that led to the fear? This realization can be a real eye-opener in explaining patterns of self-defeating thoughts, emotions, behavior, and performance that you have had for years but never knew why. You will finally be able to understand why you have continued to engage in these practices despite the fact that they have held you back in your sports participation and other areas of your life.

Third, you can't change old patterns if you don't have new patterns to replace them with. You must devise a new way to approach your sport that is positive, motivating, energizing, and in sharp contrast to the ways in which the obstacles have caused you to operate thus far. What would you like to think before a competition? What emotions would you like to feel? How would you like to perform? For example, if you have a fear of failure, you can redefine success and failure in new ways, for example, success is giving your best effort and failure is doing anything that holds you back from your goals. You can also set goals to give your best effort, take risks, and accept mistakes.

Fourth, as I note in the introduction, these changes require that you recognize that the road you are on is a bad one, identify better roads, and make the choice to take a better road. This choice isn't an easy one because you are accustomed to traveling the bad road, however bad it is. But, with a determined commitment, you can take the good road the first time, and when you do, it will be awe-inspiring because you will have overcome your greatest opponent—yourself—and be rewarded by performing better and feeling better. Moreover, every time you come to that same fork in the road, it will become progressively easier to take the good road until you get to the point that the old, bad road is covered with weeds from disuse and the good road is the only one you can travel.

OVERINVESTMENT

Overinvestment in your sport is the foundation of the obstacles discussed in this chapter. Overinvestment occurs when too much of your self-identity is comprised in your investment in your sport. Self-identity refers to how you perceive yourself and the different roles you play in your life. For example, different aspects of a self-identity can include athlete, student, friend, son/daughter, sister/brother, and so forth. You can think of self-identity as a pie consisting of pieces of different sizes, with the pieces representing the components of your self-identity (see below).

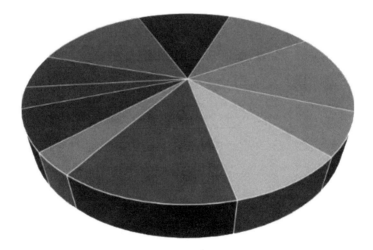

The number of pieces of pie that comprise your self-identity and the importance of each of those pieces determine the degree of your investment. Overinvestment occurs when, in this case, sports are a large piece and you have few other pieces in your self-identity pie. This overinvestment becomes harmful when your sport identity plays too large a role in how you feel about yourself, and threats to that part of your self-identity, in the form of mistakes, setbacks, and failure, are truly unsettling and are expressed as doubt, worry, and anxiety.

One good gauge of the degree of investment you have in your sport is your emotional reactions on the day of a competition. Consider what you think about and how you feel before a competition. Are you negative, uncertain, and worried? Do you feel stress, anxiety, and fear? Are you sweating? Is your heart pounding? Do you feel short of breath? Are your muscles tight and shaky? Do you feel as if you want to flee? Now consider how you feel after a competition. In the unlikely event that you have a good performance after having those reactions prior to a competition, do you feel excited or relieved? Probably the latter, because you are relieved to have avoided the assault on your self-identity that comes with failure. If you performed poorly, do you feel devastated, as if your self-identity was attacked? These "red flags" are caused by a perceived threat (as detailed in chapter 1) to your self-identity, and the cause of that threat reaction is an overinvestment in your sport. Your self-identity may now look like the pie in the following figure.

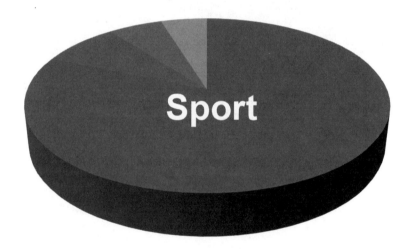

"Too" Zone

"Too" is one of the most dangerous words in sports. Doing anything "too" is not a good thing. When your self-identity is overly invested in your sport, you enter what I call the "too zone." You want to care about your sports participation, but you don't want to care too much. You want your sport to be important to you (otherwise, why do it), but you don't want it to be too important. You want to try hard in your efforts, but you don't want to try too hard.

The too zone is a direct result of the five obstacles discussed here—over-investment, perfectionism, fear of failure, expectations, and negativity. It also arises due to a preoccupation with results and self-imposed pressure, as well as pressure from others.

When you enter the too zone, your sports involvement has too big a place in your self-identity and, as a result, shifts from, referring back to chapter 1, a challenge attitude to a threat attitude, the threat being failure. Your reactions when you are in the too zone are, not surprisingly, neither pleasant nor helpful. Your sport stops being fun; you have to take it very seriously to protect yourself from the threat of failure. You overthink in an attempt to feel more in control and reduce the feelings of threat. Your confidence and motivation deteriorate because you don't believe that you can overcome the threat ahead of you. You become physically tense and anxious as your body tries to prepare for the threat.

Overthinking is just one painful reminder that you care way too much, even when you shouldn't.

—Unknown[4]

Life or Death

When you are overly invested in your sport, you turn your participation into a life-or-death encounter. Consider this somewhat disturbing scenario: Imagine you're about to begin a competition and a man approaches you and tells you that if you don't win, he'll be waiting for you afterward to kill you. How would you feel? Well, terrified. And how will you perform? In all likelihood, poorly because you will be incredibly scared. Now, of course, in reality there is no one waiting to kill you at the end of a competition. But, if you are overly invested in your sport, there is someone there who may kill another part of you, namely, your self-identity and, by extension, your self-esteem and your athletic hopes and dreams. That person, most often, is either your parents or you.

Some people think football [soccer] is a matter of life and death . . . I can assure them that it is much more serious than that.

—Bill Shankly, Scottish soccer player and manager[5]

Create a More Balanced Self-Identity

The most direct way to reduce your overinvestment in your sport is to alter the composition of your self-identity. You can do this in two ways. First, you can recognize other important areas of your self-identity that you may pay little attention to, for instance, family member or student, and gain appreciation for those roles. In doing so, you are able to gain greater validation from those aspects of your self-identity. Second, you can actively create new sources of self-identity by seeking out new roles, for example, take up a new hobby, pursue something you've been interested in for a while, or give back to your community. When you develop a more balanced self-identity, you shrink the portion of the pie assumed by your sport, lessening the impact it has on your self-identity. As demonstrated by the pie chart in the figure below, your sport will still play a dominant role in your life, but not to the point that it leads to overinvestment and an unhealthy reaction in pursuing your athletic goals.

Invest in Yourself

When you care deeply about a sport and invest time, effort, and energy into being the best you can be, it can easily lead to overinvestment. You can enter the too zone, and sports can feel like a matter of life or death. Your "survival" as an athlete depends on your ability to improve, get better results, and climb the competitive ladder. If you perform well, you continue to "live" as an athlete; if you perform poorly, you "die" as an athlete.

But, the reality is that sports are not life or death. Regardless of whether you win or lose, or achieve your athletic goals or fall short, you will survive. Of course, you will be disappointed. You will be sad, hurt, angry, and frustrated, and you will think that life is over. But it isn't. In time, you will overcome those feelings, because you will realize that no matter what happens, you will be okay. You will continue on with your life, perhaps go to or finish school, find a career, maybe get married, and have children. You will look back on your sports involvement with fondness and pride, remembering the fun you had, the successes and failures you experienced, and the many life lessons you learned that prepared you to pursue new dreams in other parts of your life.

If you can accept this reality, you will have a game-changing epiphany. You will let go of your overinvestment and be liberated from fear. You will be able to pursue your athletic goals with vigor and without hesitation. As you approach competitions, you will feel more motivated, confident, relaxed, and focused. You will be excited to compete, rather than afraid. You will feel prepared physically, emotionally, and physically. And with this reasonable amount of investment in your sport, you are setting yourself up to succeed and giving yourself a better chance of achieving your goals.

Tip from the Top: Adopt a "F&%# It" Attitude

I want to begin this tip, which has an irreverent and unprintable title, by apologizing for it. I'm not one to use profanity frequently, and, in many instances, it can certainly distract from the message you're trying to send or simply send the wrong message. At the same time, there are times when the statements "Gosh darn it!" or "Drat!" just don't do justice to your emotions. In these cases, some well-placed profanity can, in my view, best express the intensity of what you are feeling and communicate with prism-like clarity what you're trying to say.

Let me begin my explanation of the "f&%# it!" attitude by describing what it is not. This attitude doesn't mean not caring about yourself, other people, your sport, or your life. It doesn't mean not trying your best or giving up. It by no means suggests that you should surrender to the seeming uncontrollability and serendipity of life. And the "f&%# it!" attitude definitely doesn't mean bailing out on your sport or yourself.

To the contrary, the "f&%# it!" attitude enables you to engage more deeply in your sport. It liberates you to do so because, at the heart of the "f&%# it!" attitude, is being able to let go of excessive attachment to the bad consequences that you may believe your sport will cause you to experience. In other words, it means not caring too much about your successes and failures, your emotional highs and lows. The "f&%# it!" attitude involves being absorbed in the experience of your sport and being able to accept and grow from whatever your sport presents to you.

With the "f&%# it!" attitude you give up expectations, both internal and external; self-imposed and outside pressure; and any preoccupation with "what should be" or "what might happen if." You are not driven by fear or doubt, or any other negative thoughts or emotions that can prevent you from engaging yourself fully and without hesitation in your sport. You are able to

EXERCISE

CREATE YOUR SELF-IDENTITY PIE

1. Make a list of everything you can think of that comprises your self-identity.
2. Draw a circle (the pie) and slice it up into the pieces of your self-identity based on your list. The size of each slice should indicate the significance of each role in your self-identity.
3. If you believe that your self-identity is out of balance, make a list of everything you would like to have in your self-identity.
4. Draw a new self-identity pie and slice it up into pieces so that your new pie represents a healthy and balanced self-identity.

throw yourself completely and with absolute vigor into everything you do in your sport because the only thing that could hold you back—failure—is no longer an existential threat, but rather one possible outcome that, should it occur, you can live with.

The "f&%# it!" attitude means that you will embrace every opportunity that your sport presents to you, and at the end of a competition, season, or career, or on your death bed, you will have no regrets because you "left it all out there."

All I ever cared about was skiing as fast as humanly possible.

—Bode Miller, six-time Olympic ski racing medalist[6]

PERFECTIONISM

Perfectionism is one of the most frequent obstacles I see plaguing athletes. Perfectionism is a triple-edged sword (if there is such a thing). One edge of the sword drives perfectionists to be perfect, so they often reach a high level of success. These athletes push themselves to be top competitors and are often straight-A students, out to save the world on the weekends. The second edge of the sword is that striving for perfection is ultimately self-defeating because, as I will soon explain, it interferes with your pursuing your goals with commitment, confidence, and courage. The third edge of the sword is that I have never met a happy perfectionist. They can't be happy because they will never be perfect.

Perfectionism is not a quest for the best. It is the pursuit of the worst in ourselves, the part that tells us that nothing we do will ever be good enough.

—Julia Cameron, artist and writer[7]

What Is Perfectionism?

Perfectionism involves setting impossibly high standards for yourself and striving for goals that you will never, ever achieve. Yet, you believe that anything less than perfection is unacceptable. When you fail to meet those hopelessly high standards, you berate yourself unmercifully for not being perfect. Perfectionists are never satisfied with their efforts no matter how objectively well they perform, and they punish themselves for not achieving perfection. For example, after speaking to a group of elite young athletes, a girl from the audience described to me how she had won a gymnastics event at a national meet but was beating herself up for making two mistakes and not getting the score she wanted.

At the heart of perfectionism lies a threat: If you aren't perfect, bad things will happen to you—most commonly, people will think you are a failure. This threat arises because perfectionistic athletes connect being perfect to their self-esteem; being perfect dictates whether they see themselves as successful and worthy of love and respect. The price these athletes believe they will pay if they are not perfect is immense, and its toll can be truly destructive, resulting in depression, anxiety, eating disorders, substance abuse, and suicide.

By the way, you don't have to be a perfectionist in every part of your life to be considered perfectionistic. You only have to be perfect in areas that you care about. For instance, there are perfectionists in sports who don't care about their schoolwork and have messy rooms.

Perfection and Popular Culture

We live in a culture that reveres perfection. Our culture has elevated success to absurd heights, where being good is no longer good enough. Athletes must now aim for being professionals or Olympians, otherwise their efforts will have been in vain. Additionally, our athletic culture also worships at the altar of physical perfection. Athletes are bombarded by images of perfect athletes with perfect bodies who give perfect performances and never seem to fail.

Perfectionism and Failure

Although it appears that perfectionistic athletes are driven to succeed, their singular motivation in life is actually to avoid failure because they connect failure with feelings of worthlessness and loss of love (more on fear of failure in the section on the topic). Perfectionistic athletes view failure as a voracious beast that stalks them every moment of every day. If these athletes stop for even a moment's rest, they believe they will be devoured by failure, and that is simply unimaginable.

Perfectionists suffer in one of two ways. First, they often do achieve some degree of success because they push themselves to be perfect. But, because they also suffer from a profound fear of failure, they often don't fully realize their ability and achieve true success because they are unwilling to take the risks necessary to be successful. Second, admittedly, some perfectionistic athletes do attain great success, but the price they pay in unhappiness is often significant.

Perfectionism and Emotions

You might think that perfectionistic athletes experience excitement and elation when they achieve their high standards, but those emotions are far too normal for them. Like the emotional reactions to the obstacles discussed here, the strongest emotion perfectionistic athletes can usually muster is relief. Where does the relief come from? They have managed to dodge another bullet of not being perfect and can still feel okay about themselves, but not for long because they are sure to be faced with another perfectionist moment in the near future. When I asked a group of young athletes how long they think the relief lasts, a girl threw up her hand and declared, "Until the next race!"

What emotion would perfectionistic athletes who inevitably fail to meet their impossibly high standards experience? You might think disappointment. But disappointment is a normal and healthy emotion that all athletes feel when they fail, the reaction of which is to increase motivation and effort so they will reduce the chances that they will feel disappointed again. Disappointment is far too healthy and useful an emotion for perfectionists to feel when they fail. Perfectionistic athletes experience devastation after a perceived failure because they perceive it as a personal attack on who they are—successful athletes—and their value as people, since their athletic identity is such a large part of their self-identity (see chapter 5 for more). I say "perceived" failure because, objectively, they may have had a successful performance, for example, making the top 10 or landing on the podium. But what most people would perceive as a success is often viewed as a failure for perfectionistic athletes because their standards of success are so high as to be nearly unattainable.

The experience of devastation for perfectionistic athletes following a perceived failure comes with a veritable tsunami of negative emotions, including hurt, frustration, anger, sadness, humiliation, and shame. Unlike disappointment, which motivates typical athletes, devastation, with its accompanying emotional pain, has the temporary effect of sapping perfectionistic athletes' motivation and confidence. But even this energy-sucking effect doesn't last long, because their need to be perfect kicks back in, and they are back on the treadmill of striving for goals they will never achieve.

Perfectionism is just a high-end, haute couture version of fear . . . just fear in fancy shoes and a mink coat, pretending to be elegant when actually it's just terrified.

—Elizabeth Gilbert, author[8]

Where Does Perfectionism Come From?

After almost every parent talk I've given, a parent has said to me, "I swear that my child was born a perfectionist." This view may make parents feel better as they try to convince themselves that they are not the cause of their young athlete's perfectionism; however, the reality is that there is no scientific evidence that perfectionism is inborn. The research indicates that children learn their perfectionism from their parents, most often from their same-sex parent. Through their parents' words, emotions, and actions, children connect being loved and valued with being perfect. This doesn't mean that there are no inborn influences; some genetic attributes, for instance, temperament, may make children more susceptible to perfectionism. For example, someone who is born emotionally sensitive may be more vulnerable to the subtle cues of perfectionism that their parents, coaches, peers, and culture may communicate to them.

Parents pass on perfectionism to their children in three ways. Some perfectionistic parents raise their children to be perfectionists by actively praising and rewarding success and punishing failure. These parents offer or withdraw their love based on whether their children meet their own perfectionistic expectations. When the children succeed, the parents lavish them with love, attention, and gifts. But when they fail, the parents either withdraw their love and become cold and distant or express strong anger and resentment toward their children. In both cases, the children get the message that if they want their parents' love, they must be perfect. Thankfully, in my years of working with young athletes, I have only come across a few parents who were this overtly perfectionistic.

Other parents unintentionally role model perfectionism for their children. Examples of how perfectionism is communicated by these parents include pushing their children to look "just perfect," have career success, or be competitive in sports and games. Parents even teach their children perfection in how they respond when things don't go their way. Children see how their parents treat themselves when they're not perfect (not well), so they feel they must be perfect so their parents won't treat them the same way. These parents unwittingly communicate to their children that anything less than perfection won't be tolerated.

Then there are the parents who convey perfectionism to their children and are not perfectionists themselves at all; in fact, they are the antithesis of being perfect. But they are going to make darned sure their children are perfect. These parents project their flaws onto their children and try to fix those flaws in their children by giving love when their children are "perfect" and withdrawing love when they are. Unfortunately, instead of creating perfect children and absolving themselves of their own imperfections, they pass them on to their children and stay flawed themselves.

The fastest way to break the cycle of perfectionism and become . . . fearless . . . is to give up the idea of doing it perfectly—indeed to embrace uncertainty and imperfection.

—Arianna Huffington, founder of Huffingtonpost.com[9]

Excellence: The Antidote to Perfection

You should remove the word *perfection* from your vocabulary. It serves no purpose other than to make you miserable. You should replace it with the word *excellence*. I define excellence as doing well most of the time. Excellence incorporates the good aspects of perfection: achievement, high standards, and dislike of failure. Excellence still sets the bar high; it is not average, above average, or even very good—it's excellent. At the same time, excellence leaves out the unhealthy parts of perfection, for example, connecting achievement with self-esteem, absurdly high standards, unrealistic expectations, and risk aversion. And, importantly, it never connects failure with your ability as an athlete or value as a person. Excellence actually encourages you to fail—not repeatedly on the same thing due to a lack of effort, of course—because it understands that without some failure, you won't develop as an athlete and true success won't be possible. In embracing the freedom of excellence rather than the heavy burden of perfectionism, you can turn your gaze away from failure and its associated baggage and toward success and pursue it with unfettered determination and gusto.

Striving for excellence feels wonderful because you're trying your very best. Perfectionism feels terrible because your work is somehow never quite good enough.

—Unknown[10]

Tip from the Top: Let Go of Control

Perfectionists are known for having a high need for control (think control freak). Control provides them with, well, control of everything that influences their efforts at achieving perfection; the more they control, the less chance they will be imperfect or experience failure. It creates feelings of familiarity, predictability, and certainty that help to reduce the anxiety and discomfort they feel with the relentless pursuit of their unattainable goals.

At the same time, there is much in your athletic life that you can't control—weather, conditions, other people—and obsessing about not having that control is unhealthy and dysfunctional. It causes you to lose motivation and confidence because you don't believe you can be successful if everything isn't within your complete control. It causes stress and tension that prevents your body from performing its best. And it leads you to get distracted by things that you can't do anything about. Perfectionists often attempt to reestablish the perception of control and compensate for the discomfort of not being in control by latching on to superstitions and rituals that have no real impact on performance. Although comforting, these superstitions and rituals take time and energy away from focusing on those aspects of preparation that actually improve performance.

Letting go of control is important. To perform your best, you must let go of control in two ways. First, you have to let go of everything in your competitive life that you cannot control. Second, you need to give up conscious control and trust your body to do what you've trained it to do. Most sports require spontaneous and reflexive execution to be successful; there simply isn't time to think through a performance. Also, trying to maintain control of a performance results in overthinking, loss of flow, and a decline in natural coordination and timing.

I'm not saying that you should let go of all control in your athletic life. In fact, some control is healthy and functional. It increases confidence and ensures that you are as prepared as you can be by enabling you to take control of important areas that impact your performance. Appropriate control also enables you to feel relaxed and comfortable, particularly in such high-pressure situations as a big game and during crucial points in a competition. You should have three goals for healthy control of your sports performances. First, control those things that will best prepare you to perform your best. Second, accept and get comfortable with those aspects of a competition you have no control of. Third, let go of conscious control when you are performing and allow your body to do what you've trained it to do.

This last notion of accepting what you can't control is particularly important in performing your best and achieving your athletic goals. Attempting to control the uncontrollable is obviously a fruitless task. It distracts you from what you can control to perform your best. It creates a plethora of negative emotions, including annoyance, frustration, and anger. It causes anxiety and physical tension that not only feel bad, but also interfere with performance.

Accepting that which you can't control isn't about weakness, surrendering, or giving in. In fact, in an odd sort of way, it is a sign of strength where you gain control when you let go of control. When you try to control the uncontrollable, you allow those uncontrollables to control you. Those uncontrollables take control of your mind and body, thoughts, emotions, and actions. You not only fail in your attempts at control, but also, in doing so, lose control of the one thing that you must ultimately maintain control of—yourself.

When you let go of control of what you can't control, you are able to better control yourself. You are more confident and motivated. You are calm and relaxed rather than stressed, anxious, and frustrated. You are able to focus on what you need to do to perform your best. The end result of letting go is true control of your performance, where you are mentally and physically prepared to perform your best.

The irony is that often those that feel the most need for control are themselves the ones being controlled by their own fears, insecurities, and doubts.

—Carlos Felfoldi, psychologist[11]

EXERCISE

EXPLORE YOUR PERFECTIONISM

1. If you rated yourself as a 7 or higher for perfectionism in the Prime Sport Profile at the beginning of this chapter, explore your perfectionism.

   a. List the perfectionistic thoughts you have during training and competitions.

   b. Describe the emotions you feel when you have the perfectionistic thoughts.

   c. Describe how you feel about yourself when you don't live up to your perfectionistic expectations.

2. Explore what it would be like to be excellent instead of perfect.

   a. List the thoughts you would like to have during training and competitions.

   b. Describe the emotions you would like to feel.

   c. Describe how you would like to feel as you strive for excellence in your sport.

FEAR OF FAILURE

Fear of failure is the single most common cause of performance difficulties for the athletes who come to me for help. Whether they experience low confidence, precompetitive anxiety, a preoccupation with results, or severe self-criticism, in most cases, when we dig deep enough, we discover a profound fear of failure at its root. Fear of failure causes athletes to experience debilitating anxiety before they compete in their sport. It causes them to give less than their best effort and avoid taking risks while competing, and after the competition, they feel regret for not performing according to their ability.

The Meaning of Failure

Failure isn't worth fearing. In fact, it's an important part of striving toward our athletic goals. The most successful people in sports—and all walks of life—have failed frequently and monumentally on the way to success. One classic example is basketball great Michael Jordan, who didn't make his junior varsity team. What athletes come to fear is not failure itself, but rather the meaning they attach to failure. At the heart of fear of failure is the belief held by athletes that if they fail in their sport, there will be some sort of bad consequence. The most common fears among athletes are as follows:

- Disappointing their parents (and losing their parents' love)
- Falling out of favor with their friends
- Being ostracized by their peer group
- Experiencing embarrassment, humiliation, or shame
- Being viewed as worthless
- Wasting time on their efforts
- Experiencing the devastation of not achieving their goals

Athletes with a fear of failure perceive failure to be a ravenous beast that pursues them relentlessly and must be avoided at all costs. If it catches them, it will eat and kill them. When they do succeed and avoid the beast, they only experience a small and brief amount of relief because they survived one more day without being eaten by failure. As a result, avoiding failure becomes their singular motivation and goal in life.

Success isn't permanent, and failure isn't fatal.

—Mike Ditka, Super Bowl–winning coach[12]

The Cause of Fear of Failure

Athletes adopt this destructive perspective on failure from the hypercompetitive sports culture, where the constant mantra is, "You gotta win, baby!" This fear of failure is exacerbated by a broader popular culture that makes failure beyond unacceptable. For example, on television and in the movies, the losers—nerds, unattractive people, poor athletes—are teased, bullied, and rejected. With this definition of failure, popular culture has created a culture of fear and avoidance of failure. It has conveyed to people, in general, and athletes, in particular, that if they fail, they will be shunned by their peers and branded as losers for life.

Many parents have also fallen under our culture's spell of failure. They've compounded the harm that failure can inflict on children by becoming overly invested in their children's athletic lives (think Little League parents) to such an extent that their self-esteem becomes dependent on their children's athletic success (see more on this in chapter 6). Many parents also unwittingly connect their own love for and approval of their children to whether their children succeed or fail. The message young athletes often receive from their parents (however unintentionally) is, "I won't love you if you lose," either indirectly through emotional reactions (e.g., anger, frustration, disappointment, embarrassment) or directly through what they say ("Why did you play so poorly?" said with an angry tone). Athletes come to see failure as a threat to their value as people, status within their family, and place in society as a whole.

If these messages from parents persist, athletes internalize them and make them their own. At some point, they no longer need their parents to send those messages. Instead, the young athletes view themselves through the lens of their parents' criticism and send those same messages to themselves in the form of unrelenting judgment and self-criticism.

Failure should be our teacher, not our undertaker. Failure is delay, not defeat. It is a temporary detour, not a dead end. Failure is something we can avoid only by saying nothing, doing nothing, and being nothing.

—Denis Waitley, motivational speaker[13]

Avoiding Failure

If you have a fear of failure, you have learned that you can avoid failure three ways. First, you can simply quit your sport. If you don't play, you can't fail. It's no surprise that between the ages of nine and 13, 70 percent of children drop out of organized sports. The unrelenting pressure to succeed is certainly a contributing factor in this decision. Mysterious and persistent injury or illness, damaged equipment, apparent lack of interest or motivation, and plain refusal to take part are common ways in which you can avoid failure and maintain your personal and social esteem. Yet, choosing not to play is a painful decision because, despite your profound fear of failure, which may drive you to quit, at a deep level, you likely love your sport and your decision to quit can make you feel even worse for not having the strength to continue.

Second, you can avoid the perceived consequences of failure by failing but protecting yourself from the failure by having an excuse—"I would have done well, but my ankle is killing me" or "I would have done just fine, but my opponent cheated." This is called self-defeating behavior or self-sabotage. You guarantee failure, but the excuse protects you because your failures are not your fault; you can't be held responsible, and our culture and your parents and peers must continue to accept and love you.

Third, another way you can avoid failure is to get as far away from it as possible by becoming successful. But if you are driven to avoid failure, you get stuck in limbo between failure and real success—what I call the "safety zone." You are far from failure, so no one can accuse you of being a failure, for example, you finish in the top 10 in your sport but are also frustrated because a part of you knows that you can be truly successful. But to find real success, you must be willing to take risks. The problem with risks, as mentioned in chapter 1, is that they may not pay off and may result in failure. If you are more concerned with avoiding failure than pursuing success, you'll focus on the downsides of risk, and as a result, you will be unwilling to take those risks that are necessary to experience real success.

The Value of Failure

For you to begin the process of letting go of your fear of failure, you must recognize that failure is an inevitable—and essential—part of your sport. It shows you what you did wrong so you can correct the problem in the future. Failure connects your actions with consequences that help you gain ownership of your efforts. Failure teaches you such important life skills as commitment, patience, perseverance, determination, and problem solving. It helps you respond positively to the frustration and disappointment that you will often experience as you pursue your goals. Failure also teaches you humility and appreciation for the opportunities that you're given as an athlete.

Of course, too much failure will discourage you. It will cause you to question your abilities and goals. It will hurt your motivation and confidence. Too much failure can create stress and anxiety, and cause you to focus too much on the results you're not getting. As a consequence, you also need to experience success for its ability to bolster motivation, build confidence, reinforce hard work, and increase enjoyment. As you pursue your athletic goals, you must experience a healthy balance of success and failure to gain the most from your efforts.

I've learned that something constructive comes from every defeat.

—Tom Landry, Super Bowl–winning coach[14]

Not Really a Fear of Failure

As I explored fear of failure in the athletes I have worked with, I was struck by an odd paradox: These athletes have a profound fear of failure, yet they end up doing things that actually cause them to fail by doing something that ensures failure (e.g., having a pessimistic attitude, not being well prepared, or giving up without a fight), even when success is within their reach. I was stumped by this conflict. Why would athletes who fear failure so much do things that guarantee failure?

As outlined in the previous section, self-defeating behavior or self-sabotage protects your self-esteem and how others view you by providing you with an excuse for your failures: "See, it wasn't my fault, so I'm actually still really good and you still have to love me." That excuse allows you to avoid taking responsibility for the failure, protecting you from feeling like a failure. But there are four problems with this unconscious strategy. First, there is no excuse line on the results sheet. Second, even if you have an excuse, you still failed. Third, you caused yourself to fail, which makes you feel even worse. Fourth, no one really cares why you failed; the simple fact is that you did.

This contradiction led me to the conclusion that athletes don't have a fear of failure, but rather they have a fear of *total* failure. I define total failure as giving it your all and not achieving your goals. When I ask athletes if total failure is a good or bad thing, the response is unanimous and emphatic—it is the worst thing. So what is so bad about total failure? If you give everything you have and don't achieve your goals, you have to admit that you simply aren't good enough and there's nothing more you can do. And that realization is difficult to accept for athletes with big goals. For someone with a fear of failure, it is better to fail with an excuse than experience total failure because, as already stated, it allows you to avoid the consequences of total failure (e.g., disappointing others, wasting time, feeling shame) and always leaves open the possibility of succeeding in the future.

Yet, I would argue that total failure is a good (although not ideal) thing because, even though you may not reach your ultimate goal (few athletes actually do), if you did everything you could to achieve it, that's all you can really do. To put this in perspective, I define total success as giving everything you have and achieving your goal. Is total success a good or bad thing? It is a great thing! But total success and total failure have one thing in common: giving everything you've got. So your real goal is to experience "total" something, whether success or failure, because, in either case, you give it your all and what more can you do? If you don't achieve your ultimate goal, will you be disappointed? Of course. But that feeling won't last long. What will endure is the indelible pride and satisfaction you will feel at having given your best effort and performing as well as you possibly could have. Moreover, the simple reality is that giving it everything you have is your only chance to find athletic success. If you don't give your best effort, you have zero chance of being successful.

In sum, to let go of a fear of failure and free yourself to pursue your athletic goals with reservation, you must embrace the following: *"To achieve total success, I must be willing to accept total failure."* By doing so, you will have nothing to fear about failure, and as a result, you will be liberated to pursue total success with unrestrained determination and drive.

Nobody who ever gave his best regretted it.

—George Halas, six-time NFL champion coach[15]

The Real Fear of Failure

I had another epiphany about fear of failure that has taken my understanding of fear of failure to a new level. The real fear is not failure, the meaning you attach to failure, or even total failure. Instead, the real fear of failure is about the fear of experiencing the painful emotions underlying total failure that you think you will feel if you fail. If you have a fear of failure, your efforts are devoted to avoiding the unpleasant emotions that you believe will come with total failure.

So what are these emotions that are so bad you would actually cause yourself to fail (but with an excuse that protects you from these feelings)? They are devastation, depression, frustration, despair, guilt, humiliation, and shame. How's that for a list of emotions to be avoided? But your perception that you will experience these painful feelings is not as likely as you think. In fact, except in rare cases, it has been my experience that athletes do not encounter the level of emotion they believe they will feel after failure. If you experience total failure, you will certainly feel bad. You'll be hurt, sad, and disappointed. But these are far from the crippling emotions you think you will feel. They're not that intense, and, more importantly, they won't last long. If you can accept this truth, your fear of failure will surely diminish.

Nothing to Fear

There are three aspects of this perspective on fear of failure that are particularly unfortunate. First, none of the bad meanings you may attach to failure are completely accurate. Sure, there are misguided (and sometimes downright crazy) parents out there who will be angry and upset (and perhaps even withdraw their love) in the face of their children's failure. But there aren't many, and the chances are that your parents do love you no matter how you perform. Other than that, your friends will still like you, you will not be rejected by your peers, you will still be worthwhile, your time will still be well spent, and you will get over the fact that you may not achieve all your sports goals. In other words, if you fail, you will be disappointed, but you will be okay.

Second, your fear of failure is utterly self-defeating; it does you no good. It creates a win (but not really)–lose situation. You win (again, not really) by protecting yourself from the alleged painful emotions you believe you will experience if you fail. But you lose big time. You don't achieve your goals. You kick yourself for not giving your best effort. And you continue a pattern of thinking, emotions, and behavior that not only hurts your sports, but also may continue to haunt you in every aspect of your life.

Third, if you could just let go of your fear of failure and truly give it your all, that is, perform in your sport with total commitment, confidence, courage, and abandon, chances are you will find some degree of success. How much success depends on many things unrelated to what goes on between your ears. I can't guarantee that you will end up standing on top of the Olympic podium or playing in the MLB All-Star Game, but, as I often say, good things will happen. Moreover, if you risk total failure, contrary to being devastated by those painful emotions you worry about, you might actually feel such wonderful emotions as excitement, joy, pride, and inspiration. Why? Because you gave your fullest effort and left it all out there. Ultimately, that's all you can do.

I fear nothing and I regret less.

—John Cena, professional wrestler[16]

Letting Go of Fear of Failure

An article I wrote about fear of failure prompted a reader to ask the obvious question, "I now understand why my child keeps getting in his own way in his sport. He has a fear of failure! So, what can I do about it?" Let me preface my thoughts by saying that there are entire books devoted to fear of failure and how to overcome it. Also, in severe cases, psychotherapy is required. As with most things in life, there are no magic pills or quick fixes. At the same time, if you (as an athlete) or one of your children (as a parent) has a fear of failure, there are some things you and they can do to relieve the burden and begin to pursue success rather than avoid failure.

Give Your Perceptions a Reality Test

Fear of failure is about the perceptions that you hold about failure and the dire consequences that you believe will occur if you fail. But those perceptions are most likely entirely disconnected from the reality of your life. You may perceive that bad things will happen if you fail, but, in all likelihood, nothing particularly bad, aside from some disappointment, will result from failure.

For example, as noted earlier in this chapter, the main causes of fear of failure include thoughts of disappointing others, being perceived by others as a failure, and having to conclude that your efforts have been a waste of time. Yet, I'm going to argue that none of these things will happen. You can challenge these perceptions by asking your parents and friends if they will be disappointed in you (or, as a result, love you less). You can recognize the wonderful experiences and important life lessons you can learn that will benefit you later in life. I encourage you to give those perceptions a reality test and find out if your fears will really come true (I'm pretty sure they won't).

Your perception of the world around you is not necessarily the same as what is actually occurring.

—Peter Ralston, martial artist[17]

Get Support from Others

Fear of failure is a difficult obstacle to overcome on your own, so enlist family, friends, coaches, and teammates to help you get over the top. Have them encourage you when you get discouraged, challenge your thinking when you get down on yourself, provide levity when things get heavy for you, and give you hope when you don't see any. With people standing behind you, you will feel more confident, stronger, and better prepared to face your fears and pursue your athletic goals.

Be Cautiously Optimistic

If you have a fear of failure, it's hard to be overwhelmingly optimistic ("Everything will turn out great!"), at least not right away. But if you can be cautiously optimistic ("Good things could happen"), you've taken a big step in the right direction. Being cautiously optimistic involves seeing a small ray of hope when you would otherwise see gloom and doom. It means acknowledging that bad things could happen, while also recognizing the many good things that could happen. Cautious optimism means giving yourself a small chance of being successful, which opens the door to more hope, confidence, and even more optimism with every opportunity you give yourself.

Optimism is the faith that leads to achievement. Nothing can be done without hope and confidence.

—Helen Keller, blind and deaf author and activist[18]

Take Risks

As detailed in chapter 1, the very nature of sport is that you cannot perform your best without taking risks. You won't find real success unless you put it on the line. The problem is that when you take risks, you may fail. But, if you don't take risks, you are guaranteed to not perform well, which is the worst kind of failure.

I encourage you to make a commitment to taking risks for two reasons. First, by doing so you will prove to yourself that it's okay to fail. Second, you will show yourself that when you take risks, good things will happen (although not always, of course). You should start small with your risk-taking, for example, in training, where the consequences of failure are minimal, and slowly intensify your risk-taking in more important competitions. In doing so, you will get more comfortable with taking risks and see that the downsides aren't so down and the upsides really are up.

Show me a guy who's afraid to look bad, and I'll show you a guy you can beat every time.

—Lou Brock, MLB Hall of Fame player[19]

Take Your Shot

Taking your shot is inherently risky, but it is far better than never taking your shot. There's a quote from a Michael Jordan poster that goes something like this: "I've missed more than 9,000 shots in my career. I've lost almost 300 games. Twenty-six times I've been trusted to take the game-winning shot and missed. I've failed over and over and over again in my life. And that is why I succeed." Those misses didn't prevent him from continuing to take his shot and hitting far more buzzer beaters than he missed. And there is one simple fact here: If you don't take your shot, you guarantee that you will fail.

The great thing about these steps to overcome fear of failure is that they build on one another. The more you challenge your fear of failure, the more you see that your fear is unfounded and unnecessary. And, as you do so, you will learn two important lessons. First, failure is fleeting, and you will long outlive it. Second, when you let go of your fear of failure, you will perform better and be more successful than ever.

Your goal is to develop a new perspective on failure that takes away the fear. A healthier relationship with failure will free you to strive for success without reservation, take risks, and vigorously pursue your athletic dreams. In time, you will come to know in your heart that some failure is not only okay, but also essential to your athletic efforts, and it is in no way a negative judgment on your athletic goals or a poor reflection on you as an athlete or a person. In fact, your ability to persevere in the face of failure says far more about you than how you respond to success in your sport. If you can develop a healthy relationship with failure, you will be afforded a much better chance of success and satisfaction in your sport.

You can't score a goal if you don't take a shot.

—Johan Cruyff, soccer legend[20]

What Parents Can Do

If you are a young athlete with parents who are involved in your sport, this section is devoted to the influence they have had on your fear of failure and how they can help you let go of your fear. I encourage you to read the following section, as you will find it interesting and enlightening. At the same time, I'm going to speak directly to your parents, so please hand *Train Your Mind* to them and have them read this section if you believe it will help.

A basic tenet of mine about child development is that children become the messages they get the most. What this means is that children weren't born with a fear of failure. Instead, children develop their attitudes toward and beliefs about failure from the world around them. Some of those harmful messages about failure no doubt come from our hypercompetitive sports culture and overly competitive coaches. But, fear of failure in children usually comes from their parents. This happens in three ways.

First, as role models, you may react to your own failures by getting angry or despondent, increasing the chances that your children will develop a similar reaction. Second, you may send direct messages to your children that failure is simply unacceptable ("You better win today!"). And, third, you may have certain emotional reactions when your children don't live up to your expectations, for example, getting angry at them after a poor competition. In these instances, the message you are sending to your children is, "You can't lose or you'll really upset me." The subtext of this statement, which is difficult for parents to believe, is, "If I lose, my parents won't love me." And there is nothing that provokes more fear and hurt in children than that.

This is depressing, to be sure. But here's the good news: If you can send unhealthy messages to your children, you also have the power to send healthy ones. And that is where you can first begin to help your children let go of their fear of failure.

The best way to change your children is to change the world in which they live. In other words, if you can change your messages about failure, your children will receive those new messages and begin to shift how they think and feel about failure.

The following are some practical steps you can take to ensure that your messages about success and failure are healthy:

1. Look in the mirror and get feedback from your spouse about your relationship with failure and how you react to it.
2. Be aware of your emotions the morning of a competition, while your children are competing, and when the competition is over.
3. If you're unable to control your emotions while at competitions, stay home.
4. Identify any unhealthy messages you directly or indirectly send to your children about failure and the situations in which you send them.
5. Specify alternative healthy messages about failure you can begin to send to your children and the situations in which you should send them.
6. Create a plan for what you will say and the emotions you will convey so you're prepared when those situations present themselves. Other practical things you can do include avoiding discussion about results and focusing on the process and having fun. If your children talk about results, either ignore it, redirect the conversation to process and fun, or change the subject entirely (e.g., "What do you want to eat?").

If You Accept Total Failure, Good Things Will Happen

If you can accept the possibility of total failure and realize that, even if it does occur, you will be okay, you remove any threat it might hold over you. When you feel no more threat from the consequences of failure, you will no longer live in fear of it. You will feel as if a great weight has been lifted off of your shoulders and liberated you to perform your best without reservation or hesitation. You will be able to throw yourself into your sport and pursue success with absolute abandon.

This shift will allow you to live by two cardinal rules that are fundamental to athletic success. Rule number one is that, at the end of a competition, season, or life, you shouldn't ask yourself, "I wonder what I could have been?" That may be the saddest question you could ever ask yourself because there are no "do-overs" in life. You want to look back and, win or lose, be able to say, "I left it all out there." And, as I alluded to earlier in this chapter, only by leaving it all out there do you have any chance of fulfilling your goals.

Rule number two is that the one emotion you don't want you to experience is regret. Regret is defined as feeling sorry or disappointed about something that one wishes could be different; a sense of loss or longing for something gone, in other words, "Darn it, I wish I had gone for it!" In the end, you should be able to say, "I gave it everything I had." And you should experience two emotions: pride and fulfillment in having given it your all. If you can follow these two rules, you will find success in your sport and experience a healthy, successful, and happy life.

Fear of Success

A former ski racing teammate of mine sent me a Facebook comment a while back asking, "Is there a phenomenon called fear of success or something like that?" Well, in fact, there is, and it is worth discussing in this section because, in addition to fear of failure, I see fear of success frequently in my work with athletes.

You might ask, "Fear of success? Why would anyone be afraid of becoming successful? Isn't that what everyone wants?" Yet, athletes who feel threatened by achievement often harbor a fear of success. This fear is not based on achieving success itself, but rather on the ramifications of success. On the opposite side of the fear-of-failure coin, fear of success is thought of as the belief that a successful experience will lead to bad consequences, for instance, the pressure to constantly match or exceed previous achievements, unwanted attention and recognition, social and emotional isolation, and a predetermined and fixed future.

In a sense, attaining success "raises the bar" for athletes, creating greater expectations of success and more pressure to succeed. After success, people are naturally going to expect athletes to achieve even greater success more often. Furthermore, success raises the level of achievement that is considered successful. For example, based on your being a consistent top-10 finisher, your expectation of success is a top-10 finish. But if you go on to achieve several top-five results, the expectation of success becomes higher. You can assume that each time you attain a new level of success, you will be expected to reach an even higher level the next time you compete.

With each success and new expectation, the burden can grow, as the higher you climb on the competitive ladder, the more difficult it is to continue that level of success and the farther you have to fall. Fear of success increases because the pyramid of success becomes narrower the closer you get to the top. You see failure as more likely; more disappointing to others; and, ultimately, more threatening to your self-identity, self-esteem, and athletic goals.

Achieving success can also put you in the spotlight, where you may receive more attention from coaches, peers, and perhaps even the media. With this success and added recognition, you now have to deal with your own expectations and those of your family, as well as those of many others. Some athletes may not have a temperament that is suited to being on the center of attention. Athletes who are introverted, shy, insecure, or uncomfortable socially may develop a fear of success because of discomfort with this attention. Fear of success enables them to avoid the spotlight, but, unfortunately, it also keeps them from fully achieving their goals.

Peer acceptance is often important to young athletes, and success can cause them to feel or become separated from their peers. Fear of success may arise from concerns related to jealousy, rivalry, and worries about becoming socially isolated when they beat friends, teammates, and rivals. As a means of avoiding the possibility of being ostracized by their peers, athletes may sabotage their efforts to ensure they remain connected to and accepted by their peers.

Finally, one of the dangers of early success in sports is being pushed onto a future life course to which you may not necessarily aspire. For example, a gymnast may show great promise at a young age and, as a result, be encouraged by her parents and coaches to pursue gymnastics. But her real passion may be music. Showing promise in sports can cause your parents to see a bright future for you in your sport. They may direct your life toward a predetermined future without asking if that is the path you want to follow. And you may be too young to push back and so acquiesce to the pressure. Fear of success may arise from the concern that you will be required to live a life you have little interest in or motivation to pursue. The easiest way for you to circumvent this overly rigid future is to avoid the success that will lead you there.

Everything you want is on the other side of fear.

—Jack Canfield, motivational speaker[21]

Tip from the Top: Remember There's Nothing to Lose

Not long ago, an athlete I worked with told me that after a terrible first half, he ended up having a great game. I asked him why, and he said, "After playing horribly in the first half, I felt like I had nothing to lose." I asked him why he had played so poorly in the first half of the game. He said he was feeling a lot of pressure to play well and was so focused on having a good game that he didn't think about what he needed to do to play well. After the first half, he felt he had no chance of winning and just relaxed and played.

The phrase "nothing to lose" got me thinking about how it relates to fear of failure. For athletes who have a fear of failure, the opposite applies; they perform as if they have "everything to lose." That everything, as mentioned earlier, can include losing the love of their parents, losing friends, being labeled a loser, and experiencing humiliation and shame that will end their athletic dreams.

These perceptions result in a cascade of thoughts and feelings that pretty much doom you to a poor performance and cause you to:

- Maintain an outcome focus (think about the result you want)
- Harbor expectations (feel the need to have a great result)
- Feel pressure (to fulfill your expectations and the expectations of others)
- Overthink (hear unnecessary noise in your head)
- Consider the future (think about what might happen in the competition)
- Feel excessive intensity (feel overly nervous)
- Perform tentatively (act too cautiously)
- Have no fun (find no enjoyment in the experience)

With so much to lose and so many obstacles in the way, you can't help but feel threatened, unmotivated, unconfident, anxious, and unfocused. The inevitable result is tentative, cautious, mistake-ridden performances and the occurrence of the very thing you fear the most: failure.

I got to wondering what the athlete was thinking about and feeling during the second half of the game. By believing he had nothing to lose, he created a tectonic shift in his psychology from the first half that turned his performance around. Most basically, he let go of his fear of failure because he believed he had already failed. In doing so, he shed his expectations and the pressure they produced. He stopped thinking and relinquished conscious control of his performance. The athlete was totally focused on the process and the present with no thought of his poor first half or the ultimate outcome of the game (which he thought he had lost). Importantly, as he described it, he stopped thinking and just let his body do what he had trained it to do. And, even more importantly, he said, unlike in the first half, he actually had fun.

What resulted was a second-half performance entirely opposite of that from the first half. He felt relaxed, yet energized. He played aggressively and took a lot of good risks that paid off. And, not surprisingly, he played really well, enough to turn the game around and win.

Here's a realization that you need to have: You should always perform as if you have nothing to lose. Why? Because the reality is that you really don't have that much to lose. Sure, if you lose, you'll be disappointed, but as I've said before, you'll get over it. If you lose, you will still be a good person, you will still be loved and valued by others, and you will still find success in your life. In other words, if you lose, you will be okay.

The lesson here is perform as if you have nothing to lose every time you walk onto the field, course, court, or what have you. And, ironically, by performing like you have nothing to lose, you are far more likely to find the success you want so much.

Fear the one who has nothing to lose, for they have everything to gain.

—Unknown[22]

EXPECTATIONS

The dictionary defines expectations as a "strong belief that something will happen in the future; a belief that someone will or should achieve something." At first glance, an expectation seems like a good thing because it suggests that someone is capable of fulfilling the expectation and that they or others have confidence in meeting the expectation; however, upon closer examination, expectations can feel more like a burden that actually prevents you from performing your best and achieving the expectation.

First, expectations have a sense of certainty that you will get a particular result. But, as any athlete knows, there is little certainty in sport, where other people (e.g., teammates, competitors, coaches, officials), external factors (e.g., field, course, or court conditions and weather), equipment failure (e.g., a broken bat in baseball, a snapped string in tennis), and the vagaries of luck (e.g., a bad bounce, a brief distraction) can turn expectations on their head.

Second, with that sense of inevitability comes a feeling of already having fulfilled the expectation. Think of it this way: Imagine that you are eight years old and your birthday is coming up in a few months. There is a present you really want, and you tell your parents in no uncertain terms that you want it, creating the expectation that you will get the present. For the several months leading up to your birthday, you think about the item, and in your mind, you already have it. Your birthday arrives and you open your gifts, only to find that you didn't get what you were expecting. How do you feel? Devastated, of course. Why do you feel so bad? It's not because you didn't get what you wanted, but because in your mind and heart you had already gotten the item and your parents ripped it out of your hands. Therein lies one danger of expectations.

Third, there is an implicit threat hidden in every expectation, almost as if there is an invisible "or else," for example, "I expect to win . . . or else I will be terribly embarrassed." An expectation puts you in a position where you feel you must fulfill it or something bad will happen. As a result, expectations create in you a threat attitude.

Finally, expectations are all-or-nothing propositions; there is no gray area. You either fulfill the expectation and succeed or you don't and fail. This means there is only a small opportunity to succeed and a large chance of failure.

If you truly want to realize your dreams, abandon the need for blanket approval. If conforming to everyone's expectations is the number-one goal, you have sacrificed your uniqueness, and therefore your excellence.

—Hope Solo, Olympic and World Cup–winning soccer goalie[23]

Expectations and Emotions

When I ask athletes about expectations, their reactions are pretty much the same. They frown, grimace, and get uncomfortable. They say things like,

"I hate it when people expect things from me" and "When I build up expectations about a competition, I feel totally weighed down." Expectations are powerful and take an emotional toll on athletes. Like the other obstacles I've discussed, expectations produce emotional reactions that cause you to feel bad and usually result in poor performances. Before a competition, expectations create pressure to fulfill the expectations and fear that you won't, creating a threat attitude that hurts you both psychologically and physically, resulting in a poor performance. During a competition, expectations can produce a cautious mindset fueled by fear, a lack of confidence, and an inability to focus. You may perform with tension, tentativeness, and self-consciousness.

Your emotional reaction to your expectations after an event is similar to the one produced by the other obstacles discussed in this chapter. If you somehow produce a good result, your strongest emotional reaction will likely be relief, because you "dodged the bullet" of unmet expectations. When you perform poorly and don't fulfill the expectation, you will experience devastation, because, like the birthday present, the expectation of experiencing success has been ripped out of your hands.

From Expectations to Goals

I hope that I've convinced you that expectations will do you no good as you pursue your athletic goals. But, as noted earlier in this chapter, results do matter in sports, and I simply can't prevent you, as a competitive athlete in a competitive sport in a competitive culture, from thinking about results. So, my challenge is for you to think about results (at least temporarily) but also seek a better alternative to having expectations. Focus on goals, not expectations. Goals might seem little different than expectations, but they are, in fact, completely different animals.

We are actually wired to set goals, and doing so has helped us survive since we were cavepeople 250,000 years ago. Goals have been responsible for many of the great developments that have gotten us to where we are today in modern society. Goals are also deeply rewarding. As I'm sure you have experienced, setting, working toward, and achieving goals provide a sense of immense satisfaction and joy. You feel pride, inspiration, and excitement in putting forth the effort and seeing your effort rewarded. Moreover, unlike expectations and their air of certainty, goals are about the possibility of achievement if you work hard and give your best effort.

One great thing about goals is that they aren't black and white like expectations, but rather about degree of attainment. Not every goal can be achieved, but there will almost always be movement toward a goal, and that progress defines success. Thus, if you give your best effort, there is little chance of failure and great opportunity for success. When I ask athletes about goals, they convey a very different reaction. They perk up and say things like, "It means I decide to do something and want to work really hard to do it."

Here's an example to illustrate the difference between an expectation and a goal. A tennis player has the expectation of making it to the semifinals of a national tournament after getting no farther than the second round in previous years. Or that same player sets a goal of making the semifinals. If she ends up only making it to the quarterfinals, she has failed to meet her expectation; however, even though her goal wasn't fully realized, she still made it farther than ever before, meaning that she succeeded because of the substantial improvement made throughout the years.

The emotional experience of goals is also different from that of expectations. Prior to a competition for which you have set goals, you are motivated and excited to compete because you have a challenge rather than maintaining a threat attitude. After an event, if you succeeded in achieving your goal, you feel elated. If you fail to meet your goal, unlike an expectation, you certainly feel disappointed, but you also feel some pride in knowing that you gave it your all. And you remain hopeful that you can achieve the goal at the next opportunity.

If you accept the expectations of others, especially negative ones, then you never will change the outcome.

—Michael Jordan, basketball legend[24]

From Outcome to Process

So, if you're going to establish an idea related to results, set goals, not expectations. But don't stop there. There's another step that must be taken to further increase your chances of success. Once you have established goals for the results you want, shift from outcome to process and set goals for what you need to do to achieve your outcome goals. Examples include setting goals for being prepared before an event, focusing on a specific technique or a particular strategy, or playing as aggressively as possible.

There are several key elements about process goals that distinguish them from outcome goals. First, if you achieve the process goals, you are likely to achieve the outcome goals because you are more likely to perform well. Second, unlike outcome goals, process goals are entirely within your control, so you have the power to act on them or not. Additionally, because process goals are controllable, you are able to exert control over the quality of your performances and, by extension, the results you pursue.

The great mistake is to anticipate the outcome of the engagement; you ought not to be thinking of whether it ends in victory or defeat. Let nature take its course, and your tools will strike at the right moment.

—Bruce Lee, martial arts legend[25]

Six Phrases That Create Expectations (and Pressure)

Many athletes I work with don't even realize when they place expectations on themselves or hear them from others. This is a problem because if you don't know you're setting expectations for yourself, you can't change them to goals.

There are six phrases I hear from athletes that are cringeworthy because they are red flags: "I must," "I have to," "I need to," "I should," "I better," and "I gotta." Try saying these six phrases out loud and see how you feel. Just saying them causes me to tense up and feel the pressure of expectations on my shoulders. What makes these phrases so unpleasant is that, as mentioned earlier, they are followed by an implicit threat, for example, "I must do well today . . . or something bad is going to happen." What that bad thing is often depends on the meaning you attach to failure (as discussed in the section on fear of failure). But regardless of the specific threat, it feels bad and causes you to perform at a level lower than what you are capable of.

If you become aware that you are using any of these six phrases, you can replace them with much more beneficial alternatives: "I would like to," "It is my goal to," "I am working hard to," "I am directing all of my energy toward," and "I am excited to." Now, try saying these five phrases and see how you feel. When I say them, I feel positive, fired up, and motivated—clearly different reactions.

"Pressure" is a word that is misused in our vocabulary. When you start thinking of pressure, it's because you've started to think of failure.

—Tommy Lasorda, World Series–winning manager[26]

Tip from the Top: Have Confidence, Not Expectations

If you're performing well in training, it's easy to go down the bad road of expectations. You turn performing well into a bad thing by turning your success in training into expectations and pressure for an upcoming competition. You question whether you can maintain your level of performance in competitions and worry that you won't. As strange as it sounds, after a great training period, competing actually triggers a threat attitude. The result is a self-fulfilling prophecy of poor performance in competition.

But it shouldn't be this way. Quite to the contrary, performing well in training shouldn't weigh you down, but rather lift you up. Doing well in training should be a good thing; it means you're on your game and are ready to perform well in competition. It should give you confidence, not create expectations.

As for those comments from family, friends, and others when you've been performing well in training—"I know you're going to win this weekend!" "You're the best!" and "We'll be there to celebrate your victory with you!"— you need to take them for what they really are, not what they seem. They sure sound like expectations that can make you feel bad because you don't want to disappoint the people close to you. But you should reframe them for confidence as well. These words can easily be interpreted as expectations, but that's not what they are intended to be. Rather, they are really expressions of support, encouragement, and confidence in you. The words don't come out well simply because the people speaking them don't know any better.

This different perspective on the relationship between performing well in training and going into a competition triggers a challenge attitude in which you are mentally and physically prepared to continue the training success in competition. You're motivated, confident, intense, focused, and excited to be out there. The result is a self-fulfilling prophecy of good performance in competition.

I am fortunate in that I operate the best under pressure; I always perform above myself when the pressure's the highest.

—Ronda Rousey, mixed martial arts star[27]

CHANGE THE SIX PHRASES

1. Identify the situation in which you use the six phrases "I must," "I have to," "I need to," "I should," "I better," and "I gotta."
2. List the phrases you use most that create expectations and pressure.
3. List positive phrases you can use to replace the pressure phrases.
4. The next time you feel pressure in a competition, use the positive phrases.

NEGATIVITY

The four obstacles that I've just described culminate in an attitude of negativity that permeates every aspect of your sport. With the weight of these obstacles on your shoulders, you will approach everything about your sport, from practice to competitions, from a position of weakness that sets you up for failure. Your thinking will be filled with negativity, doubt, worry, uncertainty, and a lack of confidence. Your emotions will be unpleasant and unhelpful, and include fear, anxiety, frustration, anger, and despair. In training, you will hold yourself back by sabotaging yourself with shortened or skipped practices, failing to give your best, and giving up quickly. In competitions, you will perform cautiously and tentatively because the cloud of negativity won't let you give your best effort or take the risks required to perform well. The almost-certain result of this shroud of negativity will be disappointing performances and results.

That's my gift. I let that negativity roll off me like water off a duck's back. If it's not positive, I didn't hear it.

—George Foreman, former heavyweight boxing champion[28]

Enemy or Ally

Imagine you're performing in an event in which there are 80 competitors, you and 79 others. How many in the field want to beat you? Seventy-nine, of course. The odds are one against 79. Not good odds, to be sure, but the same odds as everyone else. Now imagine you are your own worst enemy in the upcoming competition. You are unmotivated, negative, anxious, unfocused, and uncertain. Now how many want to beat you? Eighty, because you have turned against yourself. And what are your chances of being successful now? Zero against 80—in other words, no chance. This scenario is what happens when the obstacle of negativity gets in your way.

Your goal as you explore negativity is to remove this obstacle (and the other four) and become your own best ally. As your best ally, you are on your own side psychologically, emotionally, and physically. You are determined, confident, fired up, focused, and ready to give your best effort. This state of positivity, in sharp contrast to negativity, provides you with the opportunity and foundation to perform your best and achieve your athletic goals. Quite simply, you are giving yourself the chance to succeed.

You can make this transition from enemy to ally, from negativity to positivity, by taking several steps. First, it's not uncommon for athletes who struggle with negativity and the other obstacles to feel that they deserve to be their own worst enemy because they aren't worthy of being their best ally. But you can't justify treating yourself the way you do with these obstacles. You need to recognize that you deserve to be your best ally, to always be on your side. You deserve to feel good about your sport and perform your best.

Second, remove the obstacles that impact you most. As I have discussed throughout this chapter, this is a simple, but not easy, task. It's simple because why would you be your own worst enemy when you can be your best ally? It's not easy because you may have become really good at being your own worst enemy to the point that it is a deeply ingrained habit. It is difficult, but possible, if you follow the suggestions in this chapter.

Third, make a conscious commitment to being your own best ally and resisting your inner enemy. This deliberate choice makes being your best ally easier because you make it your first option when faced with a situation where you would normally react with negativity.

Finally, the more you become your best ally the easier it gets, for several reasons. One, it feels good being your best ally. Two, you perform better when you are your best ally. As you spend more time acting as your best ally, you retrain your mind to the point where your dark side and being your worst enemy fade into memory.

Weight Vest

Imagine that you are about to begin a competition and someone forces you to put on a 50-pound weight vest. How will you feel and perform? Heavy, sluggish, slow, poorly. When you allow negativity and the other four obstacles to influence how you think, feel, and perform in your sport, you are wearing a metaphorical weight vest that weighs you down. Overinvestment, perfectionism, fear of failure, expectations, and negativity work to weigh you down and make you feel bad and perform poorly.

The great thing is that you have the power to remove the weight vest, because the things that are weighing you down are all in your mind, in the way you look at yourself as an athlete and the world of your sport. Your goal is to shed the weight vest so you can feel unburdened when you compete, so you can throw yourself into competition free from doubt, worry, or hesitation, with commitment, confidence, and courage. How will you feel and perform? Light, free, strong, and well.

A negative thinker sees difficulty in every opportunity. A positive thinker sees an opportunity in every difficulty.

—Chikku George Thomas, author[29]

Tip from the Top: Choose to Fight

The obstacles presented in this chapter cause you to perceive situations as threats to be avoided rather than challenges to be pursued. These threats, to your self-identity rather than your physical life, trigger our most powerful human instinct—the instinct to survive. In turn, the survival instinct elicits the fight-or-flight response, which has been hardwired into us since we climbed out of the primordial muck and, millions of years later, began walking upright.

Our "fight-or-flight" reaction is triggered when we (and all animals) perceive a situation as a threat to our existence; our sympathetic nervous system activates rapid emotional, psychological, and physical changes. Emotionally, we feel either intense fear or intense anger. Psychologically, our senses are heightened, and we're able to make faster decisions. Physically, we get a shot of adrenaline, our heart rate increases, blood flow is diverted to essential parts of the body, and we experience increased strength and stamina. Without these essential changes, our primitive forbearers would have died, their genes wouldn't have been passed on, and we wouldn't be living in the 21st century.

The fight-or-flight reaction served us well for many millennia. Unfortunately, what worked for cavepeople doesn't necessarily work in 21st-century sports. You may ask, Why would a reaction that has helped us survive, first as animals that walked the earth some 300 million years ago, and, later, as Homo sapiens for 250,000 years, fail us now? The answer lies in a change in the meaning of survival and the specific reaction that takes place when the fight-or-flight response is triggered.

Despite the fact that there aren't any saber-tooth tigers or hostile tribespeople roaming the fields, courts, courses, hills, and tracks of modern-day sports, athletes still experience the fight-or-flight response when they compete. How is this possible given that we don't necessarily face life-threatening circumstances when competing in sports (although there are physical risks in some sports that can lead to death, it is relatively rare)? This is so because the survival instinct is elicited, and the fight-or-flight reaction is triggered not by a threat to your physical survival, but by a threat to your athletic survival. Any time your self-identity and self-esteem as an athlete or your athletic goals are threatened (by failure), your survival as an athlete with big goals is in danger. If you don't achieve those goals, a primitive part of you believes you will die. Physical survival, as we typically think of it, means not dying. Athletic survival means continuing to climb the competitive ladder toward your goals.

The problem is that the typical fight-or-flight reaction doesn't work in sports. Imagine you're a caveperson on the Serengeti 250,000 years ago and are confronted by a rival tribesperson with a big club. Your survival is clearly being threatened, and your fight-or-flight reaction is triggered. Now think about which option increases your chances of survival, fight or flight? I would argue that you are more likely to live if you flee, because as long as you keep distance between you and your foe, they can't club you to death. So, because flight has served us well for so long, it has become deeply ingrained in our DNA as the best way to respond to a threat to our survival.

But what worked on the Serengeti doesn't work in the modern-day sports world. Fleeing will not help you survive as an athlete. Yet, that is your first instinct. When I say flight in sports, I don't mean literally run away from the athletic arena in which you are competing. What I mean by flight is losing your motivation, confidence, and aggressiveness, and performing tentatively, cautiously, and timidly. One thing is for sure: If you flee in sports, you lose and will experience death as an athlete.

Your only chance of athletic survival is to fight. To be clear, when I say you need to choose to fight, I don't mean hitting and kicking your opponent (unless, of course, you are a MMA fighter). Instead, I mean making the decision to give your best effort, pursue your goals aggressively, overcome any obstacles or setbacks you may face, and never give up.

Let's be realistic. There are going to be times when you get nervous, which is exactly what your fight-or-flight response is. This reaction might occur before a really important competition, when you have an opportunity for

EXERCISE

LEARN TO FIGHT

1. Move your body to break up the tension and get your blood flowing.
2. Get prepared.
3. Make a conscious commitment to fight before you enter the field of play.
4. Create aggressive imagery.
5. Use aggressive breathing.
6. Get an aggressive mindset.
7. Start the competition aggressively.

success in a big event, or when the spotlight is on you. In those situations, your natural tendency is to flee. Yet, these are the moments when you must choose to fight.

I will fight for it. I will not give up. I will reach my goal. And absolutely nothing will stop me.

—Unknown[30]

3

PrimePrep: Five Approaches to Quality Training

PRIME SPORT PROFILE: TRAINING

Instructions: Rate yourself on a scale of 1 to 10 using the five PrimePrep approaches described here.

Perspective: Having patience, persistence, and perseverance in committing the time and energy necessary to develop yourself fully as an athlete. (1: none; 10: as much as needed)

Train Like You Compete: Bringing the same focus and intensity from competition to your training. (1: not at all; 10: the same)

Consistency: Maintaining consistency in your training efforts. (1: not at all consistent; 10: very consistent)

Experimentation: Getting out of your comfort zone and trying new things. (1: not at all willing; 10: very willing)

Quality: Engaging in the highest-quality training. (1: not at all; 10: total quality)

Some sports use the term *training* to describe their athletic development experience. Runners, triathletes, ski racers, and weight lifters train to develop their abilities. Other sports use the term *practice* to describe what they do. Basketball, baseball, football, and tennis players; golfers, and swimmers go to practice to hone their skills.

In this chapter, I use the terms *training* and *train* to describe what athletes in all sports do because, although some athletes do practice their sport, there are many aspects of their sports development that are better characterized as training, for example, developing strength, stamina, flexibility, and agility. And, hopefully, they also engage in mental training.

If attitudes are part of the foundation of athletic success, then training provides its building blocks. There is little doubt that genes play an indispensable role in how far you progress athletically. (As legendary basketball coach Red Auerbach once said, "You can't teach height.") It is obvious that many sports, for instance, football and gymnastics, require certain genetically endowed attributes, for example, muscle mass and small stature, respectively. At the same time, it is equally clear that effective training is necessary to fully realize whatever genetic capabilities you were born with. For instance, technical training ensures that you possess the finely honed skills required in such sports as golf and tennis. And strength training enables you to become as strong as you are genetically capable of being.

I refer to this process of fully developing areas that impact athletic performance as quality training (as opposed to deliberate practice), and I do so for several reasons. First, the notion of deliberate practice is a goal to achieve, but doesn't provide adequate clarity on how it is accomplished. Dr. Anders Ericsson, who developed the idea, suggests the following criteria for deliberate practice:

- Maintain the motivation to focus on and direct effort toward improving performance.
- Acquire sufficient knowledge of the skill and exercise that will be practiced to ensure understanding and effective implementation.
- Receive immediate feedback about the execution of the skill.
- Exercise consistent repetition of the skill.

Although these standards are necessary for deliberate practice, they are not, in and of themselves, sufficient to engage in quality training. I define quality training as total readiness and consistent effort that results in maximal physical, technical, and mental development, resulting in optimal preparation for competitive success. This chapter explores the specific approaches for accomplishing the four essential goals of quality training:

1. Maximizing the effectiveness and efficiency of training in terms of athletes' committed time and energy.
2. Learning and ingraining physical fitness and technical and tactical skills so they can be performed automatically and consistently during competition.
3. Developing important psychological and emotional attributes and tools that can be transferred to competitive performance.
4. Garnering quality training results in athletes possessing the trained attributes necessary to achieve their competitive goals.

To accomplish these goals, *Train Your Mind* focuses on five key areas of your sport training. Additionally, later chapters identify important mental muscles and tools, for example, intensity, focus, routines, and imagery, that can further enhance the quality of training.

It's not the will to win that matters—everyone has that. It's the will to prepare to win that matters.

—Paul "Bear" Bryant, college football coaching legend[1]

PERSPECTIVE

Perspective, that is, the attitude you hold about training, sets the stage for whether your training efforts are productive and propel you toward your athletic goals or inefficient and impede your progress toward your goals. Your perspective influences three aspects of who you are and what you do, which then impact the quality of your training.

First, it influences your thoughts about training. Are your thoughts about training positive or negative? Are they resolute or halfhearted? Are they hopeful or disheartening? These thoughts about training determine your emotional reactions to your efforts, which translate into the time and energy you devote to your training. Your thoughts act as starting points in your training journey. Obviously, you want to start off on a good road when you begin training because, as a general rule, you stay on the road that you begin on.

Second, how you think about your training triggers emotions that either facilitate or interfere with your efforts. Are you optimistic or anxious? Are you calm or frustrated? Are you determined or despondent? Your emotions directly impact your training in two ways. Such emotions as inspiration, pride, and enthusiasm create an atmosphere in which you want to commit to your training with tenacity and vigor. By contrast, emotions like sadness, despair, and hopelessness set the stage for a lack of motivation, persistence, and perseverance, and cause you to give up easily. Moreover, emotions cause physiological states that influence the quality of your training. Feelings of excitement, energy, and being just plain fired up will have a positive effect on your training. Conversely, feelings of tension, lethargy, and discomfort will lead to training efforts that are minimal or nonexistent.

Third, your thoughts and emotions express themselves in the actions you take in your training. The simple reality of training is that you will get out of it what you put into it. Quality training requires a tremendous commitment of time and energy. It demands time because gaining the necessary benefits of training—physical, technical, and mental—entails massive amounts of repetition, which takes time. It requires energy because quantity of training isn't sufficient to maximize your gains in any area of athletic development. Rather, quality training requires the expenditure of enormous amounts of both physical and mental energy.

Your actions are not only expressed in terms of the time and energy you devote to your training, but also your reactions when it gets difficult.

Another simple reality of training is that it is tiring, painful, and sometimes boring. The thoughts and emotions that you connect to your training will determine what happens when you reach that point in training, what I call the "grind" (discussed in detail in chapter 4). Depending on your thoughts and emotions, you will either ease up, give up, or keep working hard in the face of the challenges.

There may be people that have more talent than you, but there's no excuse for anyone to work harder than you do.

—Derek Jeter, five-time MLB World Series champion with the New York Yankees[2]

The Three Ps of Perspective

Let's be realistic. Training can be incredibly frustrating. Why? Because nothing comes quickly or easily in sports. There are rarely sudden or large improvements in training. Rather, there is the frustratingly slow grind as you get stronger physically, better technically and tactically, and sharper mentally, resulting in better performance in competition. Also, progress isn't steady. You'll improve solidly, and then, all of a sudden, you seem to be going no-where fast. If you're lucky, you'll just plateau for a little while. If you're really unlucky, your performances will seem to go downhill, meaning you actually get worse for a while. In either case, your stagnation is often a mystery that you can't seem to solve. Then, hopefully, just as suddenly, you're back to where you were before, or better.

The slow and unpredictable nature of athletic development demands a healthy perspective on training because, without it, striving toward your sports goals would feel like an impossible journey to take. The foundation of a healthy perspective on training can be summed up with three Ps: patience, persistence, and perseverance.

Patience

Patience is defined as the "capacity to accept or tolerate delay, trouble, or suffering without getting angry or upset." Patience is essential for long-term success because, without it, you would be exasperated with the slow and in-consistent pace of your athletic development. Patience helps you accept and move through the inevitable frustration you feel when you don't progress as quickly as you would like. Patience enables you to stay positive and motivated when your training isn't going the way you want it to. The basic perspective that comes from patience is, "I will do the work and put in the time to achieve my athletic goals."

Persistence

If patience is the fuel you need to keep going in training, you can think of persistence as the engine that drives you forward in every workout and training session. Persistence involves resolute and relentless effort in pursuit of your goals. You will keep working hard for as long as it takes, and you won't give up no matter what happens. Persistence is vital in training because so much of training isn't fun, exciting, or rewarding. To the contrary, it is often tiring, painful, boring, and frustrating. Your ability to push forward every day will determine what you get from your training and whether your training efforts translate into competitive success.

Persistence can change failure into extraordinary achievement.

—Matt Biondi, eight-time Olympic gold medal–winning swimmer[3]

Perseverance

If patience is the fuel and persistence the engine, perseverance is the four-wheel drive and big, heavy-treaded tires that keep you moving onward through the metaphorical rough terrain, ruts, mud, and ice you will experience on the road to your athletic goals. The harsh reality of athletic development is that it is not a linear journey, but rather a series of ups and downs (remember my stock-market metaphor?) where you will experience failures, setbacks, plateaus, and declines along the way. Your willingness to keep slogging along and unwillingness to let the conditions slow or stop you will dictate the gains you make from your training and ultimately how far you make it in your sport.

Tip from the Top: Every Day Is a Good Day of Training

One of the most frequent comments I hear from athletes is, "I had a lousy day of training." This statement is almost always accompanied by a variety of emotions that are neither pleasant nor helpful, including frustration, anger, worry, doubt, disappointment, and, occasionally, despair. Moreover, I see that this statement hurts athletes' motivation, confidence, and focus, and, as a result, their subsequent training and competitive efforts often suffer.

A good training day is easy to identify and always welcome. You perform well technically and tactically. You learn something new that makes you better. You perform consistently, with few mistakes. You are mentally there, feeling motivated, confident, intense, and focused. You have fun while training. Most importantly, you perform really well. A good day of training can get even better when the weather and conditions are good; you're enjoying your teammates; and you're healthy and rested, and life away from your sport is going well too. After training, you're psyched and happy. As the saying goes, "It's all good."

In contrast, a bad training day is easy to recognize but most certainly not welcome. When I ask athletes why they make such a pessimistic assessment of those days, several themes emerge from their most common responses:

- *Bad technique:* "My form was terrible today."
- *Difficulty learning a new skill:* "I tried all day but just couldn't get it."
- *Mistakes:* "I was screwing up constantly."
- *Slow:* "I felt like I was in slow motion."
- *Mental:* "My head just wasn't in it today."
- *Not fun:* "It was a slog getting through the day."

These statements seem to give good cause to the conclusion that they had a lousy day of training. At the same time, I would argue that such a discouraging conclusion is both inaccurate and decidedly unhelpful as you pursue your sports goals. The problem is that this perception is defined too narrowly and actually prevents you from seeing the many benefits you get from a day that you might ordinarily decide was awful.

I believe that *every day is a good day of training.* Some days, the benefits are clear: You make technical, tactical, or performance gains. But other days, you or the conditions conspire to ensure that no matter what you do, good performance just isn't going to happen. Those days are certainly not pleasant, but they are also inevitable. The type of training day you have is determined by how you respond to it.

Let's start with one of my definitions of a bad day of training—when you turn against and give up on yourself. This is the worst kind of training day, and it can only hurt your performance. The great thing about this kind of training day is that it is completely within your control because it's all about how you think about and react to the challenges you face.

On these days, you must broaden your definition of what constitutes a good day of training aside from good technique, tactics, or good play. This narrow definition of a good day ignores another piece of the success puzzle that is essential to ultimately achieving your athletic goals—training your mind. On these so-called bad days, you have an incredible opportunity to become a better athlete by strengthening your mind while everything else feels like it is going the wrong way. You can do this in several ways.

First, I'm not asking you to say, "I'm lovin' it!" about a day when you clearly are not. That's just plain unrealistic given that there are plenty of good reasons why you are not loving it. At the same time, you can't hate it because, if you do, you will probably give up, and your training day will, at best, have been a waste, and, at worst, actually set you back. You need to find a middle ground between the extremes of love and hate. Finding that happy medium means simply accepting and dealing with the day you're having—acknowledging that it's going to be a tough day and deciding that you're going to get the most out of it.

Second, on bad days, it's easy to go to the dark side, meaning you get negative and discouraged, and may even quit. Instead, you can choose to stay positive and motivated, and to keep fighting through the challenges. Training and ingraining this more constructive reaction is important because you're going to have many "bad days" in your sports career, but you can decide whether the Force is going to be with you or you travel to the dark side (*Star Wars* again).

Third, the bad days are really uncomfortable; they don't feel good in any way. Nonetheless, these days are great opportunities for you to get comfortable with being uncomfortable. These experiences are valuable because there is a lot of discomfort in sports. Plus, the only way you're going to progress toward your athletic goals is to get out of your comfort zone. Thus, on these uncomfortable training days, it is important to embrace, rather than give in to, the discomfort until the discomfort becomes comfortable.

Fourth, sports are rife with adversity, including that created by weather, conditions, and tough competitors. Moreover, everyone in the field has to perform in many of the same conditions. Hence, it's not the conditions that matter, but rather how you perceive (threat or challenge) and react to them (fight or give up). Bad days are a great way to figure out how to perform your best (or just survive) in tough conditions. So, when you get to game day and are faced with similar bad conditions, you will have the attitude and tools necessary to respond positively and perform as well as you can (remembering that in terrible conditions, no one is going to feel good or perform their best). In fact, the athletes who minimize the deterioration of their performance on tough days are the ones who are successful despite those conditions.

Fifth, as noted earlier, so-called bad days can trigger a number of unpleasant emotions, for example, frustration and disappointment, which can make bad days even worse. But you have the opportunity to transform those emotions and generate more positive ones, for instance, pride and inspiration, which will help you stay optimistic and motivated during the rough times. Clearly, this "emotional mastery" will serve you well on the day of a competition.

Finally, reinterpreting so-called bad days in a positive way will make you a more resilient and adaptable athlete. Resilience means being able to react positively to the always-present adversity of sports. Adaptability means you're able to adjust to the difficult situation and perform your best given the tough

---

EXERCISE

RATE YOURSELF FOR PATIENCE, PERSISTENCE, AND PERSEVERANCE

1. Rate yourself on a scale of 1 to 10 for patience, persistence, and perseverance.

2. Identify training situations in which you lack the three Ps and describe the thoughts and emotions you experience in those situations.

3. Describe how you would like to think and feel in training related to the three Ps.

4. Set a goal in training of focusing on and improving the three Ps.

conditions. If you can develop resilience and adaptability, you will have a stronger mind in addressing everything that sports (and life) throw at you and give yourself the chance to perform well even on days that might otherwise be seen as bad.

The end result is simple, yet powerful. When you make every day a good day of training, you have fewer ups and downs and more fun, and you perform better and are better prepared for those inevitable "bad days."

You earn your trophies at practice. You pick them up at competitions.

—Unknown[4]

TRAIN LIKE YOU COMPETE

One of the first questions I ask athletes and coaches is, Should you compete like you train or train like you compete? By far, the most frequent response is compete like you train. This answer seems perfectly reasonable if you think about it. When you train, you're relaxed, you feel no pressure, and you are only focused on performing your best. Why wouldn't you want to do that in a competition?

And, in an ideal world, I would agree. But we don't live (or compete) in an ideal world. The reality is that there is one huge difference between training and competition: competition matters! How well you perform in training, for example, whether you win in training, doesn't matter. And the fact that competitions matter brings all sorts of baggage related to harboring expectations, focusing on results, comparing yourself with other athletes, and fearing failure. That's why so many athletes train much better than they compete. And, as we all know, one of the great challenges for athletes is translating their training performance into competitive results. This barrier is also one of the top three reasons why athletes come to me for help.

So, my initial reaction to the seemingly obvious answer that you should compete like you train is that you can't . . . unless. What's the unless? Unless you train like you compete.

One of your most significant goals when you compete should be being as prepared as possible to perform your best. Think about everything you do to prepare for a competition:

- Get a good night's sleep.
- Eat a nutritious precompetitive meal.
- Perform a physical warm-up.
- Execute a sports warm-up.
- Review your technique, tactics, and game plan.
- Follow your precompetitive routine: equipment, physical, mental.

Now, let me introduce you to two essential rules for sports success. These rules make it an absolute requirement that you train like you compete so you can compete like you train. First, whatever you do in competitions, you must first do in training. This too seems obvious, but this basic tenet is often neglected by athletes. Have you ever tried something new on the day of a competition that you've never done in training? Hopefully not, but if you have, it probably didn't work very well for you because if you haven't practiced it in training, there's no way it will work in a competition. If you want to perform technically and tactically well in competitions, you better get that technique and those tactics down in training first. The same holds true for every other aspect of your competitive preparations, whether physical or mental readiness.

Second, whatever you do in training is what you will do in a competition. Ideally, the purpose of training is to develop effective skills and habits that will translate into great performances in competitions. But here's the problem: Athletes often rehearse bad skills and habits in training. For example, if you use bad technique in training (not intentionally, of course), that's what you become good at (you get good at being bad) and that's what comes out in the competition.

Whether you practice good or bad skills and habits doesn't just apply to technique and tactics. It has a huge impact on your mental preparation as well. Here's a common example that drives me absolutely crazy when I work with athletes. As I described earlier, on the day of a competition, you go to elaborate lengths to prepare for your competitive performances. Yet, in training, I see athletes sitting around and chatting it up with their teammates before training rather than getting physically and mentally ready. These athletes are developing the habit of performing at about 70 percent focus and intensity. So what happens in competitions? They either compete at 70 percent focus and intensity or try to kick it up to 100 percent focus and intensity; however, their mind and body explode because they're not used to performing at that level.

Think about what you do in competitions to get ready, and do the same things in training. For instance, do a good physical warm-up, review your tactics, get your body moving, and do mental imagery. You don't have to go through a lengthy routine, but you should shrink it down to a one- to two-minute version of your precompetitive routine (more on routines in chapter 5).

Let's return to my original question: Should you compete like you train or train like you compete? My answer is a resounding "YES!" You should train like you compete so you can compete like you train. The more you can make training like a competition, the more you will ingrain in your mind and body the skills and habits you need to perform your best in competition, the ultimate goal of which is for your mind and body to automatically do what you do in training so you can perform at your highest level.

For me, winning isn't something that happens suddenly on the field when the whistle blows and the crowds roar. Winning is something that builds physically and mentally every day that you train and every night that you dream.

—Emmitt Smith, Super Bowl champion[5]

Tip from the Top: Fight from Start to Finish

When you compete in sports, the clock starts when the starter's gun goes off or the referee blows the whistle. But you wouldn't know it by the way many athletes approach the beginning of training. I regularly see young athletes ease into training by cruising through the first few drills or exercises to save energy and then ramping up their effort near the end of training. This habit of working their way into training is related to intensity. Sports require intensity and focus, as well as a "bring it" mindset. If you don't have this from the moment training begins, your mind and body won't be ready when they need to be, which will hurt you in competition because there's no place for easing into things when it really counts. You've got to be "all in" from the start of a competition.

To ensure that you're ready to give it everything you've got before you begin each phase of training, there are three things you need to do. First, get your intensity to the ideal level for the type of training you're doing. For example, if you're a swimmer doing stretching, you'll want to lower your intensity to foster a state of relaxation. If you're a soccer player doing footwork drills, you'll want your intensity at a moderate level to balance the physical and technical demands of the drill. And if you're a discus thrower doing squats, you'll want to raise your intensity so you can generate the most power in your lift.

Second, you want to ensure an ideal focus before you begin your training. Your focus may be on something technical or tactical, or on aggressiveness or consistency in your performance. For instance, you might focus on your spins if you're a figure skater or your receiver's routes if you're a football quarterback.

Finally, you'll want to create an ideal mindset with mental imagery and specific thoughts just before you begin to train (more on these three areas in chapters 4 and 5). The result is that you will be totally prepared at the start of your training efforts, enabling you to get the most out of them.

You have to not only start strong, but also finish strong. In addition to working their way into training, I see many athletes ease up before a drill, exercise, or practice session actually ends. This is another habit that drives me crazy. As with cruising at the start of practice, athletes are training their bodies to let up before they are really finished. How often have you seen an athlete having a good competition and then, with the end in sight, making a big mistake that costs them a victory or good result? This usually occurs because athletes think they're finished and lose focus and intensity, and stop trying. But, just as the clock starts at the beginning of a competition, it stops when athletes cross the finish line, so you need to make sure that you are focused and intense all the way to the finish. In training, always go hard until you cross the line or the coach blows the whistle.

Giving up without a fight is my number-one pet peeve when it comes to training. So many athletes have difficulties in training and just give up. It's a terrible habit. If you get used to giving up at the smallest setback in training, that is the pattern your mind and body will follow in competition. There are usually some deeper psychological issues at play here that cause athletes to give up at the slightest mistake or setback, notably perfectionism and fear of failure (refer back to chapter 2 for more). The bottom line is that when you bail out of a drill, exercise, or other training performance, one thing happens 100 percent of the time: you fail. And a failure of effort is the worst kind of preparation for competition.

You want to create the habit of fighting through all aspects of training. Of course, there will be times when you can't finish the drill because you're going all out. Those "failures" are the good kind because you are pushing yourself outside of your comfort zone. Learning to never give up after a mistake will serve you well in competition, where even the best athletes make mistakes, but they get right back in and fight to the finish.

If I can go as hard as I can in practice, make sure it's a lot harder than a fight, then the fight's going to be easy.

—Rashad Evans, MMA champion[6]

EXERCISE

EXAMINE YOUR PREPARATION

1. Describe your preparation.

   a. Before you compete.

   b. Before each segment of your training.

2. Identify the differences between the way you prepare to train and how you prepare to compete.

3. Make a list of what you need to do to be totally prepared before each training effort.

CONSISTENCY

Consistency is one of the hallmarks of great athletes, whether it's Serena Williams, Peyton Manning, LeBron James, or Simone Biles. They have demonstrated the ability to perform at an incredibly high level day in and day out, week in and week out, month in and month out, and year in and year out. It's not that other equally talented and hard-working athletes can't have great performances. Rather, it's that they can't perform exceptionally on a regular basis.

Given the obvious value of consistency in sports, the inevitable question that follows is, how do these athletes become so consistent? I would argue that competitive consistency is a direct result of consistency in their training and other important aspects of their preparations and life.

I can't remember the last day I didn't train.

—Michael Phelps, 22-time Olympic swimming champion[7]

Consistent Effort

There are three areas of athlete preparation that require consistent effort for quality training to result: physical conditioning, technique/tactics, and mental training. The notion of consistent effort in training can be expressed in several ways. First, it involves consistency in every area of training that impacts competitive performance. It's not uncommon for athletes to be consistent in some aspects of their training, most often those areas that they enjoy the most and are best at, but less consistent in other areas, generally those that aren't that fun or that they struggle with. For example, one athlete can be consistent in her on-field training but lack consistency in her conditioning efforts because she doesn't like going to the weight room. Mental training often lacks the consistency necessary to gain its benefits.

Second, you must exhibit consistency of commitment, which means putting in the required time on a regular basis. It is important that athletes have a well-structured training program that ensures they are doing the necessary work. It means showing up on time for training and finishing the training session.

Third, consistency in training involves consistency in the focus and intensity you bring to your efforts. It is key that athletes work hard in training session from start to finish. It also means doing everything that is expected of you as fully and as well as you can (in other words, with the utmost quality).

In baseball, my theory is to strive for consistency, not to worry about the numbers. If you dwell on statistics you get shortsighted, if you aim for consistency, the numbers will be there at the end.

—Tom Seaver, three-time MLB Cy Young Award winner[8]

Consistent Life

I believe that there is no distinction between you as an athlete and you as a person. Who you are as a person impacts you as an athlete. Additionally, when you walk onto the field of play as an athlete, you take your "personness" with you. My point here is that there is no line between life on the field (court, course, hill, or track) and life off the field. Your life off the field should not impact your performance on the field.

This idea is important because it suggests that for you to be consistent in your training and competitive efforts, you must begin by living a consistent life. There are four aspects of life that are most in need of consistency to support consistency on the field of play. First, you must have consistent eating habits. Because we are physical beings, what you eat has a tremendous influence on your athletic life. Your ability to consistently fuel yourself effectively and avoid food that will not optimally prepare you for performance is crucial to consistent training efforts. If your sport is a priority in your life, a consistently healthy diet that minimizes junk food is warranted.

Second, your sleep habits play an essential role in the consistency and quality of your training. Extensive research has demonstrated the effect that sleep—or lack thereof—has on the body physically, mentally, and emotionally. Despite this clear importance, an abundance of evidence shows that most people, including athletes, don't get enough sleep. The reasons for this sleep deprivation include daily stress, too much homework, overscheduling, and an excessive absorption in technology and social media. Getting good, consistent sleep takes commitment and discipline because there are so many forces pulling you away from getting enough rest. Yet, again, if you prioritize your sport, it is instrumental that you make healthy sleep choices.

Third, if you're a young athlete, chances are school is the most time-consuming activity in your life. Going to school, doing homework, and studying for exams are physically demanding, mentally taxing, and emotionally draining tasks, and they will impact your athletic life. Your ability to manage your school life consistently will pay dividends in terms of lack of stress, ability to focus, and general well-being in both your training and competitive efforts. Consistent school habits include having good study habits, preparing for exams in a timely manner, completing projects on time, not having school responsibilities hanging over your head when training and especially when competing, and generally keeping up with your school responsibilities.

Lastly, your relationships with family, friends, teammates, or coaches will have an obvious effect on your athletic life. Relationships can be affirming, calming, and pleasurable. Or they can be stressful, turbulent, and distracting. The quality and consistency of your relationships can cause you to feel cared for, safe, comfortable, and supported or insecure, anxious, and vulnerable. As with the previous aspects of your off-field life that impact your athletic life, you should ensure that your relationships support your training and competitive efforts.

Consistent Mind

Not surprisingly, given the topic of *Train Your Mind*, having a consistent mind is another essential piece of the consistency puzzle. In fact, this book is devoted to creating in you a consistent set of attitudes, mental muscles, and mental tools that will set the stage for consistent training and competitive performances.

Consistent attitudes act as the foundation for consistently excellent athletic performance in both training and competitions. They include ownership, process, challenge, long-term, and risk (refer back to chapter 1 for more details). You gain consistency in adopting and embracing these attitudes by understanding them, seeing the role they play in your life, and making relevant attitude shifts in a healthy direction. You can further support these attitudes by removing the obstacles described in chapter 2 (overinvestment, perfectionism, fear of failure, expectations, and negativity), which often prevent healthy attitudes from dominating your mental and emotional life.

Consistent mental muscles (to be examined in depth in chapter 4) include motivation, confidence, intensity, focus, and mindset. As with physical muscles, the only way to develop strong mental muscles and avoid injuring them is to commit to a consistent mental training program designed to maximally strengthen them.

Mental tools (also detailed in chapter 4) that can be used to strengthen your mental muscles consist of emotions, imagery, routines, breathing, and trust. Much like an auto mechanic had to learn to use tools to tune and repair cars, the only way for you to develop skill and comfort with the mental tools and for the tools to provide maximum value to you is to get instruction on their use and then use them a lot. By taking this approach, you learn how the tools work, when to use them, and how to get the most out of them in your training and competitive efforts.

Consistent Preparation

The final aspect of consistency that propels the world's best athletes to the top of their sport and keeps them there is consistent preparation. Whether they are preparing themselves physically or mentally, readying their equipment, or prepping with their coaches and teammates, the best athletes in the world are meticulous and unwavering in every area that can impact their training and competitive performances. Of particular note is their attention to detail in their training efforts.

Just about every athlete who aspires to personal greatness does a good job of preparing for a competition. Why? Because they know that being well prepared is an important factor in their competitive success. But sometimes you will find athletes whose training preparations are irregular at best and nonexistent at worst. The best athletes in the world have well-defined training routines (more on this in chapter 5) that ensure total preparation before every training performance. This fastidious approach helps them ingrain the best physical, technical, and mental skills and habits to better prepare them to get the most out of their training efforts, with the goal of those skills and habits translating into competitive success.

The hardest part of training is doing these workouts day after day after day. In other words: consistency. Doing a hard workout once brings small benefits. But being able to do hard workouts consistently month after month, in short, yields results.

—Charisa Wernick, professional triathlete[9]

Tip from the Top: Three Levels of Preparation

Consistency in training can have a big impact on preparation and performance at three levels: meta preparation, macro preparation, and micro preparation. Meta preparation refers to the accumulation of physical fitness, technical and tactical capabilities, and mental competencies that occurs during years of commitment to a sport. The world's best athletes became great by not only having inborn talent, but also amassing hours upon hours, days upon days, weeks upon weeks, months upon months, and years upon years of consistent, high-quality training. Years of comprehensive and consistent preparation have endowed them with a wide range of abilities, skill sets, and tools to achieve competitive success.

Macro preparation involves near-term preparation in the weeks leading up to the competition. This phase of readiness involves fine-tuning technical and tactical skills, a deescalation of conditioning intensity and attention to recovery, an increase in rest and sleep, an emphasis on healthy eating, and mental training that focuses on performance on the day of the competition. Consistent application of these strategies as game day approaches further prepares athletes to perform their best.

Micro preparation relates to your final preparations on the day of the competition. This is when you make final adjustments and channel your efforts into a laser beam of physical and mental readiness. As I will discuss further in chapter 5, your willingness to create and implement consistent precompetitive routines and habits will have a dramatic impact on your ability to perform at a consistently high level in competition. Your micro preparations on the day of the event may include, depending on your sport and start time, a morning warm-up, a precompetitive meal, a planning or strategy session with

EXERCISE

EVALUATE YOUR CONSISTENCY

1. Describe what makes you either consistent or inconsistent in the four areas of training:

   a. Effort

   b. Life

   c. Mind

   d. Preparation

2. Identify specific steps you can take to become more consistent in the areas where you found inconsistencies.

coaches and teammates, an equipment check and fine-tuning, inspection of the competitive venue, and mental preparations.

You have several goals in focusing on these three levels of preparation. First, ensuring consistency in your training and preparations early in your athletic career and during the offseason will help you establish a solid foundation of quality fitness, skills, and habits. Second, as a competition approaches, narrowing your efforts will move you a step closer to competitive readiness. Third, on the day of the competition, by carrying out your final preparations, you will feel ready to perform your best.

We are what we repeatedly do. Excellence, then, is not an act, but a habit.

—Aristotle, Greek philosopher[10]

EXPERIMENTATION

There is no instruction manual for becoming the best athlete you can be. There is no clear path to your goals. Certainly, there are established ways of training—both on and off the field of play—that have been proven generally effective in helping athletes develop and improve. At the same time, because athletes differ in many ways, simply applying a cookie-cutter approach to your athletic development is probably not the best path to your goals. In fact, it is often the innovative and "out there" approaches to training that enable athletes to take the next leap forward in their development.

Because of your uniqueness as an athlete and the ever-evolving nature of sport training, you must be open and motivated to try new things, whether physically, technically, tactically, mentally, or with your equipment. Only through experimentation will you find the precise mixture that works best for you and will allow you to perform at your highest level.

The problem is that experimentation is difficult. You're not always sure what to try. The changes you make don't always render immediate results. Your performance can decline temporarily. And you never know whether the experimentation is going to pay off with a significant increase in performance. But, if you want to become the best athlete you can be, experiment you must. As quoted in chapter 1, "If all you ever do is all you've ever done, then all you'll ever get is all you've ever got."

Close the Gap

Try this exercise: Hold your right hand open just to the right of your face, like a hatchet you are about to cut wood with. Hold your left hand in the same manner but to the left of your face. Your right hand represents how well you are capable of performing. Your left hand signifies how you are performing now. The space between your hands represents how far you have to go from where you are now to reach what you believe you can accomplish as an athlete. Slowly begin to move your left hand toward your right hand. Stop your left hand when you believe that the gap is representative of where you are now as an athlete and where you believe you can be. Your goal is to close that gap so that where you are is where you want to be.

The only way to close the gap is to constantly look for new ways to improve and push your limits—in other words, to be in a state of constant experimentation. Identify the areas in which you need to work to close the gap—physical, technical/tactical, mental, equipment, life—and make a conscious commitment to try new things and push the limits of what you are capable of. Closing the gap requires that you create and act on every opportunity you have to improve and grow as an athlete.

The willingness to experiment with change may be the most essential ingredient to success at anything.

—Pat Summitt, college basketball coaching legend[11]

Get Out of Your Comfort Zone

Here's another simple reality of sports: If you're not uncomfortable, you aren't challenging yourself, trying new things, or improving. Yet, people in general don't like to get uncomfortable, as, well, it's uncomfortable. In fact, humans are wired to avoid discomfort because when we were cavepeople, feelings of discomfort usually signaled a threat to our survival. Moreover, it just doesn't feel good. And doing what's uncomfortable often doesn't work at first. So, better to play it safe and stay comfortable, right? Wrong, because, as that Texas saying suggests, you'll never get better, and you'll never achieve your athletic goals.

The fact is that athletes associate being out of their comfort zone with feeling bad. It doesn't feel right physically or emotionally, which causes you to approach what you're doing with a negative attitude. This turn to the dark side hurts your motivation, confidence, and focus. The result is that something that started out as positive, namely, doing something to improve, turns negative. The tendency then is to avoid experimentation and return to your comfort zone. Of course, the problem is that you don't get better.

As you begin to experiment, you must change your attitude toward discomfort: It's good to feel bad! Feeling "bad" means that you are doing something different and getting out of your comfort zone. It means you're developing and improving as an athlete. And that's a good thing.

The truly powerful thing about making it a priority to get out of your comfort zone is that, as you spend more time being uncomfortable, your comfort zone grows. Through constant experimentation, what was once beyond the limits of your comfort zone becomes part of a larger and ever-expanding zone. You engage in an ongoing process of stepping outside of your comfort zone, expanding it, and stepping outside again and again. The result is a constant experience of improvement and progress toward your athletic goals.

Move out of your comfort zone. You can only grow if you are willing to feel awkward and uncomfortable when you try something new.

—Brian Tracy, motivational speaker[12]

Go to Extremes

One interesting way to experiment involves what I call "going to extremes." Our minds and bodies have evolved to be sensitive to such contrasts as hot and cold, light and dark, hard and soft. This awareness enabled primitive humans to be able to quickly judge changes in their environment that might signal a threat to their survival. The following is a modern-day example of this notion of contrasts. What do you notice when you first get into a hot tub? It's hot, of course. But what do you notice when you've been in a hot tub for a while? You no longer feel the extreme hotness of the water because your body has adapted to the heat.

With many aspects of sports training, whether physical, technical, or mental, there is a continuum between two extremes, and you perform somewhere along this continuum. Experimenting with different positions on this continuum, from one extreme to another, is one way to improve the quality of your training. Experimenting with extremes can be used in your physical conditioning efforts to see how you can give maximal effort. You can use it for your technical work to better understand, within the range of a particular body position or movement, what enables you to perform better. And you can use experimenting with extremes as part of your mental training, for instance, in identifying your ideal focus, intensity, or mindset (more on this in chapter 4).

To illustrate the use of extremes in training, let's say you are a baseball player trying to figure out your ideal balance for your stance in the batter's box. You can experiment with three different stances: weight far forward, weight equally distributed, and weight far back. During batting practice, you can take, say, 10 cuts with each stance and see how it affects your swing and contact with the ball. This sort of experimentation offers several benefits. First, it increases your awareness in the area you are working on. Second, you can see how different points of the continuum impact what you are working on. Third, you can identify where on the continuum you got the best result in terms of improved performance.

Bad versus Good Mistakes

One of the most common reasons why athletes don't like to experiment is because they will inevitably make mistakes, struggle in their training, and, yes, experience failure. But, as discussed in chapter 2, failure is an essential part of improving and progressing toward your goals. Here's another one of those simple realities of sport: If you're not making mistakes in training, you're not getting out of your comfort zone or developing as an athlete.

I make a distinction between good mistakes and bad mistakes. Bad mistakes are those you make because you are not fully committed or because you're playing it safe or giving up too easily. There is never a place in training for bad mistakes for several reasons. They prevent you from experimenting and getting out of your comfort zone. They result in poor quality training. And they create shoddy physical and mental habits that will not be effective in competition.

By contrast, good mistakes occur because you are challenging yourself and trying new things. Oftentimes, when you are first working on something new, for example, a new technique in your training, you not only take some time to learn the new technique, but also your focus on it causes you to make mistakes in your overall training performance. These mistakes are not bad. Rather, they are good because they indicate experimentation and movement out of your comfort zone. You should be happy when you make mistakes for this reason.

When you are making mistakes, as noted in the section on the three Ps, it's easy to get frustrated and want to give up. But if you can reorient your attitude to see these errors as good, they will have a different mental and emotional effect on you. You will accomplish those three Ps—patience, persistence, and perseverance—when training. You will stay motivated and calm. You will get inspired, rather than discouraged, by your mistakes. Believe it or not, you will want to make more mistakes once you are able to adopt a positive attitude toward them.

People don't want to do new things if they think they're going to be bad at them or people are going to laugh at them. You have to be willing to subject yourself to failure, to be bad, to fall on your head and do it again, and try stuff that you've never done in order to be the best you can be.

—Laird Hamilton, big-wave surfer[13]

Tip from the Top: Choose to Experiment Every Day

You want to make experimentation something you do each and every day, not periodically or when you think it will be helpful. You also want experimentation to be something you're comfortable with, not an uncomfortable experience that is looked upon with dread and aversion. You want it to be a regular and ingrained part of your overall training regimen and something you do on a daily basis to advance your development as an athlete. And, importantly, you want experimentation to be something you pursue with confidence and even excitement at the possibilities it will create in your athletic development.

One way to accomplish the goals of integrating experimentation into your training program and getting comfortable with it is to make a commitment to incorporating experimentation into your daily training schedule and life. In other words, you want to make experimentation your default in all aspects of your training.

The way to do this is to include experimentation in your weekly and daily training efforts. When you sit down at the beginning of each week and plan out your training schedule, you can identify and include one bit of experimentation in your planning. For example, during a strength session on Thursday, you're going to go for a new personal record in your squats workout. Or if you're a tennis player who prefers to stay on the baseline, you're going to serve and volley at least twice each game in a practice match. You can also make experimentation part of your daily life by, for instance, asking someone out on a date or speaking up in class.

Because experimentation may be new and uncomfortable to you, if you just make a general commitment to it (trying something new for the week), you will probably either forget to experiment or consciously decide not to because it is uncomfortable. By putting a specific act of experimentation in your training calendar and seeing it when you arrive at training, you are more likely to remember and less likely to avoid it. At first, you will have to be deliberate about this process because it is new and different. But, as you

EXERCISE

GET OUT OF YOUR COMFORT ZONE

1. Choose an area in your sport training in which you don't like to experiment and get uncomfortable.

2. Ask yourself why you like to stay in your comfort zone.

    a. Describe why staying in your comfort zone limits your development.

    b. Consider what thoughts and emotions arise when you think about leaving your comfort zone.

3. Describe the benefits of getting out of your comfort zone.

    a. Indicate what thoughts and emotions will help you experiment.

4. Schedule a time in your weekly training calendar in which you will commit to experimenting and getting out of your comfort zone.

experiment more and more, and become increasingly comfortable with it, experimentation will become more ingrained in your training habits until you find yourself experimenting and improving faster and better, without even thinking about it.

Life begins at the end of your comfort zone, so do one thing every day that scares you.

—Unknown[14]

QUALITY

Despite what many athletes and coaches believe, competitions aren't won on the day of the competition, just before the competition, or even during the competition. Rather, they are won in training in the weeks and months leading up to the event. What you do in training will determine how you perform and the outcome of the competition. Training is where you establish the physical, technical, tactical, and mental requirements of sport.

Too often, I see athletes begin training without a clear idea of what they're doing there. They have nothing in particular they're trying to improve. When this happens, athletes are not only not improving, but also making it more difficult to improve because they're further ingraining old and ineffective skills, making it harder to learn new ones.

Despite this importance, I'm constantly amazed by the poor quality of training I see athletes engage in, even at the world-class and professional levels. I see unclear intention, limited effort, ineffective focus, and little intensity. Yet, these athletes expect to perform their best in competition. That's unlikely to happen because they're not engaging in quality training, which involves maintaining the highest level of intention, effort, focus, and intensity consistently throughout a session. There are a number of strategies you can use to help you engage in quality training.

Take every practice, every game, like it's your last.

—Kobe Bryant, five-time NBA champion[15]

Goal and Purpose

You must always train with a goal and a purpose. The goal should involve an aspect of your sport you want to improve. It might be physical, technical, tactical, mental, or related to overall performance. For example, a figure skater's goal might be to improve the elevation of her jumps.

A purpose is something specific you work on in training that will enable you to achieve your goal. Using the figure skater example, her purpose might be to do six sets of plyometric exercises every other day to increase power and, in her on-ice training, emphasize explosiveness on her takeoffs. Or if a tennis player's goal is to improve his confidence, his purpose might be to use more positive body language between points.

Focus and Intensity

Another area most athletes need to work on is their focus and intensity in training. When I talk about focus and intensity, I mean being totally focused on the task at hand and being at a level of physical activation that enables your body to perform its best (more on both of these mental muscles in chapter 4). Your goal in competition is to be at your ideal level of focus and intensity.

The problem is that, too often, I see athletes training with a level of focus and intensity that is much different from the level they need to maintain during competition. When they're training, they may be at a level of 70 percent focus and intensity. In simulated competitions, for instance, in basketball scrimmages or practice rounds in golf, they may up their focus and intensity to 80 percent. Yet, when they get to a competition, they want to perform at 100 percent. But when they try to get to 100 percent, one of two things happens. Because they've been training at 70 to 80 percent focus and intensity, that's what comes out in the competition, the result of which is subpar performance. Or they try to ramp it up to 100 percent focus and intensity. But because they haven't trained at that level, their performance actually gets worse rather than better since their bodies and minds aren't accustomed to it. In either case, the result is failing to perform your best.

One objective is to have a specific focus for every training situation you are in. You determine this ideal focus by looking at your goal and purpose for the training session. If your goal and purpose relate to something you are working on technically, your focus should be on fulfilling that goal and purpose. For example, if you're a soccer player who has the tendency to lift your head on penalty kicks, resulting in the ball assuming a high trajectory and sailing over the goal posts, your goal should be to improve the arc of your penalty kicks. Your purpose would be to keep your head down as you approach and make contact with the ball. Your focus might include using imagery to see and feel proper execution before you practice your penalty kicks and developing a keyword, like "down," that you can repeat to yourself as you approach the ball and execute a kick (more on specific focusing tools in chapter 4). This gives you 100 percent focus during training to ensure that you are paying attention to aspects of your sport that will result in maximum improvement and better overall performance.

Another objective is to be at your ideal intensity in every training situation you are in. As I discuss in greater detail in chapter 4, intensity refers to the level of physical activation you feel when you perform in your sport. Because we are fundamentally physical beings, your level of intensity will have a direct impact on the quality of your training efforts and, ultimately, the quality of your competitive performance. Depending on what you are working on in your training, you will want to reach and maintain levels of intensity that might be low, medium, or high. For example, if you are stretching, you want to create a relaxed intensity. If you are performing technical aspects of your sport, you want to be at a moderate level of intensity. And if you are scrimmaging, you want to be at your ideal level of competitive intensity. You can use a variety of tools to achieve your ideal intensity, including breathing, muscle relaxation, body language, and self-talk (more on specific intensity tools in chapter 4).

By being constantly aware of your focus and intensity, and training regularly at your ideal focus and intensity, you gain several benefits. First, you ensure consistently high quality in your training efforts and reap rewards in terms of improvement and preparation for competition. Second, you ingrain that ideal focus and intensity, giving you the ability to access them as you ready yourself for competition. Third, you will be better equipped to maintain and regain that focus and intensity when you are competing.

First, you will practice mindfully and continue to improve and grow. Then, you will perfect technique and execute it unconsciously and effortlessly. Eventually, you will master it to the point where it'll be like you're watching yourself execute it as if you were a spectator of your own life.

—Georges St-Pierre, mixed martial arts champion[16]

Train for Adversity

An essential skill you need to develop to perform your best in competition is the ability to respond positively to adversity. Athletes love to train in ideal conditions, but conditions are rarely perfect in competition. Too often in practice, I see athletes develop a negative attitude, put forth less effort, or stop completely when the conditions get too difficult, for instance, rain, cold, poor training conditions, or a difficult drill.

I've heard athletes say it doesn't matter since it's just training. But they are failing to realize two things. First, as noted in the section on training like you compete, what you do in training is what you will do in a competition. If you respond poorly to adversity in training, that is the habit you ingrain and that is what will likely come out when you are confronted with adversity in competition. It is often how athletes respond to adversity, not the actual adversity itself, that determines who is successful in a competition. The reality is that every competitor experiences difficult conditions, so your opponents have to deal with them as well. What makes the difference in a competition is who is best able to respond to adversity.

The only way to compete successfully in adverse conditions is to train in them and learn how to react positively to them. This skill comes from not only understanding that the conditions will prevent you from performing as well as you would like, but also recognizing that your opponents are facing the same challenges. The goal when faced with adversity is to minimize the deterioration in your performance. Often, among those with similar ability, the one who is able to reduce the impact of the adversity on their performance will be the one who is the most successful.

Two important benefits occur when you expose yourself to adversity in training. First, experiencing adversity in training gives you the opportunity to learn to respond positively to things that stand in your way. This positive attitude starts with being determined to not let the adversity beat you. It also involves accepting that you will make more mistakes and your performance will inevitably decline somewhat. This perspective helps you overcome the frustration that can arise when confronted with adversity. As you are exposed to adversity more and more, you gain confidence and become comfortable with it, and are able to stay positive and motivated even when things get tough.

Second, by training in adversity, you come to understand the adverse conditions better and, in doing so, learn how to adapt to them. You learn how to maintain your performance as best you can given the conditions. This might, for example, mean knowing how to adjust your technique, tactics, body position, or pace to perform well in rain, heat, or mud. When you are faced with the same adversity in a competition, instead of freaking out, you have tools you can use to perform your best.

When I'm with athletes as they're training in tough conditions, one of my pet peeves is hearing them say to their coaches, "Hey coach, things are getting too hard here. Can you make it easier?" This attitude pretty much guarantees failure in a competition. In fact, if you're competing in situations where the conditions are bad, you shouldn't even begin to train until the conditions are as rough as the expected competitive conditions. Rather than looking for ideal training conditions, seek out the worst possible conditions. When the conditions are really bad, say, "Bring it on." Go for it and perform the best you can in those difficult conditions (while realizing that it isn't going to be pretty or perfect). The end result will be that when you compete in adverse conditions, you will be able to say, "I've been in these conditions before. I know what to do to perform well. This is no big deal."

Recover from Your Mistakes Quickly

As mentioned in the section on experimentation, the more you push yourself out of your comfort zone, the more mistakes you are going to make. And those mistakes certainly don't feel good or inspire confidence in yourself. Yet, it's important to realize that the best athletes in the world make mistakes all the time, whether it's Hope Solo allowing a goal, Roger Federer double faulting, Stephen Curry missing a three-point shot, or Simone Biles falling off the balance beam. One thing that makes these great athletes so great is how quickly they recover from their mistakes.

Younger or less-skilled athletes certainly make plenty of mistakes, but unlike the exceptional athletes I just noted, it usually takes them longer to recover. For example, when a young golfer double bogeys a hole, it might continue to haunt her for the next two holes, causing one bad hole to grow into three bad holes. This effect of one mistake turning into a series of mistakes or an overall poor performance occurs for several reasons.

First, the mistake hurts your confidence, which means you are less likely to commit fully to your subsequent performances. If you take a mistake as an indication of how you are performing, you will lose faith that you can perform well after the mistake. Second, a mistake can produce a range of negative emotions, including disappointment, anxiety, frustration, anger, sadness, and possibly even despair. These emotions are discouraging and demotivating. Third, mistakes can also produce a physiology that almost guarantees more mistakes and poor performance.

In the case of anxiety, frustration, and anger, you experience muscle tension, restricted breathing, and a loss of coordination, all of which impair future performance. In the case of disappointment, sadness, and despair, you will experience a let-down physiology, including low heart rate, reduced blood flow, and shallow breathing, producing a lack of the physical requirements for performing well. Fourth, a mistake can interfere with your ability to focus effectively. If you are dwelling on your past mistake, you're not focused on what you need to do well in the present in your upcoming performance. The result is more mistakes and the beginning of a vicious cycle of errors and physical, mental, and emotional deterioration that is hard to escape.

You should have several goals after making a mistake:

- Stay positive and motivated, which alone will help you let go of the mistake and get back on track.
- Accept and let go of the mistake emotionally.
- Maintain your intensity, allowing your body to be capable of a return to good performance.
- Learn from the mistake so you're less likely to do it again.
- Refocus on the present and what you need to do to return to performing well.

What to do with a mistake: 1. Recognize it. 2. Admit it. 3. Learn from it. 4. Forget it.

—Dean Smith, college basketball legend[17]

Never Give Up

A common reaction of athletes to mistakes or poor performances in training is to give up. You might shorten your workouts because you just can't get the new technique, or you stop trying because what you're working on is just too difficult. Athletes rationalize giving up by saying that training doesn't really matter. I would argue otherwise. Training counts because everything you practice either contributes to or interferes with developing effective skills and habits.

Giving up is typically caused by the perception that you have lost control of your training and there's nothing you can do to get back on track. With this perception, you lose the psychological forces that typically propel you onward after you begin to struggle, namely, confidence, motivation, intensity, and focus.

The skill of never giving up is central to your athletic success because something rather important happens each time you give up: You automatically lose. You may think that there are no real consequences to losing in training, but, as I just pointed out, they are more significant than they appear. The problem is, as described in the "Train Like You Compete" section, what you do in training is what you will do in competition. Thus, if you give up often in training, you develop the habit of giving up, and that may very well come out in competition.

You must make a commitment to keep fighting and never give up, no matter how badly things are going in your training. If you give up, you are sacrificing any chance of turning things around. Furthermore, you aren't just giving up on your performance; more painfully, you are giving up on yourself. And there is nothing worse than that. I can assure you that when you give up, you feel awful and regret having done so. But, if you keep fighting, you may not win, but at least you give yourself a chance, because anything can happen in sports. And even if things don't work out the way you want, you will still take pride in knowing you went down fighting. As the saying goes, "It's better to go out with a bang than a whimper." You want to ingrain the habit of giving your best effort and never giving up no matter what happens in training or competition.

Tip from the Top: Reach for the High-Hanging Fruit

If your athletic goals are at all high and you are competing against other individuals or teams with similar goals, you can assume that your competitors are doing the basic things everyone must do in their training to be competitive. These basics include engaging in intensive physical conditioning, improving technique and tactics, preparing and maintaining equipment, and eating healthy. You can think of these ABCs as the low-hanging fruit that you pick first as you progress, because they are easy to find, easy to reach, and sufficient for you to improve steadily early on in your athletic development. Certainly, these fundamentals are necessary to be successful, as they act as the foundation for later, higher-level development. But they are probably not enough to get you where you want to go because everyone else picks the long-hanging fruit as well. The fundamentals don't separate the great from the good. For you to gain an advantage over your competitors, you need to go beyond the basics and do what they are not doing.

The higher you climb on the athletic ladder, the more important it is for you to do more than your competitors and do things differently. You need to get to the high-hanging fruit, which is harder to reach and, as a result, infrequently picked. This means doing the small things that have a subtle yet powerful impact on your development and performance. These acts often make the difference between the winners and the also-rans. Hard-to-reach fruits include the following:

- Make your sport your absolute priority and make choices that support your efforts and goals.
- Seek out innovative training approaches and strategies that give you a competitive advantage over your competitors.
- Ensure that you get enough sleep to enable your body to recuperate from the stresses of training and competition.
- Warm up before training and competitions so you can maximize your efforts, and cool down after training and competitions to ensure complete recovery from the physical demands of your sport.
- Use training and competitive routines that guarantee maximum readiness in training and competition.
- Commit to a comprehensive, structured, and consistent mental training program.
- Experiment with equipment so you can perform even better.

This high-hanging fruit won't make a huge difference in how you perform, but you shouldn't expect big improvements as you climb higher up the competitive ladder. These minutiae may only mean improvements of a few inches or a few tenths of a second. But the closer you get to the top, these small details and improvements can mean the difference between great success and dashed dreams.

IMPROVE THE QUALITY OF YOUR TRAINING

1. Identify a goal and a purpose for your training sessions. Achieve an ideal focus and intensity before training performances.

2. Expose yourself to adversity and respond positively.

3. Be aware of your reaction to training mistakes and, if necessary, shift them to positive, process, and present.

4. Identify situations in training where you have a tendency to ease up or give up and choose to keep fighting.

Don't stop when you're tired. Stop when you're done.

—Unknown[18]

4

PrimeMind:
Five Mental Muscles

PRIME SPORT PROFILE: MENTAL MUSCLES

Instructions: Rate yourself on a scale of 1 to 10 using the five PrimeMind mental muscles described here.

Motivation: Being determined and driven to do the work necessary to achieve your athletic goals. (1: no motivation; 10: total motivation)

Confidence: Believing in your ability to perform your best and achieve your athletic goals. (1: no confidence; 10: total confidence)

Intensity: Having the ability to reach and maintain your ideal physical intensity before and during a competition. (1: not at all; 10: consistently)

Focus: Maintaining focus and avoiding distraction to perform your best on a consistent basis. (1: not at all; 10: total focus)

Mindset: Developing a line of thinking for the one to five minutes before you compete to help your performance. (1: not at all; 10: healthy mindset)

As part of my belief that mental training should be viewed in the same way as conditioning and other aspects of athletic development, I like to think of the mental contributors to sports performance as muscles. Physical and mental muscles have much in common. They can be strengthened, but only with consistent exercise. They can also become injured. Also, like the muscles in your body, your only chance for becoming the best athlete you can be is to commit to making the muscles in your mind as strong as they can be. *Train Your Mind* introduces you to five mental muscles that you must strengthen to perform your best.

Mental will is a muscle that needs exercise, just like the muscles in the body.

—Lynn Jennings, Olympic long-distance runner[1]

MOTIVATION

Motivation, simply defined, is your determination and drive to achieve your athletic goals. To perform your best, you must want to begin the process of developing as an athlete and be willing to maintain your efforts until you have achieved your goals. Motivation lies at the foundation of everything you do as an athlete. Without the desire and determination to commit the time and do the work necessary to develop as an athlete, pursuit of your sports goals will end in failure. To become the best athlete you can be, you must be motivated to do what it takes to maximize your ability.

Motivation in sports is essential for athletic success for several reasons. First, it involves putting forth consistent effort in every area of your life that affects your sports performance. It influences the effort you put into your physical conditioning, technical and tactical training, equipment preparation, and mental training. Motivation also plays a big role in how your general lifestyle impacts your sport, including sleep habits, eating habits, school or work, and relationships. Second, motivation determines your willingness to continue to work hard in the face of fatigue, boredom, pain, and the desire to do other things. Your motivation also influences whether you make sports your number-one priority in your life. To be sure, although you may love your sport, you also have competing interests, such as school or work, hobbies, and your social life. How you prioritize your sport in your life will impact the choices you make in terms of how you spend your time and energy.

Motivation is important because it is the only contributor to sports performance that you can control. There are three things that impact how well you perform. First, is your athletic ability as an athlete, which includes your innate physical talent and inborn psychological attributes. Because athletic ability is something you are born with and limited by, it is outside of your control.

Second, the difficulty of the competition influences how you perform. Contributors to difficulty include the ability of your opponents, weather, and conditions at the competitive venue (e.g., field condition). You have no control of these factors.

Finally, motivation will impact performance. Motivation directly influences the level of success you ultimately achieve. If you are highly motivated to improve your performance, you will put in the time and effort necessary to fully develop yourself as an athlete—physical, technical, tactical, and mental. Motivation also influences your level of performance when you begin a competition. If you're competing against someone of nearly equal fitness and skill, it will not be ability that will determine the outcome. Rather, it will be the athlete who works the hardest, doesn't give up, and performs their best when it counts. In other words, the athlete who is most motivated to perform their best.

Prime motivation involves an unwavering commitment to doing what is necessary to perform at your highest as you strive toward your athletic goals. It means continuing to work hard in the face of challenges, setbacks, and failure. Prime motivation ensures that your sport remains your top priority and that the choices you make in your life best serve the pursuit of your goals. It involves an ongoing determination to do your best, as well as a day-to-day dedication to giving your fullest effort in everything that will impact your sports performance.

You can motivate by fear, and you can motivate by reward. But both those methods are only temporary. The only lasting thing is self-motivation.

—Homer Rice, former American football player, coach, and college athletics administrator[2]

Effort Equals Goals?

When I speak to groups of young athletes, I always ask how many have big goals, like going to the Olympics or playing pro ball. At least 90 percent raise their hands with great enthusiasm. I then ask how many are doing everything they can to achieve their goals. Only one or two tentative hands go up. What this tells me is that there is often a big gap between the goals athletes have and the effort they are putting into those goals. It's easy to say that you want to be a successful athlete. It is much more difficult to actually make it happen. If you have this kind of disconnect, you have two choices. You can either lower your goals to match your effort or raise your effort to match your goals. There is no right answer. But if you're truly motivated to be successful, you better make sure you're doing the work necessary to achieve your goals.

We all have dreams. But in order to make dreams come into reality, it takes an awful lot of determination, self-discipline, and effort.

—Jesse Owens, Olympic 100m sprint champion[3]

Signs of Low Motivation

At the beginning of this chapter, you rated yourself on how motivated you think you are. With that assessment, you probably evaluated your level of motivation and then gave yourself a rating between one and 10 based on that belief. But motivation isn't just a perception (no athlete wants to admit that they are unmotivated) or a feeling ("Yeah, I want to be a great athlete!"). Rather, motivation is whether you actually do the day-to-day work necessary to achieve your sports goals. To help you better understand your motivation, let me identify some signs of low motivation to see if they sound familiar.

Do you often have a lack of desire to practice as much as you should? You might do the minimum of what is expected of you in your on- and off-field training, but when you have the opportunity to do a little more, you pass on it.

Do you give less than 100 percent effort in training? Unless you work one-on-one with a coach, it's easy to hide behind your teammates and not put forth full effort in the gym or on the field. I've seen athletes who are so good at giving every appearance that they're giving 100 percent (panting breathlessly, grunting, and grimacing) they could win the Oscar for Best Actor. The fact is, however, if you don't give everything you've got, you won't gain the full benefits of your training, you won't improve as well or as fast as you can, and you probably won't achieve your athletic goals.

Do you skip or shorten your training? Every athlete has days when they don't feel like training. It might be because the workouts begin at 5 a.m. or the fact that it's hot outside. And, let's be honest, even the most motivated athletes will miss a workout. There are also those days when you're just not feeling it and you rationalize that cutting your training a little short, for example, doing a few less reps in the gym or not doing a last drill won't really matter. But if you skip workouts completely or shorten them with regularity, you are doing yourself a disservice in the pursuit of your goals.

Do you make choices that aren't in the best interests of your athletic goals? As I mentioned earlier, you probably have interests that conflict with your sports participation. Maybe you would rather play your guitar, hang out with friends, spend time on social media, or watch a movie. These other options may be more fun and are certainly less tiring and painful. But the question you must always return to when faced with such choices is, Is my sport important enough for me to choose training over these other alternatives?

If you show signs of low motivation, this should serve as a wake-up call, because if you continue to exhibit these symptoms, it is safe to say that you are unlikely to achieve your sports goals (assuming that they are at all high). But you can take heart in knowing that it's not too late to find your motivation. (I was in the same situation when I was a 16-year-old ski racer, and I found my own motivation, which propelled me to compete at the international level.) You can change this pattern, tap into your motivation, and learn to work hard to embrace the "grind" and put forth efforts that equate to achieving your goals.

If you aren't going all the way, why go at all?

—Joe Namath, Super Bowl–winning quarterback[4]

Develop Your Motivation

Focus on Long-Term Goals

To be your best, you have to put a lot of time and effort into your sport. But, as noted earlier, there are going to be times—the grind—when you don't feel motivated. When you feel this way, focus on your long-term goals. Remind yourself why you're working so hard. Imagine what you want to accomplish and tell yourself the only way you'll be able to reach your goals is by continuing to work hard.

Focusing on your long-term goals motivates you in several ways. First, when you're working hard and are tired and in pain, your body is yelling at your mind to stop. If your mind listens, you will ease up or give up. So, by focusing on long-term goals, your mind is telling your body, "No, we can't stop because my long-term goals are really important to us. So keep going!" In other words, you're giving your body a reason to feel the pain it's feeling.

Second, by focusing on your long-term goals, you are taking your mind off of the fatigue and pain you may be feeling as you train. In doing so, the negatives become a little less negative and a little more tolerable.

Third, when you focus on your long-term goals, you generate such positive emotions as inspiration and pride, which can counter less-pleasant emotions like frustration, anger, or disappointment. Moreover, those positive emotions, research has shown, actually reduce your experience of pain. Thus, when you're struggling to stay motivated during a practice, training session, or workout, think of your long-term goals and tell yourself, "This is why I'm doing this!"

Have a Training Partner

It's difficult to be highly motivated all of the time on your own. There are going to be days when you just don't feel like going out there. You may be tired, stressed out, bored, or burned out, or you may just want to chill. Also, no matter how hard you push yourself, you can work harder when you have someone pushing you. That someone can be a coach, personal trainer, or parent. But the best person to fill this role is a regular training partner, someone who is at about your level of ability in your sport and who has similar goals.

Having a training partner helps you stay motivated in several ways. First, as the saying goes, "Two heads are better than one." That also includes two bodies. When you have a training partner, you don't feel as if you have to climb that high mountain alone. Rather, they are there to support you every step of the way (and you for them). Knowing you have someone to help you push forward makes it a little easier to keep climbing higher.

Second, a training partner holds you accountable. For example, it's one thing to skip a workout when you train alone. But it's going to be a lot harder to skip knowing that your training partner is there waiting for you. You can be sure he or she will be mad if you don't show up. So, even if you're not feeling it that day, you should show up and do the work because your training partner is counting on you.

Third, when you're practicing or working out and, as stated earlier, your body is yelling at you to stop, your mind isn't alone in yelling right back at your body. Rather, for example, you are on the last few reps of a set of squats or the last few laps of a sprint workout, and your training partner is right next to you yelling at you to keep going (and you're doing the same for your partner).

Train Smart

There is nothing less motivating than a training program that is exhausting, time consuming, and repetitive. Within a short period of time, you will find yourself drained, bored, burned out, and completely unmotivated. Because of this, I don't believe in training hard; I believe in training smart. Training smart means designing a training program that offers you several things.

First, it must have variety. Your program might include the necessary time in the weight room, functional conditioning outside the gym, other sports, and such nontraditional training methods as yoga or Pilates. This variety prevents boredom, and its novelty keeps you engaged, focused, and energized.

Second, you should have plenty of opportunities for rest and recovery. Most athletes don't think of rest as an essential part of training, but rather what you do when you're not training. Physical gains are not made during workouts—when the body is being torn down—but rather when the body is at rest and the stressed muscles are able to heal and recuperate. There are few things that will drain your motivation faster than a constant state of fatigue and body ache. Your body is telling your mind that it just can't keep going at that pace.

That's why it's important to build rest into your training program. This can be accomplished in several ways. Your program should be periodized with phases of high and low volume and intensity. You should also have a mandatory rest day each week where you refrain from physical activity. Moreover, when your body is feeling unusually tired, listen to it, alter your training program, and give yourself some extra time to recover.

Focus on Your Greatest Competitor

Most every athlete has a competitor they really want to beat. It might be a teammate and best friend with whom you train every day and with whom you have a friendly rivalry. Or it might be a hated adversary from an opposing team. One powerful way to keep yourself motivated is to focus on that rival when you're training. Identify your biggest competitor and put his or her name or photo where you can see it every day. Or think about him or her when training gets really hard. When you're exhausted, in pain, or just hating training in general, think about how you feel about that opponent and how much you want to crush them next time you face them. Ask yourself, "Am I doing what I need to do to beat him/her?" Remind yourself that only by working your hardest will you have a chance of overcoming your greatest competitor.

Use Motivational Cues

A big part of staying motivated involves generating positive emotions, for instance, inspiration, pride, and excitement, associated with your efforts and progress toward your goals. A great way to create those feelings is with such motivational cues as inspirational phrases and photographs. It might be a quote like, "I hated every minute of training, but I said, 'Don't quit. Suffer now and live the rest of your life as a champion,'" from boxing legend Muhammad Ali, or, "You're never a loser until you quit trying," from former NFL coach Mike Ditka. A motivational cue might be a photo of your favorite athlete or someone who exhibits the qualities you aspire to possess. The key with either is that they generate those positive emotions and thoughts that translate into increasing or maintaining your motivation, especially when training gets hard.

If you come across a quote or photo that inspires you, place it where you can see it regularly, perhaps in your bedroom, on your refrigerator door, or in your locker. Look at it periodically and allow yourself to experience the emotions it creates in you. These reminders and the emotions associated with them will inspire and motivate you to continue to work hard toward your goals.

Set Goals

There are few things more rewarding and motivating than setting a goal, putting forth the effort to reach the goal, and achieving the goal. The sense of accomplishment and validation of the effort makes you feel good and motivates you to strive higher. It's valuable to establish clear goals of what you want to accomplish in your sport and how you will achieve those objectives. Well-articulated goals act as road signs that guide you toward your final dream goal. They also act as benchmarks of the progress you are making. Furthermore, goals generate feelings of pride and inspiration that continue to propel you toward higher goals. Seeing that your hard work is moving you forward and producing results should motivate you further to realize your goals (I describe how to set goals in more detail later in this chapter).

What keeps me going is goals.

—Muhammad Ali, boxing legend[5]

Ask Daily Questions

I'm sure your life is busy, filled with activities related to your sport, school or work, hobbies, family, and friends. It's easy to get so wrapped up in life that you sometimes forget about what you need to do each day to stay on the path toward your athletic goals. One helpful way to keep your goals and efforts in the forefront of your mind is to ask yourself two questions on a daily basis. When you get up in the morning, ask, "What can I do today to become the best athlete I can be?" Asking yourself this question starts off your day in a motivating way. It helps you focus on continuing to improve as an athlete. The question inspires you to pursue your goals. It also identifies the specific actions you need to carry out to be your best.

Before you go to sleep, ask, "Did I do everything possible today to become the best athlete I can be?" This question holds you accountable for what you did or did not do that day. If you did everything possible to be the best athlete you can be, you'll feel fulfillment and pride in your efforts. If you fell short, this reality will force you to confront your shortcomings and cause you to feel disappointment and regret. In either case, the question will set the stage for what you decide to do tomorrow. These two questions serve as daily reminders of your goals and challenge you to be motivated to do your best every day.

I recommend that you write down these two questions and put them where you can easily see them.

Get to the Heart of Motivation

The techniques I've just described are effective in increasing your short-term motivation. They can get you through the hard training sessions and painful workouts. But motivation is not just about keeping at it day in and day out. It's also about staying motivated for the long haul, throughout weeks, months, and years of striving toward your goals. In that case, you need to find a reason to continue down the hard road of commitment to your sport. There are no quick fixes or strategies for staying motivated for the long-term. Rather, motivation must ultimately come from within. You have to have a personal reason for wanting to continue to put in the time and hard work in your sport. When you get right down to it, you just have to want it really bad.

Desire is the key to motivation, but it's determination and commitment to an unrelenting pursuit of your goals—a commitment to excellence—that will enable you to attain the success you seek.

—Mario Andretti, Formula One driving champion[6]

Commitment Is a Moment-to-Moment Choice

It's one thing to say you are committed to your athletic goals (talk is cheap!). But it's another to demonstrate that commitment every day in every aspect of your life. In fact, commitment is a moment-to-moment choice that involves many forks in the road, and these forks will determine your final destination as an athlete:

- "Should I do my warm-up before training?"
- "Should I do my rehab?"
- "Should I go to bed early tonight?"
- "Should I push through the pain of this workout?"
- "Should I turn off my phone so I can focus on my competitive preparations?"

There are many obstacles to those moments of commitment that I have already mentioned: fatigue, pain, boredom, the desire to do other things, and a multitude of distractions that now inhabit the lives of athletes. When you come to a fork in the road, you must decide what is important to you. You must look at each fork and decide which one you will take. The motivation you bring to your sport; your determination to achieve your athletic goals; the priority you place on those goals; and the competing forces that call for your attention, time, and energy will dictate which road you take and whether you ultimately accomplish your goals.

Commitment means staying loyal to what you said you were going to do long after the mood you said it in has left you.

—Jonathan Field, five-time martial arts world champion[7]

Set Goals

Goal setting is a simple and practical mental tool you can use to maintain a high level of motivation. For some elemental reason, people respond to goals in a deep and personal way. The experience of setting a goal, working toward a goal, and achieving a goal has a powerful emotional resonance that causes us to continue to strive higher for the goals we set for ourselves. Two aforementioned emotions, pride in putting forth the effort in pursuit of the goal and inspiration in having accomplished the goal, play a central role in the impact that goal setting has on motivation.

Aside from the deeper motivational influence that goal setting has on you, it has practical value because goals offer two essential things that fuel your motivation. First, goals provide a destination. This endpoint is important because if you don't have a destination, you're not going to have the impetus to break the inertia of where you are now. Second, having a place you really want to go doesn't have a lot of value if you don't know how to get there. Goals provide the road map for getting to your destination.

Keys to Effective Goal Setting

There has been an enormous amount of research, both within and out-side of sport, on how goal setting can be used most effectively. The acronym SMARTER (Specific, Measurable, Accepted, Realistic, Time limited, Exciting, Recorded) represents the five criteria this research has identified for getting the most out of your goal setting. (Note that there are variations on what each letter in the acronym stands for, and I have chosen those that I think are most effective.)

Specific

Your goals should be specific to what you want to accomplish. For example, if you are a lacrosse player, you wouldn't want a general goal like, "I want to improve my stick handling." Instead, you want to identify which aspects of your stick handling you want to get better at. A more appropriate goal might be, "I want to improve my passing accuracy just outside the crease." The more specific you can get, the more you can focus on what you need to do in your training to improve that area.

Measurable

One of the most robust findings in the research on goal setting is that "do your best" goals aren't very effective because they don't offer an adequate benchmark to strive for. Instead, you want to set goals that are measurable and objective. For instance, if you are a basketball player wanting to improve your free-throw shooting, a measurable goal might be increasing your free-throw accuracy from 71 to 80 percent. This type of goal clarifies your destination, but it doesn't provide directions on how to get there. As a result, you want to create a measurable goal that shows you the way. Continuing with the basketball example, a good goal might be shooting 50 free throws three times a week for the next four weeks to raise your free-throw percentage from 71 to 80 percent.

Accepted

As outlined in chapter 1, ownership of your sport is an essential part of your athletic success. Ownership is no less important in the goals you set. Goals that are set by parents or coaches will not inspire or motivate you fully because they come from outside, and you won't feel real buy-in because they aren't yours. When you set goals that you believe in, they are woven into the very fabric of your motivation and you have no choice but to strive for them. Because you own them, you can't not give your best effort in their pursuit.

Realistic

You want to set goals that are realistic, but not too realistic. Think of it this way: If you set goals that are too low, they will have little motivational value because you know you'll achieve them with little effort. Of course, you don't want to set goals that are too high because you know you can't achieve them, so you'll have little incentive to put forth any effort. You want to set goals that are both realistic and challenging—realistic meaning you can achieve them and challenging because your only chance of achieving them is by working hard. You want your goals to lie just beyond your reach, requiring that you stretch yourself if you want to have any chance of attaining them.

Time Limited

Open-ended goals haven't been shown to be effective because there is no urgency in achieving them; you can accomplish these goals when you want. The best goals are those that impose a time limit for their achievement. This timeliness acts to incentivize you to work hard right away to meet the time limit. Particularly if the goals are challenging, meaning they aren't a sure thing, you will feel highly motivated to put in the time and energy necessary to reach them when you have set a deadline. For example, if you're a cyclist and want to improve your power output, a goal might be increasing your wattage by 5 percent by doing 45 minutes of interval training three times a week for the next six weeks.

Exciting

Your motivation to strive toward your goals is driven by the emotions you associate with those goals. As a result, you want to set goals that inspire and excite you. These emotions can be the deciding factor in whether you achieve your goals when faced with setbacks, failures, disappointment, fatigue, pain, tedium, and the desire to do more interesting things. As you set goals for yourself, put them to the "excitement" test. Ask yourself whether your goals generate strong and positive emotions.

Recorded

Another robust finding in the goal-setting research is that you are more likely to stay committed to the pursuit of your goals when you write them down (not just type them into a computer) rather than simply think about them. The benefit appears to be due to several factors. First, the physical act of writing down your goals appears to imprint them more deeply in your psyche. Second, writing them down also seems to make the goals more tangible and real. Third, the explicitness of writing down your goals seems to create a greater sense of ownership, a sense of accountability that makes you feel more compelled to focus on and strive toward your goals. Fourth, a common mistake many athletes make when they complete their goal setting is to file them away and forget about them. Instead, you should take your written goals and post them where you can see them, for example, in your bedroom or locker. This constant reminder keeps your goals at the forefront of your mind and, as a result, helps you stay focused on accomplishing them.

In addition to these SMARTER criteria, there are several other guidelines that can be beneficial in setting goals that will offer maximum benefit.

Focus on Degree of Attainment

Despite the fact that setting goals has been studied for decades and we have a pretty clear picture of why, how, and when it works, goal setting is still an inexact science. What makes goal setting a less-than-precise endeavor is that it involves humans, who are, in general, unpredictable creatures. It is impossible to set goals you can be sure you can achieve, and if you can achieve them, it's hard to predict when that will happen. Because of this uncertainty in the goal-setting process, your focus when you set and strive for goals should be their degree of attainment, not absolute attainment. Let me explain.

Absolute attainment means accomplishing the goal in its entirety. For example, if you are an equestrian show jumper who has been clearing fences that are three feet tall and you set a goal of clearing 3-foot-9 fences within 16 weeks, you must clear at least that height to achieve your goal. Because of the uncertainty of setting goals, adhering to absolute attainment is a recipe for failure. Absolute attainment leaves only a small window for accomplishing the goal and a large window for failing to do so.

In contrast, degree of attainment emphasizes improvement toward the goal. Returning to the equestrian example, if, after 16 weeks, you have cleared 3-foot-3 fences, although your absolute goal wasn't attained, your improvement would be deemed a success. With degree of attainment, as long as you are showing progress toward a goal, you are on the right track. After the time frame specified in the goal has passed, you can use the information related to your improvement to modify the goal accordingly, either changing the goal outcome or simply extending the time needed to reach the goal. For example, again returning to the equestrian example, because progress was made toward the goal, you have two options. First, you can stick with the goal of clearing 3-foot-9 fences and give yourself another four weeks to achieve the goal. Or you can downgrade your goal to 3-foot-6 fences in the next four weeks. In either case, the goal will hopefully continue to motivate you to aim higher and work harder to achieve it.

Make Your Goals Public

Still another result commonly reported in the goal-setting research is that you are more likely to adhere to your goals if you make them public, meaning share them with others. You might do this by showing them to your coach, family, or friends. Or you could post them on your social media for your followers to see. By doing so, you are not only holding yourself accountable, but also allowing everyone who is aware of your goals to share in your accountability. The upside to making a public declaration of your goals is that you will receive support and encouragement from those around you, which will motivate you to work even harder. The downside is that you might not achieve your goals and have to publicly admit this failure to do so. You may feel some embarrassment for that failure. Hopefully, however, you will know that those people care about and support you regardless of the outcome, so the benefit of publicly declaring your goals will outweigh any negativity.

Review Your Goals Regularly

As noted earlier, goal setting is an inexact science in which establishing precise goals that are achievable with certainty is difficult. As a consequence, you should view goal setting as a dynamic and ever-evolving process of review, adjustment, and recommitment. You should make it a habit to review your goals on a monthly basis and compare them to your actual progress. It can also be helpful to review them with your coaches so they can provide useful feedback you can use to make adjustments that will further motivate you.

Types of Goals to Set

Goal setting involves establishing a series of goals that start with the big picture and become increasingly specific and actionable.

- *Long-term goals:* what you ultimately want to achieve in your sport (e.g., win an Olympic gold medal, play in college)
- *Yearly goals:* what you want to achieve this year (e.g., qualifying for a new level of competition [states or nationals], a ranking, won–loss record)
- *Performance goals:* what results you need to achieve your yearly goals (e.g., finish in the top 10 to qualify for a big competition, achieve certain game statistics)
- *Preparation goals:* how you need to train to reach your higher goals (e.g., physical, technical, mental)
- *Lifestyle goals:* what you need to do in your general lifestyle to reach your goals (e.g., sleep, eating habits, study habits)

Determine reasonable goals using the SMARTER guidelines, as well as the other criteria I describe. If you are unsure of which goals to set, sit down with your coaches and prepare your goals collaboratively, as they often have experience and perspective on your development that can help you set the best goals that will motivate you most.

Tip from the Top: Deal with the Grind

Hopefully you train and compete in your sport because you love it and find it a lot of fun. Improving, the competition, hanging with your friends, travel, achieving your goals, and, yes, even winning, make sports fun and exciting. But not every aspect of pursuing your athletic goals is fun. In fact, it's often hard, really hard. No matter how much you love your sport and how much fun it is in general, there are many specific aspects of being an athlete that are decidedly not fun, especially the physical conditioning. I'm thinking of those cold, early morning runs; those workouts in the rain or blazing heat of summer; those multiple sets of weights; and those incredibly intense intervals in the gym.

This is what I referred to earlier as the grind, which starts when it gets tiring, painful, and tedious—with little fun to be had. Most athletes, when they experience the grind, either ease up or give up. And we all know that no good comes from either of those reactions. But truly motivated athletes realize that the grind is also the point where their effort really starts to count, because the real physical, technical, tactical, and mental gains are made in those last few reps, laps, miles, exercises, or drills. Great athletes reach the grind and, instead of easing up, keep on going and, in fact, push harder because they know that maintaining their effort, intensity, and focus during the last moments of a training session can mean the difference between success and disappointment in the coming season.

I've heard sport psychologists and mental coaches say that you have to love the grind. I say that, except for a few hypermotivated athletes, love isn't in the cards, because there's little to love. Sweating, gasping for air, feeling fatigue down to your bones, and screaming muscles are part and parcel of becoming the best athlete you can be; however, they are decidedly aspects of training most athletes do not enjoy. But how you respond to the grind lies along a continuum. As previously stated, loving the grind is rare. At the other end of the continuum is hating the grind. If you feel this way, you are not likely to stay motivated and continue to do the work necessary to achieve your goals. My solution is that you neither love nor hate the grind; rather, you just accept it as part of the deal in striving toward your goals. The grind may not be enjoyable, but what feels even worse is failing to achieve your goals for the season because you didn't work hard enough when confronted with it. What does feel good is seeing your hard work pay off with success.

So, the next time you're training and it is *really not fun*, recognize the grind, remind yourself how important it is, and push through it. During the

---

EXERCISE

EXAMINE YOUR TRAINING AND COMPETITIVE PREPARATIONS

1. Identify areas in your training and competitive preparations in which you are not totally motivated or giving your best effort.

2. Complete the goal-setting program discussed earlier in this chapter using the SMARTER criteria for long-term, seasonal, performance, preparation, and lifestyle goals.

3. Set goals related to the specific areas you identified in number 1.

season, after you've had a few great performances, you will thank yourself for hanging tough when it really mattered.

You'll be surprised to know how far you can go from the point where you thought it was the end.

—Unknown[8]

CONFIDENCE

I define confidence as how strongly you believe in your ability to perform your best and achieve your athletic goals. Confidence is the single most important mental factor in sports. It is important because you may have the ability to perform well, but if you don't believe you have it, you won't perform up to that ability. For example, a gymnast may be physically and technically capable of executing a back somersault with a full twist on the floor exercise, but she won't attempt the skill in a meet if she doesn't have the confidence that she can successfully execute the skill.

Your goal is to develop prime confidence—a deep, lasting, and resilient belief in your ability. Prime confidence keeps you positive, motivated, intense, and focused. With prime confidence, you are able to stay confident even when you're not performing well. You aren't negative and uncertain in difficult competitions or overconfident in easy ones. Prime confidence also encourages you to seek out pressure situations and view difficult conditions and tough opponents as challenges to pursue. Prime confidence enables you to perform at your highest level consistently.

Self-confidence is the first requisite of great undertakings.

—Samuel Johnson, 18th-century English author[9]

Confidence Is a Muscle

A misconception that many athletes have is that confidence is something that is inborn and that if you don't have it at an early age, you will never have it. In reality, confidence is a muscle—much like your biceps and quads—that can be strengthened. As with any type of muscle, confidence can be developed through exercise in which you exert focus, effort, and repetition.

But your confidence muscle is actually made up of two muscles, a positive one and a negative one. If you tend to be negative in your thinking, you are strengthening your negative confidence muscle. Thus, when you compete, just like a bad technical habit, that negativity will come out and hurt your performance. In other words, you become really strong at being negative.

If you have a bad technical habit, that practice is hard to break because it's long-standing. For example, a softball player who opens her shoulders too early when swinging has probably been swinging the bat that way for a long time. She has developed a muscle pattern for swinging the wrong way. The same holds true for confidence. Your confidence muscle ingrains the wrong way of thinking.

To change negative "muscle memory" and strengthen your positive confidence muscle, you must retrain the way you think. You have to train your positive confidence muscle so that it becomes strong and allow your negative confidence muscle to atrophy so that your natural reaction is to flex your positive confidence muscle.

Vicious Cycle or Virtuous Cycle

To illustrate another influence of confidence, think back to a time when you didn't have confidence in yourself. You probably got caught in a vicious cycle of low confidence and performance in which negative thinking led to poor performance, which, in turn, led to more negative thinking and even poorer performance until your confidence was so low you no longer wanted to compete.

This vicious cycle usually starts with a period of poor performance. This poor performance leads to negative self-talk: "I'm terrible," "I can't do this," "I don't have a chance." You become your own worst enemy. You start to get nervous before a competition because you believe you will perform poorly. This anxiety hurts your confidence even more because you feel tense and physically uncomfortable, and there's no way you can perform well when you're so uptight. The negative self-talk and anxiety causes negative emotions. You feel depressed, frustrated, angry, and helpless, hurting your confidence more and causing you to perform even worse.

The negative self-talk, anxiety, and emotions hurt your focus. If you have low confidence, you can't help but focus on the negative things rather than on things that will enable you to perform your best. This accumulated negativity hurts your motivation. As bad as you feel, you just want to get out of there. If you're thinking negatively, caught in a vicious cycle, feeling nervous, depressed, and frustrated, and lacking focus, you're not going to have much fun and you're not going to perform well.

Now recall a time when you felt really confident in your sport. Your self-talk was positive: "I'm a good athlete," "I can perform well." You are your best ally. With positive self-talk, you begin a virtuous cycle of high confidence and performance in which positive thinking leads to better performance, which leads to more positive thinking and even better performance.

The positive talk helps you feel relaxed and energized as you begin competition. You experience such positive emotions as inspiration and excitement. You are able to focus and perform your best. Competing is actually an enjoyable experience. The positive thoughts and feelings motivate you to perform. If you're thinking positively, riding a virtuous cycle, feeling relaxed and energized, experiencing positive emotions, and focusing on performing your best, you're going to have fun and are likely to perform well.

A bad attitude is worse than a bad swing.

—Payne Stewart, professional golfer[10]

The Confidence Challenge

It's easy to stay confident when you're performing well, the conditions are ideal, and you're competing against a weaker opponent. The real test of confidence, however, is how you respond when things aren't going your way. I call this the Confidence Challenge. What separates the best from the rest is that the best athletes are able to maintain their confidence when they're not at the top of their game. By staying confident, they continue to work hard rather than give up because they know that, in time, their performance will come around.

As suggested in the previous section, most athletes who perform poorly get caught in the vicious cycle of low confidence and performance. Once you slip into that downward spiral, you rarely can get out of it in the short-term. In contrast, athletes with prime confidence maintain their confidence and seek out ways to return to their previous level. Every athlete will go through periods where they don't perform well. The key is to avoid getting caught in the vicious cycle, exit the down periods quickly, and return to a virtuous cycle of high confidence and performance.

There are several ways to master the Confidence Challenge:

- Develop the attitude that demanding situations are challenges to be sought out, not threats to avoid.
- Believe that experiencing challenges is a necessary part of becoming the best athlete you can be.
- Be well-prepared to meet the challenges.
- Stay positive and motivated in the face of difficulty.
- Focus on what you need to do to overcome challenges.
- Accept that you may experience failure when faced with new challenges.
- Never give up!

Why Athletes Lose Confidence

Anything that counters your belief in your ability to achieve your goals will hurt your confidence. The greatest disruption to confidence is failure. Failure can mean making mistakes in a competition, for example, missing an easy header in soccer or falling on a double axel in figure skating. Failure will cause you to lose faith in your ability and become tentative or cautious. Failure can also mean having poor results in recent competitions. There is nothing more harmful to confidence than failure because it provides evidence that any confidence you may have is unjustified.

Symptoms of Low Confidence

At the beginning of this chapter, you rated your confidence on a scale of 1 to 10, so you should have a pretty good idea of how you view your confidence. To help further your understanding of your confidence, the following are several symptoms of low confidence common among athletes.

Self-Doubt

Athletes with low confidence just don't believe in themselves. They express this self-doubt in negative self-talk or negative talk to others. Before a competition, for instance, these athletes will be thinking things like, "I'm just not going to play well today," "My opponent is looking so strong," or "I know I'm going to mess up today." Or they'll tell their coach or a teammate, "I'm not ready," "I'm not feeling it today," or "I don't have a chance." Not surprisingly, this sort of talk sets these athletes up for failure because they've become their own worst enemy, and if their opponent is against them and they are against themselves, they have no chance of success.

Anxiety

Athletes with low confidence experience intense precompetitive anxiety because they don't believe they are capable of performing well and achieving success. As such, they are placing themselves in a situation that is incredibly threatening to them, namely, almost guaranteed failure. This anxiety contributes to the vicious cycle, in which the highly unpleasant physical symptoms of anxiety—sweating, muscle tension, shortness of breath, increased heart rate—send a message to your brain that confirms the low confidence, triggers a flight reaction, and prevents the focus required to perform well. Additionally, these symptoms almost ensure performance failure because anxious athletes are simply not capable of performing their best.

Lack of Effort

Low confidence has the expected effect of reducing athletes' motivation to put forth their best effort. From their perspective, what's the point of trying hard when they know they will fail? This toxic stew of low confidence and motivation acts as a self-fulfilling prophecy of failure because, without sufficient belief in their ability to succeed and with their lack of effort, these athletes have zero chance of being successful. Moreover, low effort provides these athletes with an excuse that protects their self-esteem; they can tell themselves and others that they would have done well if they had tried harder.

Tentative Performance

Athletes with low confidence create a "perfect storm" of psychology and physiology that sets the stage for competitive performances that are cautious and tentative. These performances lack full commitment because of the absence of both confidence and motivation. They are lacking intense physical effort and exertion because their bodies aren't physiologically capable of performing their best. These performances lack the appropriate risk-taking that is essential for athletic success. The results are performances that are uncertain and lacking in determination, energy, and abandon.

If you don't have confidence, you'll always find a way not to win.

—Carl Lewis, nine-time Olympic track and field gold medalist[11]

Seven Tools for Prime Confidence

The ultimate goal of prime confidence is to develop a strong and resilient belief in your athletic ability so that you have the confidence to give your best effort, perform at your highest level, and believe you can achieve your goals in the most important competitions of your life. I have identified seven tools you can use to create a virtuous cycle that will lead to prime confidence. Each tool alone can enhance your confidence, but if you use them together, your confidence will grow significantly stronger and more quickly.

Preparation

Preparation is the foundation of confidence. It breeds confidence. Preparation includes the physical, technical, tactical, equipment, and mental parts of your sport and means putting the necessary time and effort into every aspect of your training. If you have fully developed these areas, you will have faith that you can use the capabilities gained from preparation to perform at your highest level in competition. The more of these areas you fully address in your preparation, the more confidence you will breed in yourself. When you arrive at each competition, you should be able to say, "I'm as prepared as I can be to achieve my goals." And that statement alone exudes confidence.

Mental Tools

Mental tools reinforce confidence. I encourage you to create a mental "toolbox" where you keep essential mental tools you will need in training and competition (fortunately, your mental toolbox doesn't weigh anything, even when it's filled with tools). You can use these mental tools in two ways. First, you can fine-tune yourself, making subtle adjustments to get the most out of your performances. Second, just like having a spare tire, tire iron, and jack if you get a flat tire while driving, the tools in your mental toolbox are available when you have breakdowns in your sport and need to fix a problem, for example, when you get nervous before a competition, experience a period of poor play, or have a close call go against you.

Mental tools you can place in your mental toolbox can include inspirational thoughts and images to bolster your motivation, positive self-talk and body language to fortify your confidence, intensity control to combat confidence-depleting anxiety, keywords to maintain focus and avoid distractions, and emotion-control techniques to provide calm during high-pressure situations. Both this chapter and chapter 5 offer a wealth of mental tools you can use to fix the many "flat tires" you will inevitably experience in your athletic life.

Train for Adversity

Adversity ingrains confidence. As examined in chapter 3, exposure to adversity offers many psychological and emotional benefits to athletes. Confidence is one mental area in which adversity can be a powerful developmental tool. To more deeply ingrain confidence, expose yourself to as much adversity as possible in training. Adversity can be such environmental obstacles as bad weather during soccer practice or a strong headwind in a running workout. Adversity can also involve your practice opponent, who may be a little better than you or have a style of play that frustrates you.

Training for adversity has several essential benefits. Adversity increases the belief that you can respond positively to difficult conditions because you've proven you can do so in training. It shows you ways to adapt to the adversity so you can make the same adjustments during competition. Training for adversity also familiarizes you with tough conditions, so when similar demands are placed on you during competition, you'll be confident enough to stay positive and motivated. Plus, training for adversity makes you feel tough.

Take Risks (and Succeeding)

As I described in detail in chapter 1, risk-taking is essential for athletic success. The ability to get out of your comfort zone and push the limits of your capabilities is a requirement for any athlete who aspires to greatness in sports. Risk-taking is a valuable tool for stretching yourself beyond your self-imposed limitations and, in doing so, bolstering that virtuous cycle of confidence and performance.

Just taking risks takes a certain amount of confidence because an inherent aspect of risks is that you might fail. But the consequences of failure from taking risks are far outweighed by the benefits to your confidence when you do succeed. Risk, by definition, involves pushing outside of your comfort zone and extending your perceived capabilities. Once you succeed after taking a risk, you come to believe that you can do more than you once thought, and, by extension, your confidence in those newly expanded capabilities grows. When risk-taking pays off, it's like taking a shot of pure oxygen; there is a strong emotional component, as it produces a rush of fulfillment, pride, inspiration, and excitement from the accomplishment. You feel stronger mentally and are empowered to continue to take risks and succeed.

The quickest way to acquire self-confidence is to do exactly what you are afraid to do.

—Unknown[12]

Find Support

Support bolsters confidence. It's difficult to achieve success on your own. The best athletes in every sport have many people supporting them. There will be times when things are not going well, and it helps to have people— family, friends, coaches, and teammates—who can provide support and encouragement. Although your confidence may wax and wane depending on how you're feeling, the quality of your training, and your recent competitive results, you want people in your life whose confidence in you never wavers and who you can count on to give you a "booster shot" of confidence. For example, your coach might say, "I know you can do it." Or a friend may tell you, "Hang in there. Things will turn around."

Because support is so important in building, maintaining, and regaining confidence, you should actively seek out support and build a network of people who can support you in different ways. Support can come in many forms from many different people. You need technical support from your coaches if you are struggling with your form. A conditioning expert can support you when you need help with your fitness. From family and friends, you can receive emotional support, particularly when you are in a performance slump. It's helpful to have support for your injuries from a sports medicine team, including an orthopedist, physical therapist, and massage therapist. And, of course, a sport psychologist or mental coach can support your psychological and emotional needs.

If you have people that totally support you and have your back, I feel like you have all the confidence in the world, and you believe that you can do things that most people can't achieve.

—Nicolas Cage, actor[13]

Validate Confidence through Success

Success validates confidence. The previous steps in building confidence will be for naught if you don't perform well and achieve your goals. Success validates the confidence you have developed in your ability; it demonstrates that your belief in your ability is well-founded. Success further strengthens your confidence, making it more resilient in the face of adversity and poor performance. Success also rewards your efforts to build confidence, encouraging you to continue to work hard and develop your capabilities.

But when I talk about success, I don't mean just competitive success, at least not right away. I often hear athletes say things like, "I just need a win to get my confidence back." But I would suggest that the chances of a win are low if you lack confidence. It comes down to the classic "Which comes first, the chicken or the egg" conundrum. Do you gain confidence by being successful, or are you successful from being confident? My answer to this puzzler is, "Yes!" What I mean is that both are true, but the first thing you need is the confidence that you develop using the other tools. Once you have a basic level of confidence, you can begin to use successes to further build your confidence.

One point of clarification: When I say "success," I don't mean a big victory. As I alluded to in earlier paragraphs, you can't just go out and have a big success to give yourself confidence. Your initial goal is to create little "victories" every day in training. After a workout, you should be able to say that you just "won" that day by doing what you needed to do. You do this by working hard; listening to your coach; improving technically, tactically, or physically; keeping at it even when it hurts; overcoming adversity; and elevating your game to achieve your long-term goals. With each small victory accumulated in training, you gain incrementally more confidence until you are ready for that big victory, namely, performing your best, getting a great result, and achieving your competitive goals.

Positive Self-Talk

One of the most powerful mental tools at your disposal to build your confidence is positive self-talk. What you say to yourself off the field of play, when you're training, and during competitions has an impact on what you think, how you feel, and how you perform. It often determines the quality of your workouts and the results of your performances. Whether you are inclined to have positive or negative thoughts will determine the road you travel.

Negativity is rampant in the sports world. How often do you hear "I can't do this," "I'm terrible," or some variation of those words? This negativity sucks the life and love out of your sports participation. If your talk is negative, your thoughts and feelings will be negative as well.

Negative self-talk involves thinking or saying anything that reflects a lack of confidence, for example, "I'm going to do lousy today," "I stink," or "I can't deal with these conditions." If you say these things, you're convincing yourself that you have little chance. With that attitude, you really do have no chance, because you are going up against both your opponent and yourself. You've become your own worst enemy. Your motivation will disappear. You'll get nervous and lose focus, and feel frustration, anger, and despair. You will definitely not be having fun out there.

If your talk is positive, your thoughts and feelings will be positive. Don't say, "I don't have a chance today." Say, "I'm going to try my hardest today. I'm going to perform the best I can." That will get you positive and fired up. By using positive self-talk, you'll be your own best ally. You show yourself that, despite the fact that your opponents want to beat you, you aren't going to beat you.

Positive self-talk helps you in many ways. It increases your motivation to work hard because you believe that your efforts will be rewarded. You're relaxed and focused because you know you can handle anything that is thrown at you in training or competition. Your emotions reflect your positive self-talk, as you have feelings of excitement and inspiration.

Most importantly, positive self-talk helps keep your mind strong and your body going, especially when your body starts to weaken. As your body begins to wear down late in training and competitions, it will communicate to your mind that it has had enough—"I get the point! We can stop now." If your mind listens to your body and responds with negative self-talk—"My body is so tired I can't go on," "This hurts too much to continue"—your body will take over your mind, your body and mind will give up, and you will fail to achieve your goals. Positive self-talk can help your mind assert itself over your body, so when your body is yelling at you to stop, your mind can say, "No! Keep going. That's an order!" And your body will almost always keep going.

Positive self-talk is a simple, but not easy, strategy. It's simple because all you have to do is replace your negative self-talk with positive statements. It's not easy because you may have developed some poor self-talk habits that are difficult to change. You can begin to retrain your self-talk by looking at the situations in which you tend to become negative, for example, when you're doing a really painful strength workout, you're in a competition with a tough field, or you're in a slump.

Next, figure out exactly why you become negative in these situations. Common reasons I have found include fatigue, boredom, pain, frustration, and despair. Every athlete has "hot-button" issues that trigger negativity (see chapter 2 for the most common ones). Identifying yours is an essential part of changing your self-talk. Then, monitor what you say to yourself. I've found that athletes tend to rely on their favorite negative self-talk when their buttons get pushed, for example, "Gosh, I suck," "You're such a loser," or "What's the point of even trying." Realizing what you say and how bad it is for you is an important first step in making a change. For most athletes I've worked with, there is a consistent pattern involving the situations where negative self-talk arises, the causes of the negativity, and the specific self-talk they express.

Before you go out and face those hot-button situations that typically lead to negativity, choose some positive self-talk to replace your usual negative mode. The positive self-talk should be encouraging, but it must also be realistic. If you say things like, "I love being out here," when you really don't, or "I'm feeling so strong," even when you aren't, there's no way you'll buy into what you're saying. Acknowledging the hot button but putting a positive and realistic spin on it will help you believe in what you're saying, for instance, "If I keep working hard, good things will happen" or "This really hurts, but its money in the bank for my race." By putting this tool in your mental toolbox before your buttons get pushed, you'll be able to more readily access it and have a better chance of responding more positively.

At this point, training yourself to use positive self-talk depends on your ongoing commitment to it. Because the use of negative self-talk may already be ingrained, you'll have to constantly remind yourself to be positive. Recognizing that a hot-button situation is approaching will prepare you to react and help you focus on what to say when it happens. At first, you will probably "fall off the wagon" and slip back into your old, negative ways. Simply accept it as part of the process and return to being positive once you realize the error of your ways. With time and persistence, you'll see a gradual shift away from negativity and toward positive self-talk until you realize you managed to stay positive during a hot-button situation.

Brain wave tests prove that when we use positive words, our "feel good" hormones flow. Positive self-talk releases endorphins and serotonin in our brain, which then flow throughout our body, making us feel good. These neurotransmitters stop flowing when we use negative words.

—Ruth Fishel, mindfulness expert[14]

Tip from the Top: Use Negative Thinking Positively

Even though I emphasize being positive at all times, the fact remains that you can't always be this way. You don't always perform as well as you want, and there is going to be some negative thinking. This awareness was brought to me by a group of highly ranked junior athletes I worked with not long ago. During a training camp, I was constantly emphasizing being positive, not negative (they gave me the nickname "Wizard of Pos"). One night at dinner, several of the athletes came up to me and commented that sometimes things just stink and you can't be positive. I realized that some negative thinking is normal when you don't perform well and can actually be healthy. It means you care about performing poorly and want to do better. Negative thinking can be motivating as well, because it's no fun to perform poorly and lose. I got to thinking about how athletes can use negative thinking in a positive way. I came up with an important distinction that will determine whether negative thinking helps or hurts how you perform.

There are two types of negative thinking: give-up negative thinking and fire-up negative thinking. Give-up negative thinking involves feelings of loss, hopelessness, and helplessness, for example, "It's over. I can't win this." You dwell on past mistakes and failures. It lowers your motivation and confidence, and takes your focus off of performing your best. Your intensity also drops because basically you're surrendering and accepting defeat. There is never a place in sports for give-up negative thinking.

By contrast, fire-up negative thinking involves feelings of anger and being psyched up, for example, "I'm doing so badly. I hate performing this way" (said with anger and intensity). You look to doing better in the future because you hate performing poorly. Fire-up negative thinking increases your motivation to fight and turn things around. Your physical intensity increases, and you're bursting with energy. Your focus is on being aggressive and defeating your opponent.

Fire-up negative thinking can be a positive way to turn your performance around. If you're going to be negative, make sure you use fire-up negative thinking. But don't use it too much. Negative thinking and negative emotions burn a lot of energy—energy that should be channeled in a more positive direction in your training and competition. Also, it doesn't feel good to be angry all the time.

A negative thinker sees a difficulty in every opportunity. A positive thinker sees an opportunity in every difficulty.

—Zig Ziglar, motivational speaker[15]

EXERCISE

ADDRESS YOUR NEGATIVITY

1. Identify a situation in which you become negative.
2. Identify why you become negative.
3. Write down the negative statements you say to yourself in that situation.
4. Write down positive statements you can replace the negatives with.
5. The next time you are in that situation, replace the negatives with the positives.

INTENSITY

Intensity may be the most important contributor to athletic performance once the competition begins. It's important because no matter how much strength you have in your other mental muscles—motivation, confidence, focus, and mindset—they won't help you if your body is not physiologically capable of doing what it needs to do for you to perform your best. Simply put, intensity is the amount of physiological activity you experience in your body, including heart rate, respiration, and adrenaline. Intensity is a continuum that ranges from sleep (very relaxed) to sheer terror (very anxious). Somewhere in between those two extremes is the level of intensity at which you perform your best.

The challenge with intensity is that there is not one ideal intensity for every athlete. Depending on your physical and psychological makeup, you may perform best while very relaxed, moderately intense, or bouncing off the walls with intensity. The sport you compete in also impacts intensity. Sports that have different physiological demands will have different intensity requirements. For example, sports that involve quick and powerful bursts of energy, for example, weight lifting or sprinting, need higher intensity, while sports that involve fine motor-skills or endurance, for instance, golf or marathon running, respectively, require much lower intensity.

Intensity is made up of two components. First, there is the physical experience of intensity, that is, what you actually feel in your body when you are competing. Are you calm or filled with energy? Are you relaxed or tense? Second, there is your perception of the intensity. In other words, do you perceive the intensity positively or negatively? Two athletes can feel the exact same thing physiologically but interpret those physical feelings in very different ways. One may view the intensity as excitement, and it will help his performance. Another may see the intensity as anxiety, and it will hurt his performance. At the other end of the continuum, one athlete may experience her low intensity as calm and another as lethargy.

The physical experience and the perception of intensity are affected by several mental factors. If you are not confident, feeling frustrated and angry, and focused on winning rather than performing your best, you will see the intensity as negative. In contrast, if you are confident and positive, happy and excited, and focused on performing well, the intensity will be perceived as positive.

Prime intensity is that ideal level of physical activation required for you to perform your best in training and competition. It includes just the right level of muscle activity, heart rate, blood flow, respiration, and adrenaline. Additionally, prime intensity is perceived as positive and ideal. That good physiology also has a positive influence on all aspects of your psychology.

I was so surprised. Then again, I was so relaxed in the water, it felt amazing.

—Pieter van den Hoogenband, three-time Olympic swimming gold medalist[16]

Signs of Overintensity and Underintensity

Intensity produces a wide variety of physical and mental symptoms that can help you recognize when your intensity is too high or too low. By being aware of these signs, you will know when you're not performing at prime intensity and can take steps to reach that ideal level.

Overintensity

Muscle tension and breathing difficulties are the most common signs of overintensity. Most athletes indicate that when they're too intense, they feel tension in their shoulders and legs, which happen to be the two most important physical areas for many sports, although you can feel tension anywhere in your body. If a swimmer's shoulders are tense, the motion of her strokes will shorten and she won't be able to swim with ease or power. When a high jumper's legs are tense, he loses the ability to run and jump with smoothness and explosiveness.

Many athletes also report that their breathing becomes short and choppy when they get nervous. This restriction in breathing means that they're not getting enough oxygen into their system, so they will tire quickly. I've also found that the smoothness of athletes' movement tends to mirror their breathing. If their breathing is long and smooth, so is their movement. If their breathing is abrupt and uneven, their movements are jerky and uncomfortable.

Athletes who are overly intense often exhibit poor posture and a stiff gait. Muscle tension causes their shoulders to rise and their bodies to close up. Athletes make more mistakes when they're overly intense because anxiety disrupts coordination. Overintensity interferes with motor control, which affects technical skills and movement. Athletes who are anxious also increase the pace of the competition. For example, an overly intense cyclist may go out too fast early in a road race. Overly intense athletes often look rushed and frantic. If opponents are taking their time, overly intense athletes become impatient with the slow pace.

Overintensity also negatively influences athletes mentally. Anxiety lowers confidence and causes athletes to doubt their ability. The physical and mental discomfort produces such negative emotions as frustration, anger, and depression. The anxiety, doubt, and negative emotions hurt focus by drawing athletes' attention away from performing their best and toward how bad they feel.

I've faced kicks when the anxiety has been so great that I could actually see my heart beating through my shirt.

—Jonny Wilkinson, former English rugby great[17]

Underintensity

Although not as common, athletes can also experience underintensity during competition. The most common symptoms of underintensity are low energy and lethargy. Athletes lack the adrenaline they need to give their best effort. While it is not as discomforting as overintensity, underintensity hurts performance equally because athletes lack such physical requisites as strength, stamina, and agility to meet the demands of their sport.

Mentally, underintensity undermines motivation. Athletes just don't feel like being out there. The lack of interest caused by too low intensity also impairs their focus because they're easily distracted and have difficulty staying focused on their performance.

The Line between Intensity and Tensity

The ultimate goal of prime intensity is to find the precise line between intensity (at which your body performs its best) and tensity (yes, it is actually a word; when performance declines). The closer you can get to that line, the more your body will work for you in performing your best. If you cross the line to tensity, your body will no longer be physically capable of that high level of performance.

Great athletes have the ability to do two things related to this line. First, they have a clear understanding of where that line is, so they find it and do a tightrope walk on it, maximizing what their bodies can give them. Second, they're able to stay on that line longer and more consistently than other athletes, which enables them to perform at a consistently higher level for longer periods of time.

Finding Your Prime Intensity

Your intensity is much like the thermostat that maintains the temperature in your house. You set your thermostat to the most comfortable temperature and always notice when your house is too warm or too cold because you're sensitive to changes in temperature. When the temperature becomes uncomfortable, either too high or too low, you adjust the thermostat to a more comfortable level. You can think of your intensity as your internal temperature, which needs to be adjusted periodically. You must develop a sensitivity that tells you when your intensity is no longer comfortable—in other words, if you are overintense or underintense, and it's not allowing you to perform your best. You can then use the psych-up and psych-down exercises described later in the chapter to raise or lower your intensity to its prime level.

You have several goals in developing prime intensity. First, you should be able to identify your prime intensity. Second, you must be able to recognize the signs of overintensity and underintensity during training and competition. Third, it's important to have the ability to recognize those situations where your intensity may go up or down. Finally, you must take active steps to reach and maintain prime intensity throughout training and competition.

Determining Your Prime Intensity

The first step in taking control of your intensity is to ascertain your prime intensity. You can garner information to make this determination in two ways. First, think back to several competitions where you performed well. Recall your level of intensity. Were you relaxed, energized, or really fired up? Then remember the thoughts, emotions, and physical feelings you experienced during these competitions. Were you positive or negative, happy or angry, relaxed or tense? Second, think back to several competitions in which you performed poorly. Recall your level of intensity. Remember the thoughts, emotions, and physical feelings you had in these competitions. If you're like most athletes, a distinct pattern will emerge. When you perform well, you have a particular level of intensity. This is your prime intensity. There are also common thoughts, emotions, and physical feelings associated with your prime intensity and performing well. In contrast, when you're performing poorly, there is a different level of intensity, either higher or lower than your prime intensity. There are also decidedly different thoughts, emotions, and physical feelings.

Second, you can experiment with different levels of intensity in training and see how the differing intensity impacts your performance. The following is a good exercise for learning more about your prime intensity (you can adapt it to your particular sport).

Let's say you're engaging in a series of performances in training, for example, a practice match in tennis or running plays in basketball. Break up your training performances into three segments. The first segment should emphasize low intensity. Before you begin the drill take several slow, deep breaths; relax your muscles; and focus on calming thoughts (e.g., "Easy does it," "Stay cool and calm"). As you start the drill, stay focused on remaining relaxed and calm.

The second segment should focus on moderate intensity. Before the performance, take a few deep but more forced breaths, walk around a bit, and focus on more energetic thoughts (e.g., "Let's go," "Pick it up."). Before the performance, move your body with more energy and feel your intensity increasing. During the performance, pay attention to feeling the intensity and energy in your body.

The final segment should highlight high intensity. Before the performance, take several more intense breaths, with special emphasis on a hard and aggressive exhale. Start bouncing up and down more actively, and repeat intense thoughts (e.g., "Fire it up," "Get after it"), saying them out loud with energy and force. Feel the high level of intensity and energy as you begin the performance, and focus on maintaining the intensity with constant movement and high-energy self-talk.

I encourage you to try this exercise for several days so you can see how much your intensity impacts your performance. As with comparing past good and poor performances, you will likely see a pattern emerge in which you perform better at one of the three levels of intensity, and you will likely see the same level of intensity identified in past competitions as being related to good performance. That level of intensity, your prime intensity, is the one you want to aim for in both training and competition.

With this knowledge, you will have a good sense of your prime intensity. You can then use that information to recognize when you're not at prime intensity and you need to adjust your intensity to a prime level.

I think it's playing with heart, playing with intensity, and playing with a commitment that, even if you lose, you can be proud of.

—George Karl, former NBA coach[18]

Psych-Down Exercises

It's natural to feel some increase in your intensity in a competition. You're putting yourself to the test and want to do your best. But when that increase in intensity turns to tensity and anxiety, it can hurt your performance—and that's a problem. But rather than just resigning yourself to feeling nervous and performing poorly, you can take active steps to reach and maintain your prime intensity. There are a number of simple "psych-down" exercises you can use to get your intensity back under control.

Muscle Relaxation

Muscle tension is the most common symptom of overintensity. This is the most crippling physical symptom because if your muscles are tight and stiff, you simply won't be able to perform at your highest level. There are two muscle-relaxation exercises you can use before and during competitions: passive relaxation and active relaxation. Similar to deep breathing, muscle relaxation is beneficial because it enables you to regain control of your body, makes you feel more comfortable physically, and allows your body to perform well. It also offers the same mental and emotional advantages as deep breathing.

Passive relaxation involves imagining that tension is a liquid that fills your muscles, creating discomfort that interferes with your body's ability to perform its best. As you go through the passive relaxation procedure, focus on deep and slow breathing, imagine the tension draining out of your muscles, and focus on your overall state of mental calmness and physical relaxation.

Active relaxation can be used when your body is very tense. When your intensity is too high and your muscles are tight, it's difficult to just relax them. Instead of trying to relax your muscles, do the opposite. Tighten them more, then relax them. For example, before a competition, your muscle tension might be at an 8, where 1 is totally relaxed and 10 is very tense, but you perform best at a 5. By further tightening your muscles to a 10, the natural reaction is for your muscles to rebound back past 8 toward a more relaxed 5. Paradoxically, making your muscles tenser at first results in them becoming more relaxed.

Active relaxation typically involves tightening and relaxing four major muscle groups: face and neck, arms and shoulders, chest and back, and buttocks and legs. It can also be individualized to focus on particular muscles that trouble you the most. For each muscle group, tighten your muscles for five seconds, release, take a deep breath, and repeat. As you go through the active relaxation procedure, focus on the differences between tension and relaxation, be aware of how you are able to induce a greater feeling of relaxation, and focus on your overall state of mental calmness and physical relaxation.

These relaxation procedures can also be used during a competition (for those sports comprised of a series of short performances) in an abbreviated form. Between performances, you can stop for five seconds and allow the tension to drain out of tense parts of your body (passive relaxation) or tighten and relax the tense muscles (active relaxation).

Slow the Pace of Competition

As mentioned previously, a common side effect of overintensity is that athletes tend to speed up the tempo of competition. Athletes in sports like tennis, golf, baseball, and football can rush between plays, almost as if they want to get the competition over with as soon as possible. To lower your intensity, slow your pace between plays. Simply slowing your pace and giving yourself time to slow your breathing and relax your muscles will help you lower your intensity to its prime level.

I don't psych myself up. I psych myself down. I think clearer when I'm not psyched up.

—Steve Cauthen, jockey legend[19]

Psych-Up Exercises

Although less common, inadequate intensity or letdowns in intensity can also cause your level of performance to decline. Too low intensity causes the things that enable you to perform well to disappear. Physically, you no longer

have the blood flow, oxygen, and adrenaline necessary for the strength, agility, and stamina you need to perform your best. Mentally, you lose the motivation and focus that enables you to perform well. As with the psych-down
exercises, to be used when your intensity is too high, you can use psych-up
exercises to raise your intensity when it drops.

Move Your Body

Remember that intensity is, most basically, physiological activity. The
most direct way to increase intensity is with physical action. In other words,
move your body. Walk or run around, jump up and down, do plyometric
exercises, push-ups, or squats. Anything to get your heart pumping and your
body going will raise your intensity.

High-Energy Self-Talk

One of the main causes of decrease in intensity is letdown thoughts.
Thinking to yourself, "I've got this won," "The game is over," or "I can't win
this," will result in a drop in intensity because your mind is sending messages
to your body that it no longer needs to perform. When this happens, your
performance will decline. When you start to have these thoughts, replace
them with high-energy self-talk. Self-talk, for example, "Keep attacking,"
"Close it out," and "Stay pumped," will keep you motivated and focused, and
your body will respond with more intensity.

High-Energy Body Language

It's difficult to use high-energy self-talk without also having high-energy
body language. Pumping your fist or slapping your thigh will also get you
fired up and increase your intensity.

Intensity Tools

In addition to psych-down and psych-up exercises, there are two powerful
intensity tools you can use to adjust your intensity to its ideal level: breathing
and music.

Breathing

Breathing is a key mental tool because it is the only physiological activity over which you have conscious control. You can't directly change your

heart rate or blood flow, but you can control them indirectly with breathing. Breathing is a useful tool for raising or lowering your intensity. It is also a valuable tool for improving focus and altering mindset (to be discussed later in this chapter).

When you experience overintensity, one of the first things that's disrupted is your breathing. It becomes short and choppy, and you don't get the oxygen your body needs to perform its best. Thus, the most basic way to lower your intensity is to regain control of your breathing by taking slow, deep breaths.

Deep breathing has several important benefits. It ensures that you get enough oxygen so your body can function properly. By getting more oxygen into your body, you will relax, feel more comfortable, and have a greater sense of control. This increased comfort will give you more confidence and enable you to more easily combat negative thoughts (which are often the cause of the overintensity). It will also help you let go of such negative emotions as fear or frustration and allow you to restore positive emotions like happiness or excitement. Concentrating on your breathing will also take your mind off of the factors that may be causing your overintensity and help you refocus on performing your best.

For athletes who participate in sports that involve a series of short performances, for instance, baseball, football, tennis, and golf, deep breathing should be a part of your between-performance routine (see the "Establish Routines" section in this chapter for more on routines). One place where deep breathing can be especially valuable in reducing intensity is before you begin another performance. By taking two deep breaths before you begin, you ensure that your body will be more relaxed, comfortable, and prepared for the upcoming performance.

You can also use breathing to raise your intensity. Instead of slow, deep breaths to reduce intensity, you can take shorter, faster, and more frequent breaths to increase your intensity. This intense breathing elevates your heart rate, accelerates blood flow, and releases adrenaline.

Music

Music is one of the most common tools athletes in many sports use to control their intensity. We know that music has a profound physical and emotional impact on us. It has the ability to make us happy, sad, angry, or inspired. Music can also excite or relax you. Many Olympic and professional athletes listen to music before they compete to help them reach their prime intensity and even have specific playlists.

Relaxing music is beneficial in several ways. It has a direct effect on you physically. Calming music slows your breathing and relaxes your muscles. Simply put, it makes you feel good. Mentally, it makes you feel positive and motivated. It also generates positive emotions like joy and contentment. Finally, calming music takes your mind off of aspects of the competition that may cause doubt or anxiety. The overall sensation of listening to relaxing music is a generalized sense of ease, comfort, and well-being.

Music can also be used to raise your intensity and get you psyched up and motivated. The overall sensation of listening to high-energy music (e.g., rock, hip-hop) is a generalized sense of excitement and energy.

Tip from the Top: Smile

One of the strangest and most effective tools I've come across to lower intensity is something that we do often without realizing how powerful it truly is. A few years ago, I was working with a young professional athlete who was having a terrible training session. She was performing poorly, and her coach was yelling at her. She approached me during a break feeling frustrated and angry, and her body was in knots. She asked me what she could do. I didn't have a good answer until an idea popped into my head. I told her to smile. She said, I don't want to smile. I told her to smile. She said she was not happy and didn't want to smile. I told her again to smile. This time, just to get me off her back, she smiled. I told her to hold the smile. During the next two minutes, there was an amazing transformation. As she stood there with the smile on her face, the tension drained out of her body. Her breathing became slow and deep. She said she was feeling better. In a short time, she was looking more relaxed and happier. She returned to training, her performance improved, and she made some progress during the remainder of the workout.

Her response was so dramatic that I wanted to learn how such a change could occur. When I returned to my office, I looked at the research related to smiling and learned two things. First, as we grow up, we learn the positive effects of smiling. We learn that when we smile, it means we're happy and life is good. Second, there's been some fascinating research into the effects of smiling on our brain chemistry. This research has found that when we smile, the brain releases chemicals called endorphins, which have a physiologically relaxing effect.

But for these psych-down techniques to be effective, you need to rehearse them in training and less-important competitions. The goal is to ingrain them so that when you get to a major competition where you are likely to feel nervous, you will automatically put them to use. Your intensity will decrease to a more comfortable level, and you will be better prepared to perform your best.

When I'm smiling and having fun, I perform the best.

—Simone Biles, four-time Olympic gold medal–winning gymnast[20]

EXERCISE

IDENTIFY YOUR PRIME INTENSITY

1. Identify your prime intensity using the exercise described earlier.

2. Before you are about to perform in your next competition, identify your current level of intensity in relation to your prime intensity.

3. Depending on whether it is too high or too low, use the psych-up or psych-down exercises to reach your prime intensity.

FOCUS

Focus is the most misunderstood mental factor among athletes. Most athletes think of focus as concentrating on one thing for a long time. In fact, many years ago, former Australian Open tennis champion Hana Mandlikova said that she improved her game by staring at a tennis ball for 10 minutes a day. She may have believed this worked, but, in fact, given the complexity of tennis and most other sports, it probably did little to help.

Simply put, focus involves paying attention. In sports, you can focus on things that help you perform well, for example, technique or tactics. Or you can focus on things that distract you, like who's watching, what will happen if you win or lose, or negative thoughts about your upcoming performance.

Prime focus involves focusing only on the things that will help you perform your best and avoid distractions that hurt performance. Depending on your sport, prime focus can include such external cues as your opponent, the score, time remaining, and conditions. It can also include internal cues like your technique, tactics, confidence, intensity, and mindset. Prime focus also gives you the ability to adjust your focus internally and externally as needed during the course of a performance.

For example, a football quarterback first focuses internally to select the best play based on the current game situation. As the huddle breaks and he moves over center, he widens his focus externally to survey the defensive alignment. When the ball is hiked and he drops back to pass, the quarterback focuses on the routes of his receivers until he finds one who is open, at which time he narrows his focus to that receiver before throwing him the football.

Poor focus, by contrast, involves focusing on internal and external cues that distract you from performing your best. There are two types of harmful cues. Interfering cues are those that will directly hurt your performance (negative thoughts, anxiety, or concern about who your next opponent will be if you win). Irrelevant cues are those that simply distract you from an effective focus (thinking about what you'll have for dinner tonight or the project you must finish by tomorrow).

The successful warrior is the average man, with laser-like focus.

—Bruce Lee, martial arts legend[21]

The Value of Focus

Prime focus has several essential benefits to your training and competitive efforts. First, you are far more effective in your performances because you are focused on what you are supposed to do to perform your best and, as a result, more likely to execute well. Second, you are more efficient in your training because prime focus is a key component of quality training. The more you are focused on what you need to improve, the faster you will improve. Finally, you will be more consistent in your training and compe-titions because the more consistent your focus, the more consistent your effort, execution, and performance.

You should have three goals as you develop your focus capabilities. First, you must identify those things, both internally (e.g., thoughts, emotions, physical sensations) and externally (e.g., conditions, opponent), that you need to focus on to perform your best. Second, you should identify the internal (e.g., negative thoughts, bad emotions) and external (e.g., other competitors, coaches) distractions that prevent you from focusing effec-tively. Third, you must actively and consistently focus on the good things and block out the distractions.

Obstacles to Prime Focus

There are common aspects of sports performance that can act as obstacles to prime focus. First, the most basic barrier to focusing effectively is distrac-tions that arise in your own mind or your immediate surroundings. Whether negative thoughts, anxiety, teammates talking too much, or your coach giv-ing you too much feedback, these distractions fill your mind with clutter, preventing you from focusing on what you need to do to perform your best.

Second, it is difficult to focus effectively if you don't have a clear process, that is, you don't know what to focus on. You want to develop an unambigu-ous understanding of precisely what you want to focus on to perform your best. This clear process may include technique, tactics, training or competi-tive conditions, and your opponent's playing style, among many others. With this clarity of process, you can direct your focus toward those identified areas that will result in good performance.

Third, the stress you experience before and during competitions, particu-larly important ones, also prevents effective focus. Stress impacts your focus in several ways, both mentally and physically. The stress reaction has the effect of narrowing your focus so that you can only concentrate on that one thing that is causing the stress, in this case, a big event. You develop tunnel vision to the extent that all can you think about is the enormity of the com-petition rather than widening your focus to encompass the more important aspects of the performance, for instance, preparation. Stress also produces physical changes that are uncomfortable, including muscle tension and short-ness of breath, which further narrow your focus and direct it inward.

Focus Style

One of the most important developments I've made in my work is in understanding the importance of identifying athletes' focus styles. A focus style is a preference for paying attention to certain things, particularly before a competition. Athletes tend to be more comfortable focusing on some things while avoiding others. Every athlete has a dominant style that impacts all aspects of their sports performance. This dominant style will surface most noticeably when they're under pressure. The two types of focus styles are internal and external.

Internal Focus Style

Athletes with an internal focus style perform best when they're totally and consistently focused on their sport during training or a competition. They need to keep their focus narrow, thinking only about their sport. These athletes tend to be easily distracted by activity in their immediate surroundings. If they broaden their focus and take their mind off their sport, for example, if they talk about nonsport topics with their coach before a competition, they become distracted and will have trouble narrowing their focus back onto their sport.

External Focus Style

Athletes with an external focus style perform best when they only focus on their sport when they're about to begin training or a competition. Otherwise, it is best for them to broaden their focus and take their mind off their sport. These athletes have a tendency to overthink, become negative and critical, and experience competitive anxiety. For these athletes, it's essential that they take their focus off their sport when they're not performing.

External focus style runs counter to the beliefs held by many coaches. They think that if athletes are not totally focused on their sport, they're not serious about it and won't perform their best. Yet, athletes with an external focus style don't want to think too much or be too serious, as this causes them to lose confidence and become anxious. Rather, it's best for these athletes to distract themselves by, for instance, talking to a friend or listening to music, until just before it's time for them to perform, when they narrow their focus onto their sport. These athletes perform their best when they're not thinking too much about their sport and simply allow their natural abilities and preparations to emerge on their own.

I'm one of the few gymnasts who can just block out anything. I could probably be thinking about pizza before I go and compete. A lot of people like to focus on their routines, but I feel like if I focus on it too much, I get more stressed out and I overthink, and that's when I don't do my best. I try not to think about it. I'll wave to the girls in the crowd and I'll just interact with them. I guess I'm just different.

—Simone Biles, four-time Olympic gold medal–winning gymnast[22]

Identify and Understand Your Focus Style

With this understanding, you need to identify your focus style. Are you an athlete who needs to keep your mind on your sport constantly for you to perform well? Or are you someone who thinks too much and needs to keep your mind off your sport until it's time to perform?

Recall past competitions when you've performed well. Were you totally focused on your sport or did you keep your mind off it until just before you performed? Also, recall past competitions when you've performed poorly. Were you thinking too much or distracted by things going on around you? If you're like most athletes, a pattern will emerge in which you tend to perform best when you focus one way and poorly when you focus another.

You can also try different focus styles in training and less important competitions. For example, try an internal focus style before one performance. Another day, try an external focus style. Chances are a pattern will emerge in which one focus style works and the other doesn't.

This ability to manage your focus style is most important in your normal training and competitive preparations. It is particularly important in high-pressure situations, like big events. There is a tendency for athletes under pressure to revert back to a focus style that will interfere with rather than help their performance. For instance, if you're someone who tends to overthink, you may find yourself turning your focus inward when the pressure is on. You may start to think too much and become anxious.

When you start to drift away from your ideal focus style, you must become aware that you're doing so and that you need to take steps to redirect your focus back to the style that works best for you. Continuing the previous example, when you realize that you're focusing internally too much, you should actively turn your focus outward by looking around and taking your mind off your sport.

Focus Tools

For you to focus effectively and consistently, there are a number of focus tools you can add to your mental toolbox.

Have Clear Goals and Process

A simple reality of focusing is that you can't focus on something if you don't know what you need to focus on. The first step in developing prime focus involves identifying your specific focus. You can establish this by first specifying your goal for whatever you are doing. If it's in training, you can set a technical or tactical goal. For example, a volleyball player might have as a goal improving positioning on return of serve. If it's for a competition, it might be a performance goal. For instance, if you are a 400-meter runner, your goal might be to finish the last 100 meters strong.

Once defined goals are established, you have clarity on what you want to focus on; however, you can't simply repeat that goal in your mind as you train or compete. The next step is to take those goals and create a focus process that you will focus on during your performances. In the case of the volleyball player, the process might be to focus specifically on the server's eyes and contact and early trajectory of the served ball. For the track runner, the process might involve a verbal reminder as he passes the 300-meter mark, like, "Bring it home!" repeated during those last 100 meters.

I don't focus on what I'm up against. I focus on my goals and try to ignore the rest.

—Venus Williams, seven-time Grand Slam tennis winner[23]

Identify and Limit Distractions

No matter how clear your focus goals and process may be, you won't be able to focus if you are distracted by people or things in your external and internal environments. You want to scan your training and competitive settings, as well as the thoughts and emotions that can clutter your mind, and identify the most prominent distractions that could prevent you from achieving and maintaining prime focus. Common external distractions include teammates, competitors, coaches, family and friends, media, fans, and the scoreboard. Typical internal distractions include negative thoughts, irrelevant thoughts, unpleasant emotions, and physical anxiety. Once you have identified these distractions, develop strategies to limit them. For example, if you are distracted by your competitors before an event, find a secluded place. If you are feeling anxious before a competition, listen to music and focus on your breathing to take your mind off of and lessen your anxiety.

Distractions destroy action. If it's not moving you toward your purpose, leave it alone.

—Jermaine Riley, professional soccer player[24]

Use Keywords

One of the simplest, yet most powerful, tools for focusing during training and competitions is to create a keyword you can repeat. A keyword is a short and active descriptor, ideally one word, of what you want to focus on in your sport. Whatever you're working on, think of a simple keyword. Before you begin and while you're performing, repeat the keyword to yourself (out loud if necessary). If you're saying the keyword, you have a much better chance of keeping the focus on the technique you're working on, practicing it throughout the entire performance, and ingraining it so that it becomes automatic. For instance, if you're a center in basketball and you are working on blocking out the opposing center on a rebound, your keyword might be "block," and repeating it during practice ensures that you keep it in your mind and execute it consistently.

Use Mental Imagery

Another valuable tool for focusing is mental imagery (described in detail in chapter 5). Also referred to as visualization, imagery involves seeing and feeling yourself perform in your mind's eye. Imagery offers several ways to help you to focus better. First, if you are imagining yourself in your sport, you are focusing on your performance and, as a result, blocking out unwanted internal or external distractions. Additionally, the very act of imagery strengthens your ability to focus because it takes focus to maintain imagery of your performances.

Focus on Breathing

Breathing is a key tool (also discussed in detail in chapter 5) used in a variety of mental calming and physical relaxation methods, including meditation and yoga. Much like a keyword, when you focus on your breathing, it has the effect of narrowing your attention onto yourself and blocking out distractions. Breathing also offers other mental and physical advantages. For instance, the type of breathing you use can activate the mindset (explored in the next section) that helps you perform your best. Additionally, breathing can be a helpful tool for increasing the oxygen in your system and adjusting your intensity up or down to its ideal level.

Establish Routines

Outlined in chapter 5 in detail, routines offer widespread benefits, including helping you focus on your training or competitive preparations. With this focus on your routine, you are concentrating on aspects of your performance that will assist you in performing your best. In doing so, you also block out distractions. By adhering to your routine, you ensure total readiness, and the consistency of a routine increases your comfort and confidence by creating a situation that is familiar, predictable, and controllable.

Write Messages on Equipment

Finally, an odd, yet effective, tool for helping you focus, particularly regaining an ideal focus when you become distracted, involves writing messages on your equipment. In the heat of a training session or competition, it's easy to get so wrapped up in performing that you forget to focus on things that will help you perform your best. For example, if you get nervous before an event, the physiological manifestations of your anxiety can cause you to become overwhelmed by and fixated on the physical discomfort, whether a racing heart or tense muscles. It is difficult to have the wherewithal to break free from this absorption and redirect your focus in a positive way. That's where the messages on your equipment can come in.

If, while you are distracted by your nerves, you look at messages (e.g., breathe, calm) you have written on your equipment, perhaps on your batting glove, frame of your tennis racquet, or side of your golf bag (you could even just write a message on your bare hand), they will remind you of what you should be focusing on and help you break from the unhealthy focus and regain focus on what will help you perform your best.

Tip from the Top: Three Ps

There is a simple rule you can follow that will help you identify which general areas you should focus on in your sport. I call it the three Ps. The first P is *positive*. You should focus on positive things that will help your performance and avoid negative things that will hurt it. The second P is *process*. As explained earlier, you should focus on what you need to do to perform your best, for example, technique or tactics, not that which will distract you. The third P is *present*. You should focus on what you need to do right now to perform well in the moment. You shouldn't focus on the past because you can't change it. You also shouldn't focus on the future because you can't change it

---

EXERCISE

PRIME YOUR MIND FOR TRAINING

1. Before training, do the following:

   a. Establish a goal you want to accomplish in your training (e.g., technical, tactical).

   b. Describe specifically what you will do in your training to achieve that goal (e.g., exercises, drills).

   c. Identify a simple and active keyword you can repeat to yourself before and during your training to stay focused.

   d. Before you perform, close your eyes and imagine yourself performing the way you want to accomplish your training goal.

directly. The only way to control the future is to control the present. The only way to control the present is to focus on it.

I always have on my headphones to block out all of the other distractions, and I'm just focused on doing the best I can.

—Michael Phelps, 22-time Olympic swimming champion[25]

MINDSET

Mindset is an essential and little-addressed contributor to athletic success and a mental area that has only come to light in my work with elite athletes during the past few years. Professional and Olympic athletes offer wonderful examples in the way they use different mindsets to perform at their highest level on a consistent basis.

Let me preface this discussion by clarifying that my use of the word *mindset* is different from the use of the word popularized by Stanford University researcher Carol Dweck (a perspective, I might add, that is consistent with my own and one that can also help athletes achieve their competitive goals). When I talk about mindset, I mean what is going on in your mind in the one to three minutes before you begin a competition. What happens in your mind during that oh-so-important period sets the stage for whether you are able to perform to the best of your ability.

Before I discuss the most common mindsets I have seen among professional and Olympic athletes, I would like to describe four mindsets that most interfere with an athlete's ability to perform their best. First, a doubtful mindset involves one grounded in a lack of confidence. At the beginning of a competition, if you have doubtful mindset, you are questioning (e.g., "I don't think I can do this") and negative (e.g., "I don't have a chance"). Second, a worrying mindset involves being preoccupied with "what ifs," that is, concern for the bad things that could happen in a competition (e.g., "What if I don't play well?" or "What if I get crushed?"). Third, a tentative mindset occurs when you are feeling uncertain and are not fully committed as you approach the competition. Finally, a fearful mindset is one in which you are actually afraid of performing, leading to a tense and cautious effort in competition. These mindsets pretty much guarantee poor performance and failure to achieve your goals.

Eliminate the mindset of CAN'T! Because you can do anything!

—Tony Horton, fitness expert[26]

Common Mindsets

In contrast, I have found three mindsets that the best athletes appear to use most often before a competition.

Aggressive Mindset

When I talk about an aggressive mindset, I don't mean that athletes should try to hurt their opponents. Rather, I think of aggressiveness as a mindset in which athletes are proactive, assertive, and forceful, for example, driving hard to the hoop in basketball, going for a risky shot in golf or tennis, or setting a fast pace in a marathon. This mindset is often needed for athletes to shift from solid performance to exceptional performance because it allows them to take their performance to the next level, particularly for those who aren't naturally aggressive. For example, I worked with a linebacker who was selected in the early rounds of the NFL draft. He was so gentle off the field that he wasn't able to naturally "take it to" the offense while playing. For him to be successful in the NFL, he needed to adopt an aggressive mindset.

An aggressive mindset can be valuable because many sports have become "combat sports," meaning that opponents or competitive conditions are trying to literally or figuratively beat athletes. Athletes do battle with not only opposing players and teams, but also weather and competitive conditions. Only by assuming an aggressive mindset do some athletes have a chance of vanquishing those enemies. For instance, in an interview after her first World Cup victory of the 2015–2016 season, Mikaela Shiffrin, the 19-year-old alpine ski racing prodigy who had already won Olympic and World Championship gold medals, indicated she was trying to adopt more of an aggressive mindset to help her overcome her pattern of relatively sluggish skiing in the first half of race runs.

An aggressive mindset can be developed in several ways. First, you're more likely to perform aggressively if your body is amped up a bit more than usual. You can raise your physical intensity with more movement during training, in your competitive routines, and just before you begin to compete (see the section on intensity earlier in the chapter for more details on elevating your intensity). Simply moving more and being more dynamic in your movements will help you shift to a more aggressive mindset.

Second, you can use high-energy self-talk to instill that aggressive mindset. You can see this practice in use in football locker rooms and before weight-lifting competitions. Examples include, "Let's go!" "Attack!" "Charge!" and "Bring it!" What you notice is not only what you say, but also how you say it. Thus, your aggressive self-talk should sound, well, aggressive. No pussycats here; only tigers, lions, and panthers allowed.

Third, you can incorporate an aggressive mindset into mental imagery in which you see and feel yourself performing aggressively, which, in turn, helps create more attacking thinking, focus, and feeling.

Calm Mindset

A calm mindset is typically best for athletes who get nervous before they compete. Throughout your precompetitive preparations and when you are about to begin a competition, your primary goal should be to settle down and relax, allowing your mind to let go of doubt and worry, and your body to be free of nerves and tension. Additionally, a calm mindset can be invaluable for athletes who are naturally aggressive and don't need to take active steps to get into attack mode.

A calm mindset can be created in several ways. First, it's difficult to have a calm mind if your body is anxious, so focusing on relaxing your body is a good start. Deep breathing and muscle relaxation are two good tools you can use to calm your body (see the section on intensity earlier in this chapter for more details on how to lower your intensity).

Second, calming and reassuring self-talk can ease your tension, for example, "Easy does it," "Cool, calm, and collected," and "Chillin' before I'm thrillin'." Calming self-talk can shift your doubtful, worrying, or fearful mindset, giving you the confidence and comfort to perform your best.

Third, you can use mental imagery in which you see and feel yourself being calm before a competition. This imagery has a direct physiologically relaxing effect on both your body and mind. Plus, seeing yourself performing well in your imagery has the related positive effect of increasing your confidence and narrowing your focus on good performance.

Clear Mindset

A clear mind involves having basically nothing related to performing going on in your mind before a competition. Athletes who use a clear mindset are those who can be seen talking to coaches, teammates, or even their competition before they go into action. They are often smiling, dancing around, chatting it up, or singing to themselves. They're looking around and seem completely unfazed by the fact that they are about to compete.

I have found that a clear mindset is the least common mindset among athletes and is most often found among a certain group of elite athletes. These athletes can use a clear mindset because they are incredibly talented natural athletes with years of experience that have allowed them to trust their bodies to perform their best without any interference from their minds.

A clear mind is most suited for athletes who are intuitive (they don't have to think about their sport very much to perform their best), free spirited (they go with the flow rather than being structured in their approach to their sport), and experienced (they have a lot of confidence and trust in their capabilities from many years of success).

You create a clear mindset by thinking about anything except your sport. Talking to others around you, thinking about someone or something that makes you feel good, and listening to music are several ways you can keep your mind clear, preventing it from getting in the way of your body performing its best.

I truly believe in positive synergy, that your positive mindset gives you a more hopeful outlook, and belief that you can do something great means you will do something great.

—Russell Wilson, NFL quarterback[27]

Tip from the Top: Identify Your Ideal Mindset

Identifying your ideal mindset is important because if you don't know what your best mindset is, you'll have no chance of achieving it and, as a result, little chance of performing your best. The challenge is that you may think you already know your ideal mindset because it is the one you've always used. You are comfortable with it, and it seems to work for you; however, I have found with some frequency that the mindset athletes say works best for them is often not the right one.

There are two ways you can identify your ideal mindset. First, think back to past competitive performances in which you performed really well. Recall what went on in your mind in that 30 to 60 seconds before you entered the competition. Now think back to past performances where you didn't perform up to par and remember your mindset in those competitions. If you are like most athletes, you will see a pattern in which you had one mindset when you succeeded and another when you didn't.

But you shouldn't use past experience as the only judge of your ideal mindset because what worked in the past may not work now or in the future. As you mature as an athlete, you change physically and mentally, and so your mindset may evolve as well.

The second way you can determine your ideal mindset, and either confirm or disprove your past experiences with your mindset, is to experiment with different mindsets in training. Divide a training session into three sections and try to use a different mindset (i.e., aggressive, calm, or clear) in each segment. If there is another mindset I haven't mentioned that you think might be worth trying, be sure to include that mindset in your experimentation.

EXERCISE

FORM AN IDEAL MINDSET

1. Identify negative mindsets that prevent you from performing your best.
2. Recall past competitions to determine which mindset you believe works best for you.
3. Experiment with different mindsets in training.
4. Determine your ideal mindset.
5. Commit to using your ideal mindset in training and competition.
6. Ingrain your ideal mindset so it becomes a habit.

As you experiment with each mindset, see how you feel and perform in each segment. If you are like most athletes, two things will happen. First, you will see a pattern emerge in which you perform better using one mindset over the others. If no clear winner materializes from your experimentation, continue to test the different mindsets in ensuing days of training and different training situations and conditions. If you will be competing in relatively less important competitions, you can also extend your experimentation to include them, as they will provide a more accurate gauge of your ideal mindset in competitive conditions.

If you have big competitions coming up, it's never a good idea to try anything new. Rather, stick with the mindset you are comfortable with and continue to explore your ideal mindset in training and lower-level competitions. In any case, even when you identify the mindset you believe most effective, you will still want to continue to test and fine-tune it in increasingly more competitive and demanding events.

I think anything is possible if you have the mindset and the will and desire to do it and put the time in.

—Roger Clemens, MLB Hall of Fame pitcher[28]

5

PrimeTime: Five Mental Tools

One of the challenges of helping athletes with the mental aspects of sport is that many think the mind can't change: You either "have it" or you don't, and if you don't have it, you can't get it. For example, if you don't have much confidence, well, you'll never be confident. Or, if you've always gotten nervous before competitions, you will always get nervous. If you hold this belief, I want to challenge it. Are you able to overcome physical weaknesses and

develop your fitness? Of course you can. Are you able to change bad technical habits and become more skilled in your sport? Obviously. The mind is no
different; if you put in the time and effort, you can change the way you think,
feel, and perform. You make these changes by creating a mental "toolbox"
filled with tools that help you perform your best and achieve Prime Sport.

Let me use an analogy to explain why developing a mental toolbox is so
important to your athletic success. Imagine you're driving down a road and
you get a flat tire. You pull over to the side of the road, open your trunk, and
see that you have no spare tire, no jack, and no tire iron (and no AAA!). What
does this mean for you? You're stuck where you are. But, if you had the necessary tools to replace the flat with the spare, in a short time, you would be back
on the road heading toward your destination.

The reality is that you are going to have a lot of flat tires, metaphorically
speaking, in your athletic career; they are an unavoidable part of pursuing
your own personal athletic greatness. You will feel the burden of expectation
and pressure from yourself and others. You are going to get discouraged,
nervous, and distracted. You will have difficulties mastering new skills in
your sport. And you will fail to perform up to your ability and achieve deeply
held goals. These struggles are inevitable. Only by creating your own mental
toolbox will you put yourself in a position to fix these problems. Chapter 5
explores the five mental tools I find most influential, particularly on the day of
a competition, in preparing you to perform your best and overcome the "flat
tires" you will experience as you develop as an athlete.

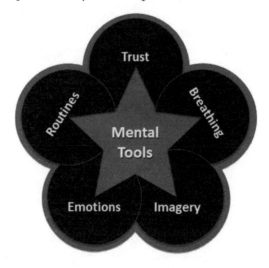

EMOTIONS

Emotions play a vital, yet often underappreciated, role in athletic performance. In fact, emotions aren't just important in sports, but also in our lives in general on a much grander scale. Emotions give our lives and our sports participation texture, depth, and richness. Often without realizing it, emotions propel you in your athletic life. If you ask yourself why you participate in sports, common responses might include that sports are fun and provide you with excitement, joy, satisfaction, pride, and inspiration.

What do these responses have in common? They're all emotions. I would also add that the reasons why you're into sports don't all involve experiencing good emotions. Rather, you may also participate in sports because of the disappointment, frustration, and stress that can result from this participation. These emotions aren't pleasant, to be sure, but when you experience them, they trigger such reactions as determination, drive, resilience, and perseverance, which can lead to even stronger positive emotions because of the challenges you overcome and the good feelings generated by these accomplishments. As a result, emotions are an essential piece of the Prime Sport puzzle.

An athlete experiences the emotions of pain and elation through triumph and defeat, through teamwork and individuality, as nothing more than a human being . . . that is the true glory of sport.

—Aimee Mullins, Paralympian[1]

Emotions: Weapons or Tools?

Unfortunately, you can't just feel the positive emotions, like happiness, gratitude, and hope. Think of emotions as two sides of the same coin; you can't experience the good emotions without also being willing to experience the emotions that don't so feel good. So, it's not really a matter of whether emotions feel good or bad, but rather the effect they have on the way you think and react. Too often, the so-called negative emotions act as weapons. These emotions are typically experienced as being negative (e.g., fear, worry, despair), unpleasant, seemingly uncontrollable, overwhelming, hurtful to one's psychology (e.g., decreased motivation, confidence, and focus) and physiology (e.g., anxiety, apathy), and disruptive to one's training and competitive performances. They just plain feel bad.

But emotions are not just phenomena you experience in reaction to your sports participation. Rather, they can also be used as tools to promote athletic success. In this case, emotions can be experienced as being positive, pleasant, controllable, moderated, helpful to one's psychology and physiology, and helpful to one's training and competitive performance. And they can feel good. From this perspective, you should have several goals as you gain experience in using your emotions as tools.

First, you should be willing to experience the broad range of emotions common in sports. You can't cherry pick your emotions, meaning you can't just feel the good emotions—happiness, excitement, and inspiration—while avoiding the so-called bad ones—anger, exasperation, and sadness. You have to be willing to experience and accept the entire range of emotions you will experience in your athletic life.

Second, you want to recognize those situations that tend to trigger the bad emotions and understand where they are coming from (e.g., overinvestment, fear of failure, expectations). Refer back to chapter 2 for an explanation of the obstacles that are frequently related to emotions that interfere with your athletic efforts. In this process of recognition and understanding, you can learn to let go of their impact and no longer fall victim to them.

Third, rather than keeping your emotions bottled up inside, you can learn to express them, particularly the unpleasant ones, in healthy ways. For example, instead of throwing a tantrum after a poor first half, you can channel your anger into intense motivation and an aggressive mindset that will allow you to have a strong second half. In making this shift, you are transforming those emotions from weapons that hurt you into tools that help you, that is, to invoke the well-known adage, from swords into plowshares.

Mentally tough athletes are not emotionless: They are just skilled in subordinating emotions to the greater requirements of winning competitions.

—Ellis Cashmore, author of *Making Sense of Sports*[2]

Understanding Your Emotional Life

Of the mental areas that impact your athletic life, emotions are perhaps the most difficult to understand. We, of course, experience emotions all the time. Yet, we don't often know what causes them or how to deal with them effectively. To increase your understanding of your emotions, there are four things you should know about them.

Emotionality involves the degree to which you feel emotions. Some people don't seem to feel emotions very strongly. We think of them as being rather stoic or made of Teflon (life just slides off of them). Others feel emotions deeply, experiencing intense highs or debilitating lows. Still others lie somewhere between the two extremes. Emotionality has been shown to be largely genetic; you are born somewhere along the continuum.

Expressiveness is related to the degree to which you express your emotions outwardly. Many people confuse expressiveness with emotionality. Yet, some people can be very emotional but turn their emotions inward and not express them. Hence, others can't tell what they are feeling. As with the other qualities of emotions, you lie somewhere on a continuum between being openly and intensely expressive ("wearing your heart on your sleeve") and hiding your emotions from others ("holding your emotions close to the vest").

Direction involves how positive or negative your emotions are in relation to your athletic life. Do you mostly experience pride, fun, inspiration, and joy in training and competitions? Or, do you chiefly feel anger, frustration, worry, and fear? Obviously, if you tend to gravitate toward the negative side of the continuum, you'll want to take a close look at what is causing the negative feelings and either figure out how to make a shift in the positive direction or perhaps consider whether sports participation, which is causing such an unpleasant emotional experience, is right for you.

Control means how well you are able to consciously regulate your emotions in a way that not only feels good to you, but also helps you perform your best in your sport. In other words, it is the degree to which your emotions act as weapons against you or tools for you. An essential part of achieving Prime Sport involves learning to control your emotions in a way that fosters high performance and positive feelings about your efforts.

The Negative Emotional Chain

One of the great obstacles you will experience as an athlete, particularly in your training efforts, can be summarized as what I call the negative emotional chain. The negative emotional chain involves a linked series of unpleasant and interfering emotions you experience as you face the inevitable challenges of developing as an athlete and oftentimes making unsteady progress toward your goals. The three emotions are frustration, anger, and despair.

Frustration

Frustration may be your most significant obstacle to achieving your athletic goals. Every athlete, ranging from juniors and age-groupers to Olympians and pros, has experienced the feeling of frustration when they're not able to do something, whether physically, technically, tactically, or competitively: You feel stuck, become tense, lose focus, and grow discouraged. The best way I can describe the feeling is, "AAARRGGHH!!" It is a truly infuriating emotion.

But what is frustration precisely and what causes it? Simply put, frustration arises when the path toward your goal is blocked, whether the goal is setting a new PR in your squats, nailing a new technique, or getting a good result in competition. Frustration is an emotion you probably experience frequently. And it can be really disheartening and, well, frustrating.

Most people think of frustration as a bad emotion, but it is actually more complex than that. The fact is, frustration is hardwired into us to help us survive. It starts as a good emotion because, when you get frustrated, you're motivated to remove the obstacle that is blocking the path toward your goals. You try harder, and that extra effort can, if the obstacle isn't too big, result in clearing that path, enabling you to alleviate the feeling of frustration and continue on down the road.

There is a problem that often arises when you become frustrated, preventing you from clearing the way to your goals: There is a tendency to continue doing what you were doing before but more and harder, relying on the "magical thinking" that you will somehow wear the barrier down by sheer will and persistence. Unfortunately, this strategy violates Albert Einstein's famous law of insanity—doing the same thing over and over, and expecting different results. Thus, your well-intentioned efforts can actually increase, not decrease, your frustration, leading you to the next link in the negative emotional chain.

You must have long-term goals to keep you from being frustrated by short-term failures.

—Charles C. Noble, English politician[3]

Anger

If, despite your best efforts, you are unable to clear the path toward your goals and relieve your frustration, your frustration can morph into anger. Most people also believe that anger is a bad emotion; however, like frustration, it has both positive and negative sides. Anger starts out as being potentially helpful because it too is motivating. When you're angry, you want to go after the thing that is causing your anger. So, you direct your energy toward ripping down that barrier that is blocking your path. Again, if the barrier isn't too difficult to overcome with the added energy of anger, turning up your emotional volume from frustration to anger may be just what you need.

Unfortunately, more often than not, anger can turn into an emotion that hurts your performance. Feelings of anger are like those of frustration but exponentially more intense. Your body becomes tense, you lose your coordination, and the quality of your effort declines. Your focus narrows to the extent that you miss important cues that might otherwise help you surmount the roadblock. And your ability to think and focus becomes clouded by the anger, so you aren't able to make good decisions about how to approach the obstacle. The likely result is that the barrier will remain in place, you will remain stagnated along the path to your goals, and you will move on to the final link in the negative emotional chain.

Anger is only one letter short of danger.

—Eleanor Roosevelt, former first lady of the United States[4]

Despair

If you aren't able to clear the obstacle from your path, your emotions will shift to the final link of the negative emotional chain: despair. You have tried and tried again, and still can't remove the barrier, so the natural inclination is to quit. You feel out of control, helpless, and hopeless. What's the point of continuing to try if nothing you do works? The unfortunate outcome is immediate and irreversible failure to make progress toward your goals that day.

When you experience despair, everything that would normally be required to overcome the initial cause of the negative emotional chain reverses direction. Psychologically, you lose your motivation, confidence, and focus. The physical parameters related to athletic success, including energy, blood flow, oxygen, and adrenaline, drop precipitously. The result is that you lack the mental and physical abilities to remove the roadblock.

It has been my experience that if you move from frustration to anger to despair, continued efforts that day usually fail. You are, quite simply, finished for the day. And if you experience the negative emotional chain on a regular basis—sinking repeatedly into despair—you will likely lose your motivation and be unwilling to make a sustained effort in the future. As you descend the negative emotional chain link by link, you come to believe that you can no longer control your emotions when faced with difficulties in your sport, that your actions have little effect, and that you will progressively lose confidence in your ability to achieve your goals.

Breaking the Negative Emotional Chain

Despite the powerful influence that frustration can have on your training and competitive efforts, you were probably never taught how to deal with your frustration in a constructive way (it should be a required part of your sports training). Your goal is to learn to stop the negative emotional chain at frustration by responding positively to the frustration when it first arises. There are several steps you can take.

Take a Break

When frustration first arises, immediately take a break from the situation that is causing the frustration. By doing so, you create physical distance from the source of the frustration, and that distance also results in emotional distance in which the frustration naturally diminishes.

As a part of taking a break, there are two more useful steps you can take. First, noted earlier, frustration causes an increase in physiological intensity, including muscle tension and choppy breathing. To relieve these unpleasant symptoms of frustration, you want to change your physiology by taking deep breaths and relaxing your muscles. Second, do something during the break that fosters emotions that are the opposite of frustration. Listen to music, be goofy, or talk to friends. This step lessens the uncomfortable physical symptoms that accompany frustration and generates emotions like happiness or fun, which can counteract the feelings of frustration, reducing their influence on you.

Another great way to counter the feelings of frustration is to engage in something at which you know you can succeed. For example, if you can't get something technically, focus on and practice something you are good at, feeding your feelings of confidence and generating such positive emotions as pride and hope.

Finally, when you get frustrated, it can be helpful to have a snack or something to drink. Hunger and thirst can contribute to vulnerability and frustration because your body is in a weakened and needy state. Refueling can give you the energy you need to resist the pull of frustration and help you perform better, making it less likely that frustration will resurface.

Gain Perspective

Having an unrealistic perspective on your training and competitive efforts can set you up for frustration even before you begin to train or compete and exacerbate your susceptibility to frustration after you've begun. This perspective revolves around the belief that you can reach your goals quickly and easily. Unfortunately, as discussed in chapter 1, nothing of value comes without significant time, effort, and energy.

To prevent this self-fulfilling prophecy from occurring, you can use the three Ps detailed in chapter 3: patience, persistence, and perseverance. When you begin to experience frustration, remind yourself that progress takes time and that you should hang in there no matter what occurs. You can also commit to persisting for as long as it takes and persevering through the inevitable ups and downs you will experience as you pursue your athletic goals. This long-term perspective may not remove your frustration completely, but it will lessen it, allowing you to more easily take the additional steps I recommend before returning to the source of your frustration.

You can also look at your confrontation with frustration as an opportunity to become tougher and more resilient. The reality is that the pursuit of your athletic goals is a frustrating process because it is long and difficult, with many setbacks and failures. Experiencing frustration gives you an opportunity to embrace the frustration and learn how to deal with it in a positive and constructive way. You can think of frustration as emotional adversity, another form of adversity explored in chapter 3. When you allow yourself to be exposed to it and learn how to respond positively to it, you become a better athlete, more capable of dealing constructively with this emotional adversity in the future.

Patience, persistence, and perspiration make an unbeatable combination for success.

—Napoleon Hill, American author[5]

Identify the Cause

By this point, you will have relieved yourself of most of the physical, psychological, and emotional expressions of frustration. But you still aren't ready to return to the task of confronting the cause of your frustration because that cause is still there, and if you reengaged it now, you would simply become frustrated again. The next step, then, is to identify the cause of your frustration. If you can understand the specific problem, that is, what produced your frustration, you have the opportunity to find a solution and, in doing so, remove the obstacle that originally led to your frustration.

Find a Solution

With the cause identified, you are only one step away from being able to return to the situation that caused your frustration in the first place. Now that you know what the obstacle is—it may be physical, technical, tactical, equipment, or mental—you are in a position to find a solution. Sometimes, the solution is obvious and easy to put into action. Other times, it is too big to act on. In this case, it can be useful to break down the bigger problem into smaller, more manageable problems. Moreover, if you can't figure out the cause of your frustration yourself, ask your coach for help.

If All Else Fails

The reality is that you can't always immediately clear the obstacles to your goals. Thus, continued efforts in pursuit of those goals on any given day would be futile and discouraging. The barriers may just be too great to surmount on that day. If you feel as if you have exhausted every resource, you have two options. First, you can change your goals to ones you feel capable of striving for and achieving that day. For example, you can shift your focus to another area of your development where you believe you can make progress.

Second, there are going to be days when you just aren't going to make any progress toward your goals and continuing to try without success will just discourage you more and actually hurt your efforts in the long run. In this case, it may be wise to deliberately "give up" and choose to fight another day. If you choose this path—and it should be your path of last resort—do something else productive, whether it be conditioning, schoolwork, or something you enjoy that will take your mind off the day's frustration.

Disappointment versus Devastation

It never feels good to have a poor performance. When you perform badly, you feel bad. It's natural to experience negative emotions in reaction to results that don't live up to your expectations. But the specific negative emotions you experience will have a big influence on how that subpar performance affects you in the near term and the future. I have found that athletes can have one of two emotional reactions to unsatisfactory results: disappointment or devastation.

Hard days are the best because that's when champions are made.

—Gabby Douglas, Olympic gymnastics champion[6]

Disappointment

No one likes to be disappointed. You feel sad and defeated. Your heart aches for the opportunity lost and the goal not achieved. Certainly, disappointment is not a pleasant emotion; it feels really bad, in fact. But that doesn't mean it should be avoided at all costs. To the contrary, disappointment is actually a healthy and positive emotion that plays an essential role in the pursuit of your athletic goals. Disappointment is an emotional reaction to a failure of a situation, specifically one in which you perform poorly or have an unexpected loss in competition. Disappointment occurs when you are unable to fulfill some hope, goal, or expectation. It involves feelings of thwarted desire and loss.

Disappointment is hardwired into us to help when we are confronted by failure. It girds your resolve and mobilizes your resources to do better in the future. What's your natural reaction to disappointment? If you're like most athletes, after a brief period of discouragement, your disappointment morphs into determination and drive to overcome the situation that caused the disappointment and prevent it from happening again.

When you experience disappointment after a performance in which you did not do well, you should let yourself feel the emotion fully, even if it doesn't feel good. Allowing yourself to feel the disappointment in all its power will enable you to use the energy to motivate you so you don't feel that disappointment again. Your newfound understanding of disappointment will also take some of the sting out of the experience and make it easier to use it as a positive force in your athletic efforts.

After "falling off the horse" with a poor result, you will naturally encounter a brief period of letdown. But you must pick yourself up and get back on the horse—that is, get back to pursuing your athletic goals with renewed determination and intensity. By putting the disappointment behind you and directing your focus to the present and the future, you can experience a better way of feeling in response to failure and find new ways to overcome your setbacks and return to your journey to your goals.

Rather than allowing the disappointment to dishearten you and cause you to feel bad about yourself, you can use the experience to reaffirm your capabilities by showing yourself that you can conquer your failures and disappointment. As difficult as it may seem, you want to view disappointment as training for adulthood (because you're going to experience plenty of disappointment as a grown-up). You want to accept that failure and disappointment as an inevitable and unavoidable part of life. What matters is how you react to it.

Devastation

Unfortunately, some athletes will perceive poor performances not as disappointments that are experienced as relatively minor and temporary setbacks, but rather devastating assaults on who they are and what they are capable of. This occurs because, unlike disappointment, which is seen as a failure of a situation (in this case, a failure of a competition), devastation is experienced as a perceived failure of self, meaning the failure is felt as a direct reflection on themselves as athletes and people.

Devastation in response to a discouraging performance is experienced when athletes are overly invested in their sport (discussed in chapter 2, most specifically in the section on overinvestment). In other words, how they perform in their sport is too connected to their evaluation of their value as athletes and worth as people. Devastation is a truly harmful emotion that not only hurts future performance, but also is overwhelmingly painful. It can last for days, weeks, months, or even years after the unsatisfying performance (depending on how important the failure was; for example, a poor result at the Olympics could last for a long time).

What makes devastation such a destructive emotion is the natural reaction you can have afterward. This reaction, unlike disappointment, actually increases the likelihood of more failure and more devastation in the future. Devastation is, in fact, a general emotional state that is comprised of a veritable plethora of awful emotions that can include pain, embarrassment, humiliation, shame, fear, grief, dejection, despair, jealousy, pity, bitterness, loneliness, and self-hate. Now that is one depressing list of emotions!

This tsunami of hurtful emotions doesn't just make these athletes feel really, really bad. It also does damage to their motivation and confidence—they plummet—and causes them to feel incompetent and inadequate as both athletes and people. These reactions then have the effect of killing their passion for their sport—devastation is the opposite of fun—and their determination and drive to overcome the poor performance. These athletes are hit so hard by a substandard performance that they want to flee from the painful experience. They withdraw socially, mope around, look deflated, and feel sorry for themselves for far longer than they should. The problem with this type of reaction to failure is that you automatically lose. Yes, poor performances and unsatisfying results can take the wind out of your sails, but it shouldn't be that painful.

Experiencing devastation should be a big red flag for you. It should tell you that you have one of the obstacles mentioned in chapter 2 (overinvestment, perfectionism, fear of failure, expectations, negativity) blocking the path to your goals. Moreover, you need to follow my recommendations for reducing your investment in your sport to a healthier level. In doing so, you will moderate your reactions to setbacks, mistakes, and failure from devastation to disappointment. As you make this shift, you will also be able to use those obstacles to your advantage by increasing your resilience, motivation, and confidence. Finally, you will perform better and be happier as well.

We need to continually challenge ourselves to "do better" but never to the extent that we experience negative emotions as a function of anxiety or excess stress—physically, mentally, or emotionally.

—Warren Gray, college basketball coach[7]

Emotional Risk

In chapter 1, I discuss the importance of risk as an attitude that is essential to performing your best. There are many types of risk athletes can take, with physical, technical, and tactical risk being the most obvious. But perhaps the most important and, well, risky risk is emotional risk. The notion of emotional risk ties in with the issues explored in chapter 2, related to obstacles that get in the way as you pursue your athletic goals, for example, overinvestment, perfectionism, and fear of failure. At the heart of these topics is the excruciating pain you think you will feel, what I term "total failure," if you give it everything you have and still fail to perform your best and achieve your goals. That is the emotional risk I'm talking about: Your willingness to fully put yourself out there knowing that taking this immense risk may not always pay off.

If you want it, go for it. Take a risk. Don't always play it safe or you'll die wondering.

—Unknown[8]

Emotional Risk Mitigation

As you prepare for a competition, you do everything you can to mitigate the emotional risk you are taking. There are many things you can control to help you accomplish this goal, and the more things you can control, the less the emotional risk. You have a good precompetitive meal, prepare your equipment, do your warm-ups, study strategy and tactics, and do mental imagery—everything you can think of to be as prepared as you can be to perform your best. Wanting to perform your best is certainly one reason for your extensive preparation. But another is to reduce the emotional risk you will be taking when you begin the competition. The better prepared you are, the better your chances of performing well and succeeding. And the better your chances of success, the lower your emotional risk.

Unfortunately, you can't remove the emotional risk completely because there are many things in sports you can't control. Examples include weather; court, course, field, track, or hill conditions; other competitors; and officials. Then there is that thing athletes call "bad luck," which is sometimes used to explain unforeseen events in a competition. These uncontrollables can hurt your performance, and you can't do anything about them. Despite your best efforts, the emotional risk remains.

As detailed in the section on fear of failure in chapter 2, many athletes further reduce the emotional risk of failure in ways that protect them temporarily but ultimately prevent them from finding success and achieving their sports goals. They engage in self-sabotage or self-defeating behavior (e.g., not being totally prepared, feigning injury, not giving their best effort), which ensure failure but provide them with an excuse that protects them from the emotional risk. This produces a "win"–lose–lose scenario. They "win" (in quotes because it's not really winning) because they protect themselves from experiencing the painful emotions they associate with total failure. But they lose by not performing well or achieving their goals. And they lose again because they feel awful for not having the strength to take the emotional risk and not giving their best effort.

Instead, you want to create a true win–win–win scenario. You win by taking the emotional risk of being totally prepared and giving your best effort, increasing (but not guaranteeing) your chances of success. You also win because you are more likely to perform your best and get the results you want. Finally, you win because you feel great that you were mentally strong enough to take the emotional risk rather than "wimping out."

Make Emotional Risk a Lifestyle Choice

Taking emotional risks is, well, risky and, as a result, uncomfortable. When it comes to that moment when you have to make the decision whether to take the emotional risk, it can be difficult, because so much of your mind and body are telling you not to. You don't want to make taking an emotional risk into a spontaneous, last-minute decision. If you do, you will probably play it safe and not take the risk. You want to make an emotional risk a nondecision— that is, it's just what you do.

To that end, the easiest way to make emotional risk a habit in your sport is to make it a lifestyle choice; it is simply the way you live your life. To not take emotional risks would be inconsistent with your values and goals in sports and life. You can create this default of emotional risk in several ways. First, you can do your best to remove the obstacles (overinvestment, perfectionism, fear of failure, expectations, negativity) so that failure isn't so threatening to you. By doing so, you free yourself to take emotional risks because those risks aren't as risky.

Second, you can constantly expose yourself to challenging situations in which failure is a possibility. You can do this in your sport by trying new techniques and tactics that may or may not work, experimenting with new approaches to performance, and pushing the limits of what you think you are capable of in training and competitions. The more you expose yourself to emotional risk, the more familiar and less threatening it will become, the more confident you will become that the emotional risk will pay off with success, and the more you will learn that will enable you to see your emotional risks rewarded in the future.

Third, as you ingrain the habit of taking emotional risks, you will find that what was once uncomfortable is becoming increasingly comfortable (although emotional risk may never feel completely comfortable; if it did, it wouldn't be a risk).

As emotional risk simply becomes what you do, you will learn several invaluable lessons that further gird you to take more emotional risks. You learn through experience that the consequences of failing aren't as painful as you thought they would be. Yes, you feel bad, but it's more disappointment than devastation. You also learn that when you take emotional risks, good things happen more often than not. Additionally, you see that if the emotional risk doesn't pay off, there are still some good feelings to be had, with one example being pride, because you overcame your greatest obstacle—yourself—and survived. The more you take emotional risks, the more you learn that it feels far better to take them and fail than to not risk at all.

The key to facing fear and taking risk is to start small. Get some practice and you'll discover you get better at facing fear.

—Georges St-Pierre, mixed martial arts champion[9]

Become an Emotional Master

A key message in this section is that emotions play an essential role in your athletic life. Sports can evoke a wide range of emotions, from inspiration, pride, exhilaration, and satisfaction, to fear, frustration, anger, and panic, often in a short time span during training or competition. I emphasize the impact emotions can have on you because it has been my experience that they ultimately dictate your ability to perform your best and achieve Prime Sport (defined, if you recall, as being able to perform at a consistently high level in the most challenging conditions). Your ability to perform well consistently is often determined by the consistency of your emotions—as your emotions go, so go your performances—and your ability to master them. Your ability to respond positively to the inevitable challenges you will face in training and competition is, again, often impacted by your emotional reactions to those challenges. Because of this influence, being able to master your emotions gives you the power to use emotions as tools to facilitate, rather than weapons that hurt, your athletic performance.

Emotional Master or Victim?

Many athletes believe that they are just the way they are emotionally, that they have little control of their emotions, and that there is nothing they can do to gain control of them. If their emotions hurt them, well, they have to accept the situation because they can't do anything about it. I call these athletes *emotional victims*, because their emotions control them, they don't believe they can do anything about how they feel, they possess unhealthy and unproductive emotional habits, and their emotions hinder their ability to perform well and achieve their goals.

Despite these perceptions, my work has shown that you are capable of becoming an *emotional master*. You can gain control of your emotions and develop healthy and productive emotional habits. And your emotions can facilitate your ability to perform well and achieve your goals.

Choosing your emotions is a simple, but not easy, task. It is simple choice, because if you have the option to feel bad and perform poorly or feel good and perform well, you will certainly choose the latter option; however, emotions are tricky, as your hardwired temperament, emotional obstacles, and old emotional habits can lead you down the bad emotional road and cause you to respond emotionally in ways that are unhealthy and result in poor performance. Choosing your emotions is based on being aware of when old emotional habits arise and stepping in with a positive emotional response that will lead to good feelings and successful performance.

Emotional Mastery

Emotional mastery is not about not feeling, avoiding, or suppressing your emotions. The reality is that emotions are such powerful forces that, despite our best efforts to keep them under wraps, they have a way of emerging and hurting us in both subtle and obvious ways. Emotional mastery involves allowing yourself to fully experience the emotions you feel, identifying the emotions you are feeling, understanding where these feelings come from (both external causes and internal perceptions), and expressing your emotions in healthy ways that foster performance and happiness.

The process of emotional mastery begins with recognizing the negative emotional reactions that hurt your sports performance. When you start to feel negative emotions during training or a competition, be aware of what they are, for instance, fear, frustration, or anger. Then identify the situation that is causing them, for example, a series of mistakes, being criticized by a coach, or feeling a lack of support from a teammate.

After the competition, consider the underlying cause of the emotions. This might require you to examine the emotional habits you've developed since you were young. The attitudes and obstacles explored in chapters 1 and 2, respectively, will help you identify those unhealthy emotional habits.

If the emotions are strong and you find that they hurt you both in your sport and other parts of your life, you might consider seeking help from a sport psychologist or other qualified mental health professional (much of my work focuses on clearing these emotional obstacles). Such guidance can assist you in better understanding your emotional habits, how they may interfere with many aspects of your life, and how you can learn new emotional responses that will better serve you in your sport and your life.

To continue the process of emotional mastery in training and competition, specify alternative emotional reactions to the situations that commonly trigger negative emotions. For example, instead of yelling, "I am terrible!" when feeling frustrated after making a mistake in training, you could slap your thigh and say, "Come on, better next time!" which should generate feelings of hope and determination. Or, instead of screaming at the referee and getting ejected from a game after getting angry because of a disputed call, you could turn your back and take several deep breaths. These positive emotional responses will help you let go of past mistakes, motivate you to perform better next time, generate positive emotions that will give you more confidence, and allow you to focus on what will help you raise the level of your performance.

Recognizing that emotional mastery is about developing emotional tools, this positive reaction will not be easy at first because your negative emotional habits are well ingrained; it is difficult to change a bad technical habit. But, with commitment, awareness, control, and practice, and the realization that you will feel better and your performance will improve with a positive response, you will, in time, retrain yourself to have positive emotional habits. You will transition from an emotional victim into an emotional master, with the tools to not only perform better, but also be much happier.

Courage is resistance to fear, mastery of fear, not absence of fear.

—Mark Twain, author[10]

Tip from the Top: Fun Is a Mental Tool

Fun isn't something most people think of as a mental tool. Fun is, well, fun, and something you have, not something you do. Yet, it is one of the most powerful tools you can put in your mental toolbox. It affects you psychologically and emotionally, and, as a consequence, can have a real and positive impact on your athletic performance.

Why is fun so beneficial? It generates potent positive emotions, including happiness, joy, excitement, and contentment. These emotions counter negative emotions like fear, frustration, and anger. Fun also produces positive changes in your physiology, including a reduction in stress, anxiety, and tension, and, depending on the type of fun, an increase in relaxation and physical comfort or adrenaline, heart rate, and blood flow. These changes in emotions and physiology directly affect how you think, feel, act, and perform in any given training or competitive situation.

Do you ever think about the past or future when you're having fun? Decidedly not. Fun is about being in the present. It encourages you to stay in the moment when training and competing as you begin to focus on the past or future. Fun also provides perspective by reminding you why you participate in your sport: because it's fun. It can lift the heaviness and seriousness that sports can often cause in athletes by bringing lightness and joy to training and competing. Isn't that what sports should really be about?

Given that fun is a mental tool you can use to feel and perform better in your sport, you have to be able to do things that will trigger fun. This process starts by remembering why you participate in your sport and specifically what makes it fun. You might do it because it's fun to push yourself or to be part of a team, master new skills, rise to the challenge of competition, and, yes, get great results and win.

Once you know what is fun for you in your sport, you can also incorporate fun into your training and competitive experiences. You can goof around

---

EXERCISE

CONTROL YOUR EMOTIONAL REACTION

1. Identify a sports situation in which your emotions interfere with your ability to perform your best.

2. Label the specific emotion you experience (e.g., fear, frustration, anger).

3. Describe what about the situation causes your emotional reaction.

4. Specify your thoughts, your emotional reaction, how your body feels, and how these responses impact your performance.

5. Understand the cause of the emotion.

6. Create an alternative emotional reaction to the situation in case it resurfaces.

   a. Specify more positive thoughts.

   b. Label the emotion you would like to feel.

   c. Identify how you want your body to feel and how you will achieve that feeling.

7. When you are in that situation again and you feel yourself begin to have a negative emotional reaction, choose the alternative plan you have devised.

8. Continue to use this plan until it becomes a habit.

during breaks in training, keep things light as you prepare for a competition, stay connected with your teammates, and do more of what you enjoy most in your sport. You can also make your sport more fun by making your life more fun. Make sure you have fun in other parts of your life, including with your family and friends, at school, and in other activities in which you participate. As I mention in chapter 6, not everything about your sport is going to be fun, but if you can actively make much of what you do in your sport fun, you're giving yourself another powerful tool in your mental toolbox to perform your best and achieve your athletic goals.

The rewards are going to come, but my happiness is just loving the sport and having fun performing.

—Jackie Joyner-Kersee, three-time Olympic track and field gold medalist[11]

IMAGERY

If you do anything to work on the mental side of your sport, it should involve mental imagery. Why, you ask? Because there is no more powerful mental tool than imagery, and it can have a huge impact on your sports performance. I say this with such conviction not because of my work as a sport psychologist or because I studied it in school. Rather, I believe in the power of imagery because of the profound effect it had on me when I was young and aspiring to become one of the best alpine ski racers in the world.

One summer I took a course at a local college that introduced me to the power of imagery. I applied it to my ski racing as part of my final project for the class and continued to use it the following fall and into the competitive race season. The results were nothing less than spectacular. From doubt came confidence. From distraction came focus. From anxiety came intensity. From timidity came aggressiveness. From inconsistency came consistency. From good skiing came really fast skiing. And, most importantly, from decent results came outstanding results, and I went from being an okay ski racer to one who earned an international ranking.

When I studied imagery in graduate school, I learned why it is so powerful. Imagery is used by virtually every great athlete, and research has shown that, when combined with actual practice, it improves performance more than practice alone. In my decades of mental training work with professional, Olympic, collegiate, and junior-elite athletes, imagery has been the tool I have emphasized the most and had the greatest impact on athletic performance. The bottom line is, if you aren't using imagery on a regular basis away from your sport, in training, and to prepare for competitions, you're not doing everything you can to achieve your athletic goals.

I am a big believer in visualization. I run my races mentally so that I feel even more prepared.

—Allyson Felix, six-time Olympic sprint champion[12]

What Is Mental Imagery?

To be sure you understand precisely what imagery is, let me describe it for you. Many athletes, coaches, sport psychologists, and mental trainers call imagery visualization. Although I use the term *imagery*, you can use them interchangeably. At the same time, while the seeing part is important, I want to emphasize the importance of another key contributor to the power of imagery: feeling. Effective imagery isn't just something that occurs in your mind. It is also a psychological and physiological phenomenon in which you reproduce the actual athletic experience in your mind and body. Moreover, it impacts you in your sport in every way: psychologically, emotionally, physically, technically, and tactically. You can think of imagery as weight lifting for the mind because it strengthens every mental muscle.

Keys to Quality Mental Imagery

There are six factors that impact the quality of mental imagery: perspective, vividness, control, feeling, speed, and total experience. You can develop each of these areas to get the most out of your imagery.

Perspective

Imagery perspective refers to where the "imagery camera" is when you do imagery. The internal perspective involves seeing yourself from inside your body looking out, as if you are actually performing your sport. The external perspective involves seeing yourself from outside your body, as if you are on video. Research indicates that one perspective is not better than the other. Most people have a dominant perspective with which they're most comfortable. Use the perspective that's most natural for you and experiment with the other to see if it helps you in a different way.

Here's an exercise to test where your camera is. Close your eyes and imagine yourself performing your sport for 15 seconds. Is your imagery camera internal or external? Now try it the other way and see what happens. Some athletes can switch easily from one camera view to another. But most athletes find that it takes a lot of effort to change views and that they quickly revert to their comfortable camera view.

Vividness

Vividness involves how clear your images are. Are your visual images blurry or high-definition? Are your feelings vague or sharp? It's not uncommon for athletes who first begin to do imagery to say that their imagery isn't very good. It's important to emphasize that imagery is a skill that takes practice; the more you do it, the better you get at it. Additionally, thanks to the widespread use of video in sports these days, it's easy for you to gain an accurate and vivid visual image of how you perform in your sport and translate it into your own imagery.

Here's an exercise to experiment with the vividness of your imagery. Close your eyes and imagine yourself performing in your sport for 15 seconds. If the image isn't as sharp as it could be, watch 15 seconds of yourself in your sport on video and then immediately repeat the imagery segment. Do this several times. You will likely see an improvement in your imagery vividness, and you can continue to use this exercise until your imagery is consistently clear and sharp.

The key to effective visualization is to create the most detailed, clear, and vivid a picture to focus on as possible.

—Georges St-Pierre, mixed martial arts champion[13]

Control

Have you ever been doing imagery and keep making mistakes? For example, a basketball point guard might see the ball stick to the court while dribbling, or a golfer might see her ball pop out of the cup. This problem relates to imagery control, which is how well you're able to imagine what you want to imagine.

It's not uncommon for athletes to perform poorly in their imagery. This occurrence seems odd to most athletes, because shouldn't you be able to imagine whatever you want to imagine? But I have found that this lack of imagery control is very common (in fact, I struggled with it when I first started using imagery as a ski racer), and I believe I know why. Imagery bypasses the conscious mind and taps into deeply ingrained beliefs athletes hold about themselves. When you make a mistake in your imagery, it can be a reflection of several issues. An error can reflect a fundamental lack of confidence in your ability to perform the way you want, even in your mind's eye. (This was my biggest problem as a ski racer, and it improved significantly as I learned to control my imagery.) A mistake may also indicate that you haven't fully learned and ingrained a new technique or another aspect of performance. Finally, it might suggest that you don't fully understand some important aspects of what you are trying to imagine.

The following is an exercise to assess and improve your imagery control. Close your eyes and imagine performing your sport for 15 seconds. If you performed without errors, great. But if you made mistakes in your imagery, you shouldn't just let them go. If you do, you'll further ingrain the negative image and feeling, which will make it more difficult to retrain and gain more control of your imagery. Instead, when you perform poorly in your imagery, immediately rewind the "imagery video" and edit it until you do it correctly.

I use visualization to think about the perfect technique. If I can get that perfect image in my head, then hopefully it'll affect my physical performance.

—Jessica Ennis-Hall, Olympic heptathlon gold medalist[14]

Feeling

As previously indicated, feeling is, for me, the most important part of imagery. I mean two things when I talk about feeling in your imagery. First, when you do imagery, I want you to feel it in your body as if you are actually performing. In fact, what you are trying to do is fool your body into thinking you are actually performing your sport. Many athletes I have worked with have found that their bodies move unconsciously when they imagine themselves in their sport. Moreover, there is scientific evidence that, when you do imagery, you are actually triggering your muscle memory in the same way as when you are physically performing (although not at the same level of muscle activation). This occurrence may explain why research has shown that athletes can learn new sports skills using imagery alone, without actual physical practice.

Second, when you do imagery, I want you to feel your performance on an emotional level. For example, if you feel calm and contented before you actually compete, you should recreate that serene feeling in your imagery. In contrast, if you get nervous when you compete, you should feel nervous before you compete in your imagery (and then use mental tools to relax yourself). Because you can reproduce your emotional reactions in your imagery, you have the opportunity to ingrain positive reactions and retrain negative reactions in your imagery, which will then translate into your actual competitive performance.

Here's an exercise to assess and explore how much you feel physically and emotionally in your imagery. Close your eyes and, while imagining yourself performing your sport for 15 seconds, focus entirely on feeling your performance in your body—in your muscles, breathing, and movements. Next, repeat the imagery with a focus on the emotions you want to experience when you compete. Then combine the two types of feelings into another 15 seconds of imagery. In a final 15 seconds of imagery, take those two kinds of feelings and add in visual imagery in which you combine all three modes of imagery.

Before the [Olympic] trials I was doing a lot of relaxing exercises and visualization. And I think that helped me to get a feel of what it was gonna be like when I got there. I knew that I had done everything that I could to get ready for that meet, both physically and mentally.

—Michael Phelps, 22-time Olympic swimming champion[15]

Speed

The ability to adjust the speed of your imagery will enable you to use imagery to improve different aspects of your sports performance. Slow motion is effective for focusing on technique. When you first start to work on technique in your imagery, slow the imagery down, frame by frame, if necessary, to see

yourself executing the skill correctly. This "slo mo" is no different from beginning to learn a new technical skill during a training session. In both cases,
slow motion enables you to focus entirely on the new skill without the usual
distractions, maintain control of your movements, and repeat the skill until it
becomes progressively more automatic.

As you see and feel yourself performing well in slow motion, you can
increase the speed of your imagery until you can perform well in "real-time"
speed. Doing imagery in real time allows you to get comfortable with the
speed at which you want to perform in competition.

Finally, what I call "fast forward," when you imagine yourself performing
as if your mental video is on fast forward, can also be a beneficial part of imagery. This accelerated imagery is helpful because it forces you to not think
too much, trust your body, and just react.

You can continue to use the different imagery speeds at different points
in your season. In the offseason, you can use slow motion to deeply ingrain
good technique and tactics. As the season approaches, you can use fast
forward to instill trust and quick reactions. As you enter the competitive
season, you can shift to real time to prepare for the actual experience of
performing in your sport.

I have found that an athlete's relationship with time in their imagery is
related to how much experience they have. Athletes with less experience
tend to either perform in their imagery slower or faster than real time. For
instance, when a certain exercise or segment of a performance takes 45 seconds to actually execute, it takes some athletes only 15 seconds to complete it
when using imagery, while other athletes aren't even half way through when
the 45 seconds are up. In contrast, experienced, high-level athletes are able to
imagine themselves performing in almost precisely real time. For example,
a world-class figure skater imagined herself performing her long program
within one to two seconds of the four-minute limit. And a 400-meter runner
imagined himself running within a few tenths of a second of his personal best.

The following is an exercise to experiment with your use of different
speeds in your imagery. First, imagine yourself performing in your sport for
15 seconds in slow motion. In this imagery, see and feel yourself executing
proper technique and tactics. Next, imagine yourself for 15 seconds in real-
time speed and see if you can maintain your form and quality of performance.

Then, in the last 15 seconds, imagine yourself at fast-forward speed, allowing your body to perform without conscious interference.

Total Experience

The best imagery involves the complete, multisensory reproduction of the actual sport experience. You should duplicate the sights, sounds, physical sensations, thoughts, and emotions that you would experience in an actual competition. As you practice and gain comfort with the use of imagery, you can incorporate more aspects of your actual sports performance. Your goal is to make your imagery as close to the actual athletic experience as possible.

Here's an exercise you can use to develop that total experience in your imagery. Break down your imagery into four 15-second segments with five-second pauses in between. In each segment, focus on the following modes of imagery separately: visual images, physical sensations, thoughts, and emotions. Then, during the course of another four 15-second segments, starting with the visual images, add in another mode, so that by the end you have incorporated all four into one total imagery experience.

You may find that your imagery is lacking in one of the areas I have described. If so, don't be discouraged. You're no different than most athletes when they first start using imagery. Imagery is a skill, and just like any other skill, it takes time and effort to understand and develop. My own personal experience and work with athletes suggests it can take up to several months to get comfortable with and gain complete mastery of your imagery.

You are creating the sights and sounds and smells, the atmosphere, the sensation, and the nerves, right down to the early morning wake-up call and that feeling in your stomach. It helps your body to get used to performing under pressure.

—Jonny Wilkinson, former English rugby great[16]

Developing an Off-Sport Imagery Program

As detailed in the introduction, the key to getting the most out of your mental training, in this case, your mental imagery, is to approach it the same way you do your conditioning and on-field training. In other words, your imagery program should be comprehensive, structured, and consistent. You wouldn't expect to get stronger by lifting weights once every few weeks. You wouldn't expect to get better technically by practicing your sport once in a while. The same holds true for mental imagery. The only way to gain the many benefits of imagery is to develop an imagery program that looks similar to your conditioning efforts.

Set Imagery Goals

Set specific goals for the areas you want to work on in your imagery. Goals can be technical, tactical, or mental, or involve overall performance. For instance, you might focus on a technical change, being more relaxed and focused, or just going for it in your sport. Before every imagery session, you should choose a goal you want to achieve and have that be your focus for the entire session.

Climb the Imagery Ladder

Create a ladder of training and competitive scenarios in which you will be performing. The ladder should start with training in a simple setting and progress to more demanding training situations, less important competitions, and more important events, leading up to the most important competition of the year.

Begin your imagery on the lowest level of the imagery ladder, focusing on your imagery goal. Stay at that rung until you are able to accomplish your imagery goal consistently, that is, to see and feel yourself performing the way you want. When this is achieved, stay at that step for several imagery sessions to reinforce and ingrain the positive images, thoughts, and feelings. Then work your way up each rung of the ladder until you're achieving your imagery goal and performing the way you want in your imagery at the top of the imagery ladder.

Training- and Competition-Specific Imagery

Choose training and competitive situations that are appropriate for your level of athletic development. In other words, if you're a high school soccer player, don't imagine yourself playing in a World Cup game against the Messi or Marta. Also, choose a specific competition in a precise location with particular conditions for each imagery session. Reaching your imagery goals in a variety of competitions, settings, and conditions will have the result of more deeply ingraining positive images, thoughts, and feelings related to your performance.

Imagery Content

Each imagery session should be comprised of your preperformance routine and your performance in training or competition. If you compete in a sport that is short in duration, like sprinting or wrestling, you can imagine an entire performance. If you compete in a sport that is lengthy, for example, golf, tennis, or soccer, you can imagine yourself performing in four or five key parts of the competition.

Imagery Sessions

Imagery sessions should be done three to four times per week (imagery shouldn't be done too often because, as with any type of training, you can get burned out). Each session should last about 10 to 15 minutes. Set aside a specific time of the day when you will commit to doing your imagery (just like you do for your physical training), and make it a normal part of your daily routine. If you don't, you're likely to forget. I recommend that you set your smartphone calendar to send you a reminder until it becomes a habit. Find a quiet, comfortable place where you won't be disturbed. Sit or lie down and begin your imagery session.

Imagery Journal

One difficulty with imagery is that, unlike physical training, the results aren't tangible. An effective way to deal with this problem is to keep an imagery journal. These logs should record key aspects of each imagery session, including the quality of the imagined performance, any thoughts and feelings that occur (positive or negative), problems that emerged, and what you need to work on for the next session. An imagery journal enables you to see progress in your imagery, making it more rewarding and increasing your motivation to stay committed to it.

Visualize this thing you want, see it, feel it, believe in it. Make your mental blueprint, and begin to build.

—Robert Collier, American author[17]

In-Sport Imagery

In addition to the many benefits you will gain from imagery away from your sport, you can get even more by incorporating imagery directly into your training sessions and competitive preparations. Research has shown that when you combine actual practice with imagery practice, you learn and perform better faster.

In-sport imagery can primarily be used in two places in training and competition. Before you begin an exercise, drill, or practice performance, close your eyes and take 15 seconds to see and feel yourself performing the way you want in the upcoming performance, with your specific goal in mind. This approach offers several benefits. First, it blocks out distractions like people talking around you. Second, it narrows your focus onto what you want to accomplish. Third, it primes your mind and body for the upcoming performance. Fourth, the positive images, thoughts, and feelings you experience in the imagery boost your motivation and confidence because you are seeing yourself succeed before you perform. Fifth, imagery helps you reach your ideal intensity before you begin. The overall benefit is being more mentally and physically prepared to perform your best in that exercise, drill, or performance, which will increase the quality of your effort and the benefits you gain from your efforts.

The second place you can use imagery during training and in competition is after you've just performed or, if you compete in a sport with a series of short performances, like tennis, golf, baseball, or football, between performances to encourage improved performance in your next effort. When you finish an exercise, drill, or performance, immediately close your eyes and imagine your just-completed effort. If you just had a successful performance, you want to remember it. Doing imagery right away in which you "replay" your good performance ingrains the good images and feelings you just experienced even more deeply.

If you made some mistakes or performed poorly, the last thing you want to have are images and feelings of that less-than-ideal effort. Yet, that is what will remain if you just move on to your next task in training. Instead, immediately close your eyes and "replay and edit" the performance, correcting the mistakes and replacing the negative images and feelings with a successful imagined performance and the related positive images and feelings.

The Power of Mental Imagery

So, here's the deal. I can't guarantee that an imagery program is going to result in a quantum leap in your sports performance like it did for me in my ski racing many years ago. But I will say that if you commit to an imagery program that is comprehensive, structured, and consistent, there's a darned good chance that you will be better prepared mentally than you were last year. And if you combine the imagery program with an intensive physical conditioning regimen and quality training in your sport, I can say with confidence that, after a few months of committed imagery, you'll be able to say, "I'm as prepared as I can be to perform my best and achieve my goals."

A major element in mental training is visualization. . . . Visualizing a positive outcome can create a pattern of success.

—Grete Waitz, former marathon world-record holder[18]

Tip from the Top: Move Your Body with Your Imagery

One of the most common sights you see when professional and Olympic athletes use imagery before training or a competition is that they move their bodies with the imagery. In other words, as they imagine themselves performing, they are also simulating the movements they are executing in their mind's eye. You see it with gymnasts rehearsing their routines, golfers preparing for a shot, and basketball players practicing their free throws. For some athletes, the movements are subtle; for others, the movements are more active; and for still others, the movements appear to mirror actual movement patterns. There is no evidence that one approach is better than another; rather, it is a matter of personal style, feel, and comfort.

Combining imagery sensations with the actual physical sensations has several important benefits. First, this practice brings the imagery out of the mind and into the body. Second, it connects and aligns your imagery with the motor programs for the movements. Third, it makes the imagery more real because of the experience of the more robust physical sensations over and above the imagined sensations. Fourth, it more directly fires the motor programs, priming them for a successful performance.

The following is an exercise you can use to figure out whether and how much moving with your imagery can help you. Close your eyes and imagine yourself performing in your sport for 15 seconds while keeping your body still. After a 10-second break, repeat the imagery, this time moving your body subtly to simulate your imagined performance. Finally, after another 10-second break, repeat the imagery but with active physical simulation of the movements. See which feels better and enables you to perform better in your mind's eye. You may also want to use this exercise in the course of several days to ensure that your immediate impressions were accurate.

I visualize what I'm going to do on that day, walk out to the fight. I'll go over and over it inside my head so when I do actually do it, I've been there 100 times before so it's nothing.

—James Te Huna, mixed martial arts champion[19]

ROUTINES

Routines are one of the most important aspects of sports you can develop to improve your conditioning, training, and competitive performance. They benefit your efforts by:

- Ensuring total preparation in your efforts
- Enabling you to be physically, technically, tactically, and mentally ready to perform your best
- Ingraining effective skills and habits that make it easier to transition from training to competition
- Training your mind and body to react the same way regardless of the importance of the competition
- Creating consistency, familiarity, predictability, and control

I don't know a world-class athlete in any sport who doesn't use routines in some part of their training efforts and competitive preparations.

Routines are most often used before competitions to make sure that you are prepared to perform your best. They can also be valuable in two other areas. Routines can be developed in training to ensure that you get the most out of your practice time, giving you clear purpose, ideal intensity, and a productive focus. Routines are also important between performances to help you get ready for subsequent performances (for sports comprised of a series of short performances).

There are a lot of things in sport that you can't control, for instance, weather conditions and your opponent. Ultimately, the only thing you can control is yourself. Routines can increase the control you have of your performances by enabling you to directly prepare in every area that impacts your sport, namely equipment (is your gear in optimal condition?), your body (are you physically and technically warmed up?), and your mind (are you at prime focus and mindset?).

Routines also allow you to make your preparations more familiar and predictable, and, as a result, more comfortable, since know you have systematically covered the areas that will influence performance. Routines can also help you expect the unexpected. In other words, as part of your routine, you can plan for any eventuality that could arise during a competition. If you can reduce the things that can go wrong and be prepared for those things that do, you'll be better able to stayed focused and relaxed before and during a competition.

Winning can be defined as the science of being totally prepared.

—George Allen, Super Bowl coach[20]

Routines versus Rituals

Some sport psychologists and mental trainers use the term *ritual* in place of routine. I don't like this term, because it has connotations that go against what routines are trying to accomplish. Remember, the goal of routines is to totally prepare you to perform your best in the gym, training, and competition. Everything done in a routine serves a specific and practical function in that readiness process. For example, a physical and technical warm-up and a review of tactics for an upcoming competition are essential for total preparation.

In contrast, a ritual is associated with superstitions and is often made up of things that have no practical impact on performance, for instance, wearing lucky socks or following a specific route to the competition site. Routines can also be adjusted should the need arise. For example, if you arrive late to a competition, you can shorten your routine and still get prepared. Rituals, however, are rigid and ceremonial. Some athletes believe that rituals must be done or they will not perform well. In sum, you control routines, whereas rituals control you.

I had only one superstition. I made sure to touch all the bases when I hit a home run.

—Babe Ruth, baseball legend[21]

Gym Routines

Most sport psychologists and mental trainers work with athletes on the mental side of their sport in an office setting (usually one hour per week), providing them with mental tools they can use during training and competition. This approach makes about as much sense as a coach offering their athletes technical instruction in an office and then telling them to go out onto the field, course, or court and work on it in training. In either case, the transfer from inside to outside isn't good.

I have found that the most productive work I do with athletes is during their actual training sessions. I'm able to go to training with them and show them how to incorporate mental training—intensity, focus, imagery, and routines—while they're practicing.

But, in the last few years, I have discovered an even better setting in which athletes can begin to develop their mental muscles: the gym. Yes, using mental exercises and tools as part of your physical conditioning program is a great way to begin to strengthen those mental muscles and learn to use the mental tools discussed in chapter 4 and this chapter.

Think of it this way: Both a drill in practice and, for example, a set of squats are physical performances that share many attributes. They both involve strength and technique. They hurt, especially at the end. And, most importantly, they require certain mental muscles and tools to maximize the gains you make from them.

A great thing about beginning your mental training in the gym is that it is a much less complex environment than in your sport training. Thus, it is easier to exercise and strengthen the mental muscles. You have fewer variables, fewer things to think about, and, importantly, fewer distractions that can prevent you from focusing on and strengthening your mental muscles.

Conditioning, sport training, and competition also have similar phases of execution. There is the preparation phase, where you get yourself physically and mentally ready to perform your best. There is the performance phase, where you are doing your best to perform at the highest level possible. There is the conclusion phase, where you may be in pain and your body is telling your mind (often in a very loud voice) to either ease up or stop because it hurts too much. Finally, there is the completion phase, where you evaluate your performance and see what you can do to improve.

What you need to do mentally for your sports training and in competition also applies to each set of a workout. You must be highly motivated to give your best effort, even when you get tired or begin to really hurt. You have to have confidence that you can, for instance, lift a certain weight or do a particular number of reps. You need a certain mindset to perform the exercise well, for example, an aggressive mindset to attack a lift or a calm mindset for stretching. You must have the high intensity necessary to explode upward with the weight in a lift or the low intensity to get the most out of yoga. You have to be focused on good technique so you execute properly and don't risk injury.

There are several benefits to using mental training in the gym. First, because you will be more mentally prepared for your workouts, you'll give more effort, have more quality in that effort, and, as a consequence, make greater gains in your fitness. Second, you'll be able to work on the mental tools before you get to your sports training, making the incorporation of the tools into your training and competitive preparations go faster and smoother. Finally, once you are using mental tools in your physical conditioning, training, and competitive routine, you'll ingrain them so deeply that when you get to that big event, those well-practiced mental habits will come out and enable you to perform your best.

Now that I've (hopefully) convinced you of the value of using mental training in the gym, you're probably wondering exactly how you can begin to include it into your workout regimen. There are five key mental areas you can incorporate into your conditioning that can transfer over to your sports training and competitive efforts: commitment, confidence, mindset, intensity, and focus.

Commitment

For you to get maximum gains from your conditioning, you must want it bad, otherwise your body's desire to avoid pain will overwhelm your desire to make fitness gains. Before each exercise, make a conscious commitment to put your best effort into it from start to finish: "I'm doing this!" This commitment is particularly important at the end of a set, when you need to finish strong in the face of the inevitable pain you feel to get the most out of the exercise.

Confidence

Say something positive that will give you a confident state of mind toward the exercise (e.g., "Ten reps at 225 pounds, I feel strong!"). This is especially important when doubts creep into your mind as you're doing a new exercise that you're not that skilled at or you're going to be attempting a weight you've never lifted before.

Mindset

Particularly in strength training, a passive mindset just isn't going to help you get the most out of your conditioning. In a way, you're competing against the exercise; it wants to stop you from lifting the weight or completing the required number of reps. You have to attack the weight and impose your will on it. Otherwise, near the end of the set, your body will tell your mind to stop, and your mind will listen. Adopting an aggressive mindset from the first rep to the last can make a big difference, particularly with the last few reps, when it gets hard. Tell yourself, "I'm attacking this lift!"

Intensity

Different types of conditioning exercises require different levels of physical intensity to get the most out of them. If you don't have the requisite intensity for a specific exercise, you won't get the most benefit from it. For exercises that require strength and power, "rev your engine" before every set by jumping up and down, taking some aggressive breaths, and using "psych-up" self-talk (e.g., "Let's do it!). When doing low-intensity exercises like stretching or yoga, relax your muscles, breathe deeply, and use "psych-down" self-talk (e.g., "Let's be calm and easy").

Focus

Simply put, if you're not totally focused on your best execution and effort in an exercise, you will fail to perform it well and gain its greatest benefits, and you might also hurt yourself. Before each set, stop talking to people, take a deep breath to direct your focus onto the exercise, take five to 10 seconds and imagine yourself doing the exercise well, and then repeat a keyword (see the section on focus in chapter 4 for more details) that reminds you of an important thing you need to do to perform the exercise well (e.g., "straight back" or "attack").

Because mental training is new and not a part of your conditioning routine, you'll probably forget to use it from time to time. Don't beat yourself up about it if you don't remember every time. At first, you'll need to be reminded to use the mental tools during each set. I recommend taping a sheet of paper to the wall or mirror of your workout space that says something like, "MENTAL TOOLS!". When you see it, you'll be reminded to do it. Before you know it, the mental tools will become so ingrained that you will use them automatically without needing reminders.

Training Routines

Once you've developed a gym routine that is well ingrained, you can translate those habits of preparation into a training routine that you use in your sport. For you to get the most out of your training efforts, you should develop a brief training routine that will ensure that you're totally prepared for every drill, exercise, and practice performance. Your training routine is simply a sport-specific version of your gym routine in which you get yourself prepared physically and mentally.

Your training routine should only take a short amount of time—one to three minutes—to complete, but it will prepare you to get the most out of your training efforts. It will also lay the foundation for using a routine before and during competitions. Remember, for your training routine to become effective, you must use it consistently.

If you only give 90 percent in training, then you will only ever give 90 percent when it matters.

—Michael Owen, former English soccer star[22]

Competitive Routines

The next step in developing effective sport routines is to create a competitive routine that is an extended version of your gym and training routines. The goal is the same: to be prepared to perform your best. The difference is that a competitive routine is usually much more detailed and thorough, may have a few more components, and usually takes longer to complete.

There is no one ideal routine for everyone. Competitive routines are individual. Every great athlete will have a different routine, but the routines will have common elements. You have to decide what to put into your routine and how to structure it. Developing an effective competitive routine is a progressive process that requires time so you can find the one that works for you.

Focus and Intensity

Focus and intensity are two areas you must consider in developing your competitive routine. You should know whether you have an internal or external focus style and what level of intensity you perform best at. With that in mind, you want to plan your competitive routine so that you have prime focus and intensity when you begin a competition.

The most important thing is how a guy prepares himself to do battle.

—Hank Aaron, Hall of Fame baseball player[23]

Focus Needs

The goal in your competitive routine if you have an internal focus style (see chapter 4 for a reminder about focus style) is to put yourself in a place where there are few external distractions and you can focus on getting yourself ready to compete. To maintain that narrow focus, go through your competitive routine in private, away from other people and activities that could distract you.

An external focus style means you need to keep your focus wide during your preparations so you can keep your mind off of the upcoming competition and avoid thinking too much. The goal in your competitive routine if you have an external focus style is to put yourself in a place where your focus is drawn outward and you're unable to become focused internally and think about the competition. Your competitive routine should be done where there is enough activity to draw your focus away from what's going on inside your head. To widen your focus, go through your competitive routine while surrounded by teammates, other competitors, and activities that can draw your focus outward.

Intensity Needs

You'll also want to build your competitive routine around your intensity needs. The intensity component of your competitive routine should include

checking your intensity periodically as the competition approaches and using psych-up or psych-down techniques to adjust it as needed (see chapter
4). You'll need to set aside time in your routine when you can perform these
techniques. As you approach the competition, you'll want to move closer to
your prime intensity. The short period just before the competition should be
devoted to a final check and adjustment of your intensity.

If you perform best at a lower level of intensity, you want your competitive
routine to be carried out at an easy pace and include plenty of opportunities
to take a break and slow down and relax. You'll want to be around people
who are relaxed and low key as well. If you're around anxious people, they'll
make you nervous too.

If you perform best at a higher level of intensity, you want your competitive routine to be done at a faster pace, with more energy put into the components of your routine. You will want to make sure that you are constantly
doing something. There should be little time during which you are just
standing around and waiting. You'll also want to be around people who are
energetic and outgoing.

Design a Competitive Routine

The first step in designing a competitive routine is to make a list of everything you need to do before a competition to be prepared. Some of the common elements you should include are meals, a review of competitive tactics,
a physical warm-up, a technical warm-up, an equipment check, and mental
preparation. Other more personal things that might go into a competitive
routine include going to the bathroom, changing into your competition
clothing, and using mental imagery.

Decide the order in which you want to do the components of your list as
you approach the start of the competition. Consider competition activities that
might need to be taken into account. For instance, where you will eat your
precompetitive meal, the availability of a warm-up area, or the team warm-up
might influence when you accomplish different parts of your routine.

Next, specify where each step of your routine can best be completed. For
example, if you like to be alone before a competition, is there a quiet place
you can go to get away from people? You should use your knowledge of the
competition venues at which you often perform to determine this part of
your routine.

Finally, establish a time frame and a schedule for completing your routine. In other words, how much time do you need to get totally prepared? Some athletes like to get to the competition site only a short time before they compete. Others like to arrive hours before. These decisions are personal; you must find out what works best for you.

Once your competitive routine is organized, try it out at competitions. Some things may work, while others may not. In time, you'll be able to fine-tune your routine until you find the one that's most comfortable and best prepares you for competition. Lastly, remember that competitive routines only have value if they're used consistently. If you use your routine before every competition, in a short time you won't even have to think about doing it. Your competitive routine will simply be what you do before each competition to ensure that you are prepared to perform your best and achieve Prime Sport.

The separation is in the preparation.

—Russell Wilson, Super Bowl–winning quarterback[24]

Between-Performance Routines

Many sports, including baseball, football, tennis, and golf, are comprised of a series of many short performances with breaks of various lengths in between. For these sports, whether between at-bats in baseball, downs or possessions in football, or points in tennis, being well-prepared for the first performance is not enough. Routines can be invaluable in ensuring that you are prepared for every performance within a competition. One thing that separates the great athletes from the good ones is their ability to be not only prepared at the start of a competition, but also consistently ready for each performance within a competition. By being prepared for every performance, you can be sure to avoid giving your opponents "free points" because you weren't ready.

The time between performances is essential in maintaining consistent competitive performance. What you think, feel, and do between performances often dictates how you perform. You must take control of this time to be sure that you're prepared when the time comes to act. To do this, I use a four-step between-performance routine called the Four Rs: rest, regroup, refocus, and recharge.

Rest

Immediately after the conclusion of a performance, take several slow, deep breaths and let your muscles relax. This is especially important after a long or demanding performance in which you became fatigued and out of breath. It's also important to recover as much as possible to be ready for the next performance. Deep breathing and relaxing also help you center yourself and better prepare for the next R.

Regroup

This phase of the routine addresses your emotions between performances. Particularly when you are not performing well or the competition is at a critical juncture, you may feel a variety of emotions, for example, excitement, frustration, anger, or despair. Regrouping allows you to gain awareness of how your emotions are impacting you and, if they are affecting you negatively, master them so they help rather than hurt you in the next performance. If you are emotional after a poor performance, you may feel frustrated and angry. You should give yourself more time to regroup and let go of the unhealthy emotions. Because of the powerful influence emotions have on your performance, your ability to "get your act together" emotionally between competitions may be the most important thing you can do to prepare for the next event.

An important realization that can make regrouping easier is that specific performances within a competition are not directly related to one another. In other words, the chances of being successful in the next performance are in no way associated with how you performed in the last performance. For example, a poor parallel bars routine by a gymnast has no direct bearing on how he will perform on the pommel horse. Or a bad tee shot in golf doesn't mean a golfer will hit a poor second shot.

One thing that connects performances are the emotions attached to the last performance. If you're frustrated or depressed about your last performance, you increase your chances of doing poorly in the next performance because negative emotions usually interfere with good performances. In contrast, if you have positive emotions, or no emotions at all, about the last performance, you increase your chances of succeeding in the next performance because positive emotions will make you more motivated and confident, which, in turn, will enable you to perform better. Using the time to regroup will enable you to let go of and replace the negative emotions with positive ones or none at all, increasing your chances of having a successful performance.

Refocus

There can be a tendency during competitions, especially in pressure situations, to focus back on the last performance or forward on the possible outcome of the competition, neither of which will help you perform well in the moment. This is a form of outcome focus in which you're focusing on the outcome of the last performance or the possible result at the end of the competition. When this happens, you need to return to a process focus for the next performance. During the refocus phase, you should first evaluate your present situation, for example, the score, how you've been performing, and tactics. Then, focus on what you need to for the next performance. Your focus may be technical, tactical, or mental. The important thing is to begin the next performance with a clear focus on what you want to do to perform your best at that moment.

Recharge

If your body is not prepared, you won't be able to perform your best. Just prior to beginning the performance, you should check and adjust your intensity. If you need to lower your intensity slow your pace, take deep breaths, and relax your muscles. If you need to raise your intensity increase your pace, take some short, intense breaths, and jump up and down. The goal in this phase of your competitive routine is to ensure that your body is prepared to perform your best in every performance within the competition.

Every athlete acquires routines as a way to help control nerves.

—Hope Solo, Olympic and World Cup–winning soccer goalie[25]

Tip from the Top: Don't Let Others or Circumstances Dictate How You Perform

As previously mentioned, there are many external forces that can impact your athletic performance. Social factors can include teammates, competitors, coaches, and officials. Situational forces can include the conditions of the competitive venue and weather. These influences can wreak havoc on the best-laid plans and most thorough preparations because they are largely out of your control. They can cause dramatic and negative shifts in your psychology, including a decline in motivation and confidence, a loss of focus, and a cautious mindset. These forces can also hurt your physiology, resulting in stress, shifts away from your ideal intensity, and muscle tension. Your goal is to not allow others or the circumstances to dictate your performance.

Routines are a powerful tool at your disposal to minimize the effect that these forces have on your competitive efforts. When you follow a well-practiced routine, you marshal your resources to resist those influences. As I just discussed, although there are many forces outside of your control on the day of a competition, there is one thing you can control—you. A routine allows you to actively take control of all aspects of your preparation. It makes whatever situation you are in, regardless of the presence of those uncontrollable forces, feel more in control and manageable, mitigating the impact of the factors that are outside of your control.

Your routine focuses you on yourself, rather than those external forces. The consistency of your routine makes the situation, however uncontrollable or uncertain, feel more familiar and comfortable. The rhythm and predictability of your routine enables you to maintain your ideal psychology and

EXERCISE

CREATE A ROUTINE

1. Create a routine for the gym, training, and competitions.
2. Include the following areas in these routines:
   a. equipment (if you participate in a gear-intensive sport)
   b. physical (warm-up, breathing, ideal intensity)
   c. mental (imagery, keywords, mindset)
3. Begin to use and get comfortable with the routines in their respective settings.
4. Fine-tune the routines until you are comfortable with them and believe they prepare you to perform your best.

physiology, even in the most adverse conditions and most pressure-packed competitive situations. And knowing that you are doing everything you can to be prepared to perform your best builds your confidence and belief in your ability to overcome those factors outside of your control.

I have a certain routine and certain preparation for these big matches that works for me, again. Everybody is different. But I have been—I will try to follow that kind of routine and get myself in that state of mind where I'm able to get the best out of myself when it's most needed.

—Novak Djokovic, top-ranked tennis player[26]

BREATHING

Breathing may be the most underrated tool in your mental toolbox. In fact, you may have never even thought about your breathing in your athletic life because it is something that you do without conscious thought every moment of your life. Breathing is, of course, essential for living. It supplies your body with the oxygen that is necessary for it to function. That very purpose means that breathing can also have a significant impact, good or bad, on your athletic performance, where your body must not only maintain a minimal level of functioning, but also be able to function optimally.

It's not uncommon for athletes to either breathe too shallowly or inadvertently hold their breath while competing. This unconscious practice has several effects that hurt your ability to perform your best. Because you are not getting the oxygen you need, you tire more quickly, your muscles become tense, you lose motor control, your balance shifts back, and your center of gravity rises. The net result is that you are physiologically incapable of performing to your fullest ability.

Because of this influence, breathing can also be a powerful tool that has both physical and psychological benefits in your sport. Most basically, you can ensure that you get the oxygen your body needs to perform, which, in contrast to the problems a lack of breathing can cause, means you will have more energy, your muscles will be more relaxed, you will maintain motor control, your balance will stay centered, and your center of gravity will stay low. You can also use breathing as a means of adjusting your intensity to an ideal level (more on that shortly). The net result in the case of active breathing is that you will be physiologically capable of performing your best.

Breathing also has value mentally and emotionally. Because breathing is the only thing physiologically that you can control directly, maintaining active control of your breathing enables you to counteract stress, anxiety, and fear, and instill a sense of confidence and calm. You can also use breathing as a focusing tool; if you are focused on your breathing, your attention is directed inward rather than on distractions around you. Moreover, because breathing can be used as a tool for overall control of your body, you can use it to create a sense of rhythm and flow in your sports movements. For example, a baseball pitcher can use breathing in different ways based on the type of pitch he wants to throw, or a golfer can use breathing to control her club-head speed. Breathing is also one way you can adjust your mindset just before you compete.

Breathing should be more than simply an automatic physiological action that you do constantly without any thought. Instead, your goal should be to make breathing a tool to help you be optimally prepared to perform your best consistently and a purposeful habit that you do actively to maximize performance.

I don't care who you are, you're going to choke in certain matches. You get to a point where your legs don't move, and if you can't take a deep breath, you start to hit the ball about a yard wide.

—Arthur Ashe, tennis legend[27]

Types of Active Breathing

As I just suggested, breathing can be used as a mental tool in different ways to accomplish different goals. There are three types of breathing you can do that can impact you differently physically, psychologically, and emotionally. Deep breathing involves long and slow breaths. It is best used when you are feeling stressed, anxious, rushed, and unsettled. Deep breathing can be used to center yourself amid the chaos of competitive preparation and help you refocus when you become distracted. It can also instill feelings of calm and relaxation.

Aggressive breathing involves breaths that are deep but have a more vigorous exhale. It is best used when you need to get yourself fired up to confront a tough opponent or overcome difficult conditions. This type of breathing offers several benefits. First, it increases your physiological intensity by getting your blood and adrenaline flowing. Second, it generates feelings of excitement and energy; you get more pumped up. Finally, aggressive breathing creates a more forceful and determined mindset in which you want to assert dominance over the conditions or your competitors.

A helpful tool to ensure that you are breathing actively is to puff your cheeks out with each exhale. Pushing your cheeks out gives you physical feedback that you are, in fact, breathing by feeling tension in your cheeks as the air passes from your lungs and out your mouth. It also gives coaches visible feedback that you are breathing when you should be.

When to Use Breathing

As with all mental tools, breathing won't be effective if you don't use it actively on a regular basis and make it a consistent part of your athletic life. There are specific places in your training and competitive efforts where breathing can become an invaluable tool to help you perform your best.

As Part of Your Routines

Build breathing into your gym, training, and competitive routines. As you progress through these routines, make breathing an integral part of them. For example, during your physical warm-up, use breathing—whether deep or aggressive—to help you reach your ideal intensity. When you are getting mentally prepared in your routine by, for instance, doing imagery of how you want to perform, add breathing into your imagined performances.

During Performances

As mentioned earlier, it's not uncommon for athletes to inadvertently hold their breath while performing, producing physical and mental states that are decidedly not conducive to optimal performance. Whether you are doing a set of squats in the gym, working on something technical in training, or giving your best in competition, you want to include breathing in your efforts. When you exert yourself, simply exhale with either deep or aggressive breaths (depending on your needs at that moment). At first, you will need to be very conscious of your breathing because it hasn't yet become a habit. But, with repetition, this habit of using breathing as a tool will become ingrained, and before you know it active breathing will simply be what you do when you perform.

To Recover from Performances

If your conditioning or sport requires any type of physical exertion, for example, a set of squats, a point in tennis, a 400-meter run, a play in football, or a drive to the goal in soccer, you're going to be tired when you've finished. At this point, a quick and complete recovery is essential to maintaining a high level of performance. The most noticeable symptom of a hard effort is that you will be out of breath. What typically happens is that you simply wait until your breathing moderates at its own pace. This process can be slow, and it may not give you time to fully recover and get ready for your next performance (particularly in such sports as tennis and football, which have short breaks between sets and plays, respectively). To regain control of your body and recover from tiring performances faster, you can actively take control of your breathing with deep and deliberate breaths. Using breathing as a tool in this way will enable you to reclaim control of your breathing, get more oxygen into your system when it's needed most, and speed up your recovery and return to physical equilibrium in preparation for the next performance.

When you are negative, nervous, or distracted, breathing is a powerful tool in preventing your mind and body from going the "dark side" and turning against you. When you go negative before a competition, it's usually because you don't feel in control, prepared, confident, or comfortable in some way. Since breathing is the one physical function you can directly control, you should use it to your advantage during those moments when you're not feeling good mentally or physically. Focusing on your breathing increases your sense of control, which, in turn, increases your confidence and your comfort with the competitive situation. Breathing also has the direct effect of relaxing your body, counteracting the stress or anxiety you may be feeling. Finally, when you're focusing your breathing, you are diverting your attention away from distractions and onto something that will help you feel better and be better prepared to perform your best.

Tip from the Top: Breathing as a Performance Trigger

One thing I've observed countless times when watching professional and Olympic athletes in action is that when they are preparing to perform, almost without exception, they take some sort of noticeable breath before they do such things as assume their stance in the batter's box in baseball, hit a shot in golf, serve in tennis, settle into the starting blocks in swimming or running, set up for a penalty kick in soccer, or shoot a free throw in basketball. Their preperformance breathing can be deep and slow or shorter and intense. These athletes may take one to three breaths. And their breathing appears to be the last thing they do before they perform.

I have asked the high-level athletes I work with why they breathe in this way, and their answers are remarkably similar: They say it helps them feel prepared to perform their best. But when I ask them to be more specific, their responses are much more nuanced and interesting:

- "It's my final cue to channel all of my mental and physical energy into being my best."
- "Deep breathing makes me feel like I'm settling my body deeply into the ground, allowing me to explode upward."
- "It triggers a happy feeling that I need to feel for me to play well."
- "Breathing just before I go gets the last bit of nerves and tension out of my body."
- "My two intense breaths get me really fired up, so I just charge out there."
- "I need to get angry before I play, so a couple of aggressive breaths are a constant reminder to get mad."
- "My breathing clears my mind, allowing me to trust my body to do what I've trained it to do."

While these reasons vary, the common theme is that breathing acts as a trigger to activate their performance. These triggers take them to their final stage of readiness, in which the mind and body work together to produce an outstanding performance.

You can use breathing in the same way. I encourage you to experiment with two aspects of breathing as a performance trigger. First, what do you need to feel to be ready to perform your best? Do you need to feel calm or fired up? Do you want to be focused on something technical or something mental? Do you want to be happy or angry? Second, once you know what you want to think or feel at that last moment before you perform, you can decide what type of breathing will best achieve that goal—one deep breath,

---

EXERCISE

MAKE BREATHING PART
OF YOUR PERFORMANCES

1. Build breathing into your performance efforts (whether in the gym, training, or competitions).

   a. As you go through your routines and prepare to perform, use active breathing to reach your ideal intensity, narrow your focus, and find your ideal mindset.

   b. During performances, use active breathing to maintain intensity, focus, and effort.

   c. After performances, use active breathing to recover more quickly and fully.

---

two long but intense breaths, or perhaps a series of shorter and more aggressive breaths.

Once you understand what kind of breathing will provide you with the best performance trigger, you can incorporate it into your gym, training, and competitive routines. In doing so, you make this active breathing the final step in your preparations that will enable you to perform your best.

Sometimes the best thing you can do is not to think, not wonder, not imagine, not obsess. Just breathe and have faith that everything will work out for the best.

—Unknown[28]

TRUST

The four mental tools I have described lead directly to trust, the mental tool that is essential just before you perform. You may normally think of trust as a mental tool. Yet, your ability to use it effectively is fundamental in maintaining a high level of performance in your sport. You can use trust as the final mental tool to bring together everything you've done thus far in your preparations to channel your efforts into a mental and physical state of complete readiness.

If my mind can conceive it and my heart can believe it—then I can achieve it.

—Muhammad Ali, boxing legend[29]

What Is Trust?

You can think of trust as a deep belief in your capabilities as an athlete based on both your natural abilities and your preparations during conditioning, sport-specific training, mental training, and other areas that impact your sports performance. This trust offers several essential benefits. First, you develop a fundamental faith that good things will happen for you as an athlete. Although there are no guarantees of success on any given day, this faith creates confidence, optimism, and hope that, if you stay committed and give your best effort, you will experience success at some point. Trust also helps you view competitive situations without doubt, worry, or fear because, with this trust, you don't have any concerns worthy of those negative thoughts and emotions. The ultimate benefit of trust is that, when it comes time for you to perform, it allows you to reduce your thinking to a minimum or even turn off your mind completely, freeing up your body to do what you've trained it to do.

Trust because you are willing to accept the risk, not because it's safe or certain.

—Ritu Ghatourey, Indian writer[30]

Build Trust

Trust is developed progressively throughout time and based on an accumulation of many aspects of your athletic life. It starts with a basic belief in yourself and all that you bring to your sports efforts: innate abilities, physical and mental capabilities, knowledge and understanding of your sport, and passion and drive to be your best and achieve your athletic goals.

You must also have trust in your coaches. So much of what you come to believe about yourself comes from the people who coach you. If they express belief and trust in you, it's much easier to gain trust in yourself. Relatedly, you need to have trust in the training system that your coaches have created for you. Your training system includes your physical conditioning program, sport-specific technical and tactical progression, nutrition, and, of course, mental training program. For you to have a deep trust in your ability to perform your best when it matters most, you need to believe that the system you are using will lead you there.

If your sport involves extensive use of equipment, whether tennis racquets, golf clubs, skis and boots, cars, motorcycles, boats, or bicycles, trust in your equipment is also vital. Without believing that your equipment will enable you to do what you want to do in your performances, you won't have complete trust in yourself and, as a result, will likely hold back from a full effort. Your equipment can impact your trust in several ways.

First, you must believe that the equipment you use is capable of allowing you to perform your best. For example, if a golfer believes that his driver is too stiff and takes away from his feel during his swing and contact with the ball, he will probably be worried about his ability to control the ball and hit to his target area. The result could be a tense body, poor focus, and a tentative swing. Second, you have to trust that your equipment is optimally prepared so it will allow you to perform the way you want, for example, having a well-tuned snowboard, motorcycle, or race car. Third, trust is particularly challenging when your equipment has failed you, for instance, a flat tire on a bike or a broken vaulting pole. If you don't believe that your equipment can stand up to the demands you place on it, you may have a nagging apprehension that it will fail you again, preventing you from trusting it and giving your fullest and most committed effort.

Perhaps the most important contributor to trust is your preparations leading up to the "moment of truth." So many different types of preparation go into achieving a precise state of readiness that will lead to success: physical conditioning, sport-specific technical and tactical training, competitive simulations and rehearsals, nutrition, sleep, equipment testing and preparation, mental training, meetings with coaches and teams, and precompetitive routines. It's important just before you enter the competitive arena that you are able to say, "I'm as prepared as I can be to perform my best." This is reflective of the fact that you have found trust, the final piece of the athletic success puzzle.

When you make a commitment, you build hope. When you keep it, you build trust.

—Malika E. Nura, educator[31]

Tip from the Top: Sports Are Like Sleep

Have you ever tried to sleep when conditions are preventing you from doing so? You lie in bed and tell yourself that you have to sleep and try your best to do so, but it doesn't work. Why? Because sleep can't be forced. So, how do you fall asleep? You create an external and internal environment that will allow sleep to come. Externally, you make sure your room is quiet, dark, and warm. You have a comfortable bed, pillow, and comforter (maybe even a teddy bear or blankie). Internally, you take deep breaths, relax your body, and clear your mind. Having created this environment within and outside of yourself, you trust your mind and body to accept the sleep that will naturally follow.

How are sports like sleep? You can't *try* to perform well. Trying is associated with a lack of trust and the need to control everything. Yet, great athletic performances can't be controlled or forced. To the contrary, the more you try, the worse you will perform. A lack of trust in your ability to perform well creates overthinking, muscle tension, and the attempt to control your body in the hopes that you can make it perform the way you want it to. But that just doesn't work.

EXERCISE

LEARN TO TRUST YOURSELF

1. Practice trusting yourself in training.

   a. Be well prepared.

   b. Clear your mind.

   c. Let your body do what you've trained it to do.

Just like sleep, you want to create an external and internal environment that you have, through experience, come to trust will allow great performances to emerge naturally. The external environment has two levels. First, as a foundation, it includes having a good training schedule leading up to the competition, being organized, and getting the support you need from others. Second, on the day of the competition, it involves having your equipment optimally prepared, being warmed up, and being surrounded by a supportive coach and teammates before the start of the event.

The internal environment also has two levels. First, going into the competition, you should be healthy (no injuries or illness), rested, in top physical condition, and well fueled, and you should be experiencing minimal stress. You should also be well trained with solid technique and tactics. Second, on the day of the competition, internal means having a healthy perspective about the competition, having clear goals, and having fun. It also means being mentally prepared—that is, being motivated, confident, energized, focused, and happy, and having a mental toolbox you can access when needed.

Creating environments that encourage good performances can't be left to chance. Instead, trust in these environments comes from a quality training plan, eating well, getting the proper amount of sleep, keeping up with schoolwork, and, in general, being disciplined and diligent about everything that can impact your sport.

On the day of the competition, there are two tools you can use for further developing the environments that lead to trust. First, mental imagery primes your mind and body for optimal performance, ingrains successful images that translate into more confidence, and focuses your mind on what you need to do to perform well. Second, total preparation for a competitive routine includes executing a good physical warm-up, making sure your equipment is prepared, reaching your ideal intensity, narrowing your focus onto what you need to do to perform your best, and using your ideal mindset. A structured and consistent competitive routine can be the final piece of the athletic performance puzzle, ensuring that you have created those ideal internal and external environments, which lead to a complete trust in your capabilities and, in turn, allow you to give your best performance.

6

Prime Topics for Athletic Success

In *Train Your Mind*, I provide a comprehensive approach to mental preparation for athletic success. I identify the five primary areas that comprise my Prime Performance system, as described in the first five chapters, which I believe are important for you to focus on in your mental training. Using these five areas and chapters as the structure, I offer useful information and practical tools you can use to ensure that you are mentally prepared to perform your best on the day of a competition.

But there are many other important aspects of mental preparation worthy of discussion that don't readily fit into the five areas and chapters. This chapter explores some of these areas.

PERFORM YOUR BEST IN BIG EVENTS

In the introduction, I introduce two important goals. First, you should aim to achieve Prime Sport, which means performing at a consistently high level in the most challenging conditions. This goal involves maintaining a high level of performance day in and day out, week in and week out, and month in and month out. Second, you want to perform your best in PrimeTime, which is the biggest competition of the season, in difficult conditions, against your toughest opponents. These events are the ultimate standard by which you measure your success as an athlete. Depending on your age, level of competition, and ability, PrimeTime can mean a state, sectional, or national high school championship. Or it can mean a collegiate playoff game, the Olympics, or the World Series. Whatever your example of PrimeTime, you want to enter the event prepared and ready to perform your best on this biggest stage of your athletic life.

Your ability to perform your best in PrimeTime depends largely on how you think about the big event. In this section, I share some ideas that can help you approach the important competition with a frame of mind that will set you up for success.

The physical aspect of the sport can only take you so far. In the Olympic Games, everyone is talented. Everyone trains hard. Everyone does the work. What separates the gold medalists from the silver medalists is simply the mental game.

—Shannon Miller, Olympic gymnastics gold medalist[1]

The KISS Principle

In sports, you will have some pretty complicated experiences. There are so many things you put into your sport and so many things you get out of it as well. There are also many contributors to athletic success—physical, technical, tactical, equipment, mental, weather, conditions, and team, just to name a few. Additionally, there are numerous things that can go wrong leading up to, preparing for, and during a big competition. There are usually more people involved, more things to do as an athlete, more responsibilities to more people, and a lot more distractions. These complications can lead to more complications inside your head, including doubt, worry, expectations, pressure, and stress. And this tsunami of complications can overwhelm you and lead to a disappointing performance in PrimeTime.

The KISS principle is my antidote to these complications. Most people know the KISS principle as "Keep it simple, stupid"; however, I prefer to define it as "Keep it simple, smart." If you're smart, you'll keep your preparations for and participation in the big event as simple as possible and have a much better chance of performing up to your ability and ending the day satisfied with the result.

You can invoke the KISS principle in several ways. First, identify the things that have the most impact on your performance and of which you have control. For the controllables, do everything you can to gain control of them so they impact you in good ways. Moreover, identify the things that are either not that important to your performance or of which you have no control. For those things that carry little importance or for the uncontrollables, do your best to ignore them because, by definition, they are either not a concern or there's nothing you can do about them, respectively. Furthermore, if you pay attention to them, they will affect you negatively.

Second, identify the key areas you need to focus on that are most important for you to perform your best. Throw everything else out the window. Make sure you pay attention to those key areas and address them the best you can.

Finally, remind yourself why you're there. It's easy to get caught up in the hoopla of a big competition, whether it be the attention you're getting (e.g., from family and friends, fans, or the media), the activities related to the event (e.g., banquets, press conferences), or the talk about winning. When you go to the "dark side," think about why you're really there: for the fun, the excitement, the opportunity to show yourself how good you can be, and the satisfaction of giving your best effort, regardless of the outcome. If you can adhere to the KISS principle leading up to that moment when you enter the competitive arena, you will set yourself up to perform your best and increase your chances of finding success.

My thoughts before a big race are usually pretty simple. I tell myself: Get out of the blocks, run your race, stay relaxed. If you run your race, you'll win . . . channel your energy. Focus.

—Carl Lewis, Olympic track and field gold medalist[2]

Dance with the One Who Brung Ya

Yes, I realize this is bad English, but it conveys an important message. Too often, when athletes are preparing for a big competition, they feel the need to do something different, something special—that they need to "raise their game" because the event is so important. In fact, that is the worst thing you can do. To the contrary, you want to keep doing exactly what you've been doing to get to the big competition, hence the expression, "Dance with the one who brung ya."

You should never do anything new or different for an important competition for several reasons. You won't be familiar with your new approach, and as a result, it may cause discomfort and uncertainty. Because it is different, you can't be entirely sure it will work, hurting your confidence when you need it most. And the break from your usual patterns may cause stress and anxiety because you will be out of your usual rhythm and flow.

Dancing with the one who brung ya means sticking with the fundamentals of what has worked in past competitions. You should maintain good eating and sleeping habits. You should continue your usual conditioning program, although dialing it back to ensure you stay rested. You should stick with the training and competitive routines you have used to prepare in the past. And you should make sure you have fun because, as mentioned in an earlier chapter, you will feel relaxed if you're having fun, which is the best way to enter a big competition.

Don't change for change's sake.

—Ray Allen, NBA player[3]

Two Approaches to Performing Your Best in Big Events

You've worked hard all season. You've earned a place in the competition you've been aiming for all year. But getting there isn't enough; you want to perform your best in the "big one." Continuing to improve your technique and sticking with your usual physical conditioning maintenance program will help. But whether you succeed in achieving your goals at these all-important events ultimately depends on what happens between your ears as the events near. Approaching these competitions with the right attitude is key to performing your best.

The problem is that important competitions can play mind games with you. Instead of just wanting to do your best, you *really* want to do your best. Your focus can shift from, "What do I have to do to perform well?" to "What will happen if I don't perform well?" Goals can turn into pressure-laden expectations. An enjoyable challenge becomes a threat to fear. If you go to the "dark side," you lose before even entering the competitive arena.

I've never been afraid of big moments. I get butterflies, I get nervous and anxious, but I think those are all good signs that I'm ready for the moment.

—Stephen Curry, two-time NBA MVP[4]

There are two schools of thought on how to prepare for a big competition. One approach is to try to ignore the fact that it is big and simply say, "It's no big deal so there is nothing to get worked up about." For example, in preparation for an upcoming world championships, the coaching staff of a national team had their athletes train in isolation, keeping the media away so they didn't get distracted by the press or buy into the expectations outside forces can often impose before big events. The coaches and athletes wanted to treat the world championships like just another event and ignore the hype surrounding the competition.

The risk of this approach is that big competitions are hard to ignore, even if the athletes are kept isolated. By ignoring the reality of the situation, you are failing to prepare yourself for the magnitude of the event, which will inevitably hit you sooner or later. You will have to face the hyped expectations—usually from family and friends—at some point, but you won't be mentally prepared to handle the inescapable pressure that comes with the big event.

The other school of thought argues that big events can't be avoided, ignored, or downplayed. Rather, athletes must face the reality of these competitions and do what they can to respond positively to the unavoidable expectations and pressures. Another national team coaching staff assumed this approach in preparation for the same world championships. Given the popularity of the sport in their country, there was nowhere for them to hide. This approach has athletes say, "This event is a big deal, so let's figure out how to deal with it positively." With this approach, you must acknowledge that your upcoming competition is huge and not to be taken lightly.

You must establish an attitude that will enable you to achieve your goals. ("I am going to believe in myself, stay grounded, and focus on what I need to do to perform my best.") This attitude helps you deflect the external and self-imposed pressures, and enables you to maintain a positive and healthy perspective and focus as you approach big events. You need to figure out what you need to do to be prepared to perform your best (e.g., training, physical conditioning, mental preparation, social activities). You also should recognize what and who might interfere with your preparations (e.g., too much time with family and friends). Finally, you must take deliberate steps to ensure that you maintain the attitude and do the things you have learned to achieve success.

The risk of this approach is that, despite your best efforts, you won't be able to deflect the expectations and pressure. Instead of inoculating yourself against the pressure, you will actually succumb to it. What we can learn from this is that there is no one ideal approach. You must look at how you have handled big competitions in the past. If you performed well using one approach, stick with it. ("If it ain't broke, don't fix it!") But if it didn't work before, don't expect it to work next time. In this case, you will want to do something different. Regardless of the approach you take, the goal is to enter a big event feeling motivated, confident, relaxed, and focused. If you feel that way, you will perform your best and, most likely, achieve the goals you have set for yourself.

Four Keys to Performing Your Best in Big Events

What do you need to do to be prepared to perform your best on the day of a big competition? If you ask the top 10 men and women in any sport, you will probably get 20 different answers. But, having asked this question of many professional and Olympic athletes, I have found five themes that underlie their responses.

Control or Not to Control

The life of an athlete can be stressful. There are many things you might worry about that can cause you to become distracted, anxious, frustrated, and just plain irritated, and all of these things will hurt your ability to perform your best when it counts most. Unfortunately, many athletes worry about the wrong things. They get stressed out about things they can't control. In your athletic life, there are some things you should think about and others you shouldn't. Things you should pay attention to are those things you can control, including your physical condition, effort, attitude, thoughts, emotions, behavior, equipment, and preparation. These things are within your control, so by thinking about them, you can ensure that they are working for you rather than against you.

At the same time, the things in your athletic life you have no control over yet still may worry about include competitors, coaches, officials, parents, and the competitive venue and conditions. If you think about these things, you're creating stress, wasting energy, and preventing yourself from focusing on aspects of your sport that will actually help you perform your best.

The next time you find yourself stressing out before a big competition, ask yourself one question: "Is the thing I am stressing about within my control?"

If it's not, let it go and focus on things you can control. If it is within your control, rather than worrying, do something about it.

You have no control over what the other guy does. You only have control over what you do.

—A. J. Kitt, ski racing world championship medalist[5]

Have a Game Plan

Getting prepared for a big competition doesn't just mean doing what you need to do physically, technically, tactically, and mentally. It also involves having a clearly defined and understood plan of how you will perform your best and achieve your goals in the event. There are two components to an effective game plan. First, you need to decide what you need to do to perform your best. Contributors to this aspect of your game plan might include identifying your strengths and devising a competitive strategy that will play to those strengths, determining what pace you want to set in the competition, and establishing what you need to do before and during the event to ensure that you are committed, confident, and comfortable.

Second, your game plan should include information about your opponent, whether another competitor (e.g., tennis, fencing, boxing), a group of competitors (track and field, swimming), or a team (volleyball, basketball). The more you know about their strengths and weaknesses, the more you can devise a strategy that will play to their weaknesses and avoid their strengths.

As the saying goes, "The best-laid plans of mice and men often go awry." This paraphrase from poet Robert Burns certainly applies to sports. You can have a great game plan in theory, but it doesn't always work out in reality. As a result, in addition to your plan A, you should also devise a plan B in case plan A doesn't work. Although you can never predict with certainty how a plan will play out, you can base your plan B on other possible scenarios that might occur during the competition. For example, a lacrosse team's plan A might focus on their opponent's supposed weakness, based on a scouting report that revealed they are easily intimidated by an attacking style of play. But, once the game begins, they may see that their opponent is defending well, neutralizing their aggressive style. In this case, they should have created a plan B beforehand that allows them to shift to a more defensive and counterattacking style.

I never left the field saying I could have done more to get ready, and that gives me peace of mind.

—Peyton Manning, former NFL quarterback[6]

Be Flexible and Adapt

As I'm sure you've experienced in your own athletic life, competitions don't always work out the way you expect. For instance, your opponent may be better than you thought, you might not be able to perform the way you wanted, or you may be confronted with conditions you didn't prepare for. The result is that you are on your way to a disappointing defeat. Clearly, if you continue to approach the competition the same way, you will be violating the law of insanity (doing the same thing over and over, and expecting different results) and are pretty much guaranteeing failure. Unfortunately, athletes can be reluctant to change in the middle of a competition, particularly a big one. Sticking with a known strategy is familiar and comfortable, even if it isn't working. By contrast, changing strategies is risky because you can't be sure the new plan will work.

In these unexpected situations, if you want to have any chance of "snatching victory from the jaws of defeat," you have to be flexible and adapt as quickly as possible. Recognize and acknowledge that your present approach isn't working and that it will likely not work if you continue on your current path. Second, either shift to plan B or identify a different approach that takes into account the realities of the current competitive situation. Third, make a full commitment to the change, and throw everything you have behind your new plan.

Enjoying success requires the ability to adapt. Only by being open to change will you have a true opportunity to get the most from your talent.

—Nolan Ryan, MLB Hall of Fame pitcher[7]

Expect the Unexpected

A major source of stress for athletes is the unexpected things that can come up on the day of a big competition. The natural reaction to unexpected events is to, well, freak out. You worry, lose confidence, become anxious, and get distracted. In this mental and physical state, you have little chance of performing your best and achieving the results you want.

During the course of a big competition, many things can go wrong. On the way to the event, the airline might lose your equipment, you may get lost during the drive or get stuck in traffic, or you might get a flat tire or run out of gas. At the event, your equipment could break, start times might be delayed, or routines may be disrupted. If you're not prepared for these unexpected occurrences, you're going to stress out and probably perform poorly.

There are two ways to deal with the unexpected. First, expect the unexpected. Take a sheet of paper, and on the left side, make a list of the things that can go wrong at a big competition. Think travel, weather, gear, and competitive schedule, for starters. On the right side, list solutions to these problems. For example, if you break a piece of equipment, you should have a replacement or know someone beforehand who you can borrow a replacement from. Or, if your start time is moved up, you can do a shortened version of your competitive routine. Using this strategy, you prevent yourself from stressing out by preventing the unexpected event from being, well, unexpected.

Of course, you can't anticipate everything because of the natural uncertainty of sports. Thus, the key is how you react to unexpected occurrences (e.g., you're running late and you might miss the start of the competition). You have two choices here. Either experience the aforementioned freak out, which I'm sure you would agree doesn't do you any good. Or you can accept that these things happen; focus on staying positive and calm; look for the best solution to the unexpected event; and stay focused on your goal for the day, which is to perform your best. I can assure you that you will feel and perform much better if you can keep your cool.

Obstacles don't have to stop you. If you run into a wall, don't turn around and give up. Figure out how to climb it, go through it, or work around it.

—Michael Jordan, NBA legend[8]

Tip from the Top: Be an Artist

There's a place for being a scientist in your athletic life. What I mean by scientist is that there are times when you need to be logical, rational, analytical, organized, and methodical in your pursuit of your goals. You need to be in control and focused on every detail, making sure every "t" is crossed and every "i" dotted. As a scientist, this attention to detail helps you feel more prepared, confident, comfortable, and in control. Being the scientist is usually best when you are planning, organizing, and preparing for a big competition.

When you arrive at the important event, it's time to set aside being a scientist and shift to being an artist. Tapping into the artist in you enables you to be spontaneous, creative, emotional, and inspired in your performance on the big stage. Just as a painter uses her palette of paints and the sculptor uses his clay, you are using the competitive arena to express yourself as an athlete by painting a picture of exceptional performance. As an artist, you trust your capabilities and preparations, give up conscious control, and allow your mind and body to do what you've trained it to do.

Don't think. Thinking is the enemy of creativity.

—Ray Bradbury, science fiction author[9]

OVERCOME PERFORMANCE SLUMPS

Performance slumps are one of the most common, yet mysterious and frustrating, phenomena in sports. Typically viewed as unexplained drops in performance, slumps are a source of concern for athletes and coaches. Despite their visible place in the collective psyche of the athletic community, little is known about the causes of or cures for performance slumps; however, I have worked extensively with athletes who are suffering from performance slumps and will share how athletes and coaches can identify, prevent, and overcome them.

Slumps are like a soft bed. They're easy to get into and hard to get out of.

—Johnny Bench, 14-time MLB All-Star[10]

What Is a Slump?

The term *slump* has been used to describe a wide variety of performance declines. As a result, there is no clear definition of what a slump really is. For example, *Webster's New Collegiate Dictionary* defines a slump as a "period of poor or losing play by a team or individual." But this definition lacks precision. Several factors must be considered in defining slumps.

First, ability is important; that is, if a team is always lousy, their poor play would not be considered a slump. As such, current performance must always be compared to a previous level of play. Second, the length of the decline is relevant. For instance, a baseball hitter who goes 0-for-4 may not be in a slump, but if he goes 0-for-25, he probably is. Third, a common aspect of a slump is that there seems to be no apparent explanation for the decline. If there is an obvious reason for the drop in performance, for example, an injury, it would not be a slump. In defining a slump, these factors must be taken into consideration. Because of this, a slump is more accurately defined as an unexplained drop in performance that extends longer than would be expected from the normal ups and downs of competition.

When you're in a slump, you're not in for much fun. Unslumping yourself is not easily done.

—Dr. Seuss[11]

Identifying a Slump

An inherent part of sports participation is that performance will naturally vary during the course of a season. In other words, it is rare for athletes to maintain a consistently high level of performance. As a result, most performance declines are simply a typical part of the ups and downs of competition. So, the question is whether a decline is a slump or just a natural drop in the performance cycle.

The first step in determining whether a decline is a slump is to evaluate your average level of performance—that is, how do you usually perform? For statistically oriented sports like baseball and basketball, this can be measured by plotting performance to date on a graph. Normal variation can be determined by seeing the ups and downs that commonly occur during the season. Recent performance can be compared to the normal variation. If the current decrease is unusually low, it may be a slump. Finally, you should take a superficial look at the causes of the decline. If there is no obvious cause of the decrease, it is safe to say the athlete is in a slump.

Slump? I ain't in no slump . . . I just ain't hitting.

—Yogi Berra, MLB Hall of Fame catcher[12]

Causes of Slumps

The causes of performance slumps can be grouped into four general categories. First, perhaps the most common cause of slumps is a physical problem. These difficulties include fatigue, minor injuries, and lingering illness. Second, slumps may be due to subtle changes in technique that occur during the course of a season. These changes may be in the execution of the skill or the timing of the movement.

Third, slumps may begin with changes in an athlete's equipment (e.g., loosening of string tension on a tennis racquet or using a baseball bat with a different weight). Particularly in those sports that require elaborate equipment, there is a precise balance between equipment and technique. As a result, a slight change in equipment may alter technique, hurting performance. Fourth, slumps can be caused by psychological factors. Furthermore, the mental contributors may be related to or independent of the athletic involvement. For instance, a particularly poor performance may hurt confidence and increase anxiety, which could lead to a prolonged drop in performance. In contrast, issues away from competition, like family difficulties, financial problems, and school struggles, may impair concentration, increase stress, and decrease motivation, resulting in a performance decline.

Recommendations for Preventing Slumps

The best way to deal with slumps is to prevent them from happening. Slumps can be prevented by paying careful attention to the potential causes and taking steps to avoid those causes.

Physical

As mentioned earlier, many slumps begin with physical difficulties. More specifically, slumps are often caused by the normal physical wear and tear of the competitive season, which isn't as noticeable as injury or illness. As a result, you can reduce the likelihood of performance slumps by paying attention to various factors that influence your physical state.

One important area that can be addressed is physical condition. Quite simply, if you are well conditioned, you will be less susceptible to fatigue, injury, and illness. Consequently, a rigorous physical training program during the offseason and a physical maintenance program during the competitive season will help minimize slumps due to physical breakdown.

Second, a significant part of slump prevention is rest. In other words, physical deterioration can be lessened by actively incorporating rest into your training and competitive regimens. Adequate rest can be assured in several ways. Days off can be built into the weekly training schedule. For example, in sports with weekend competitions, having mandatory Mondays off is a good way to ensure that you recover from the prior week's training and the stresses of the previous competition.

Third, you can reduce the quantity and increase the quality of training as the season progresses. This approach will allow you to maintain a high level of health and energy through the end of the season. This is especially important in sports that have lengthy seasons, namely baseball, tennis, and golf.

Fourth, planning a responsible competition schedule can also prevent slumps. Perhaps the most demanding aspect of sports involvement is the actual competition. Competing in too many events is both physically and mentally draining. You and your coaches need to select the competitions that are most important for you to participate in and avoid scheduling events that serve no specified purpose in your seasonal competitive plan.

Fifth, scheduling time off about three weeks before an important competition, particularly when it is near the end of the season, can help ensure a high level of performance. This strategy allows you to get extra rest, recover from previous competitions, overcome nagging injuries and illness, recharge mentally and emotionally so you enter the big event excited to compete, and prepare for the final push toward that competition.

Most fundamentally, the best way to reduce the likelihood of a slump due to physical causes is for you to listen to your body. You need to acknowledge fatigue, injury, and illness, and when they are evident, they should be dealt with immediately.

Technical

Slumps that are caused by technical changes can also be prevented by taking steps to maintain sound technique, which results in strong performance.

First, technique is best developed during the offseason, when the primary focus is on technical improvement and there is adequate time to fully acquire the skills; therefore, technically induced performance slumps may be prevented by minimizing technical work done during the competitive season. Working on technique may not only disturb the technique that is producing good performance, but also hurt performance by reducing confidence and distracting you from performing your best. In addition, maintaining a video library of good technique and performances can be used by you and your coaches to remind you of proper technique and compare current techniques with past methods.

Equipment

The best way to prevent equipment-related performance slumps is to maintain your equipment at its highest performance level. You should pay attention to how long you have been using your equipment, ensuring that it isn't worn out and remains capable of allowing you to maintain your level of performance. For example, tennis racquets should be restrung before their tension changes, or if a favorite baseball bat is broken, it should be replaced by another with identical weight and balance.

Mental

Performance slumps that are caused by psychological factors can be addressed on two levels. First, for those difficulties that arise directly from competition, it is important that you engage in a regular mental training program. This approach will strengthen your mental muscles, including motivation, confidence, intensity, focus, and mindset, making them more resilient to the negative psychological effects of periodic poor performance. A structured mental training program will also ensure that you have a well-stocked mental toolbox filled with tools that are readily available to fix any issues that arise. In addition, following a poor performance, you will need to actively combat the resulting negative psychological effects by flexing your mental muscles and using these mental tools. This will prevent you from getting caught in a self-perpetuating vicious cycle of negativity and poor performance.

Second, for those difficulties that occur away from your sport, you should work them out as quickly and effectively as possible. Whether this involves such occurrences as family conflict or difficulties in school, actively seeking out support and finding solutions can reduce the impact these events have on your athletic life. Moreover, you can use the previously discussed mental muscles and tools to leave these difficulties off the field of play, so that, at least during training and competition, you are able to maintain proper focus and intensity, preventing a drop in performance.

My motto was always to keep swinging. Whether I was in a slump or feeling badly or having trouble off the field, the only thing to do was keep swinging.

—Hank Aaron, MLB Hall of Fame player[13]

A Slump-Busting Plan

It is essential that slumps be addressed in an organized and systematic way. When you are in a slump, you should look at each cause and determine the best way to alleviate it. The attitude you have about getting out of the slump will also be a factor. Oftentimes, athletes and coaches believe that athletes can just jump out of their slump; however, the fact is that it takes time to get into a slump and time to get out of one. You should be prepared to put in the necessary time and effort to return to your previous level of performance.

Take a Timeout

The first thing you need to do as part of your slump-busting plan is take some time away from training and competition to give yourself a change of scenery and people. This timeout offers several benefits. First, slumps usually produce strong negative thinking and emotions, which only make them worse. Taking a timeout enables you to let go of the negative thoughts and emotions, and regain a positive attitude toward your performance. The timeout acts as an emotional vacation and provides you with much-needed perspective on how to move forward with better performances.

Second, slumps can be draining physically and emotionally. Consequently, a timeout allows you to recover and recharge your batteries. This restoration will further assist in your return to competitive form.

Third, the timeout gives you the opportunity to devise an organized plan to overcome the slump. The time away from your sport will enhance your ability to view the slump objectively. You can then use this information to alleviate the slump in the shortest time possible.

Set Goals

A crucial part of the slump-busting plan is to develop an organized program aimed at alleviating the slump. This program is based on setting a series of specified goals. As with all goals, these should rely on the SMARTER (Specific, Measurable, Accepted, Realistic, Time limited, Exciting, Recorded) goals outlined in chapter 4.

The Return-to-Form Goal

The return-to-form goal defines the ultimate purpose of the slump-busting plan. In particular, this goal indicates the level of performance to which you want to return. For example, a baseball player in a slump at the plate might make his return-to-form goal hitting at his preslump batting average.

Causal Goals

Causal goals focus on the level of performance associated with the particular causes of the slump. If there is more than one cause of a slump, it is important that a goal be set for each cause. For instance, if a slump has been caused by an injury and maintained by a loss of confidence, separate goals should be set for rehabilitating the injury and rebuilding confidence.

Daily Training Goals

Once the causal goals have been established, you should set daily goals to achieve the causal objectives. Daily training goals specify what you need to do in your regular training to relieve the causes, thereby alleviating the slump. For example, if a cause involves a technical problem, it is up to you and your coaches to decide the best way to resolve the technical flaw and, more specifically, what to do in training to work toward the causal goal. Additionally, these goals should ensure that you progress toward your causal and return-to-form goals in an incremental and constructive way.

Daily Performance Goals

Frequently, athletes are unable to take time off to work on their slump due to their competitive schedule. Because of this, they must keep performing while trying to relieve the slump. This situation is difficult because it forces them to keep performing at a subpar level. Daily performance goals provide a level of performance to work toward that, while below the return-to-form level, is above the current slump level. These goals act to motivate you and reinforce rather than discourage your efforts by furnishing realistic levels toward which you can aim. They also provide a positive and improving orientation that will help in resolving the slump.

We're not even thinking about (the postseason) right now. We've been in a slump, so we're taking things day by day. We aren't looking to the future because we haven't addressed the present.

—Cartier Martin, professional basketball player[14]

Tip from the Top: Find a Sport Psychologist

If the slump you find yourself in is severe and resisting your best efforts to overcome it, I recommend that you seek out a qualified sport psychologist. A significant component of a performance slump is the negative emotional chain (i.e., frustration, anger, despair; see chapter 5) that can develop. Working with a sport psychologist can give you the opportunity to air your thoughts and emotions to an objective observer and allow them to provide effective coping skills that will help you better deal with the stress and concerns of being in a slump.

EXERCISE

ADDRESS YOUR POOR PERFORMANCE

1. When you are in an extended period of poor performances,

   a. Determine if you are in a slump.

   b. Examine possible causes and identify the likely cause.

   c. Take some time off from your sport, if possible.

   d. Create a slump-busting plan with specific goals.

   e. Be patient and stay committed to performing your best.

THE PSYCHOLOGY OF INJURY

The sad reality of competitive sports is that many young athletes either have or will hurt themselves so seriously that it will end their seasons and potentially their careers. The good news is that surgical and rehabilitative technology has become so advanced that a full physical recovery from an injury that two decades ago might have been career-ending is now commonplace.

But another reality of physical injuries is that the mind gets "injured" as well. When you sustain an injury you can experience a loss of motivation and confidence; feel stress and anxiety; become preoccupied with the injury and have trouble focusing; and experience a myriad of emotions, including fear, frustration, anger, sadness, and despair. Yet, little attention is paid to how the absence of "mental rehab" can prevent athletes from returning to or improving on their preinjury level of performance. The following are some ideas about how injured athletes can ensure that their minds recover as fully as their bodies.

Work hard. And have patience. Because no matter who you are, you're going to get hurt in your career, and you have to be patient to get through the injuries.

—Randy Johnson, MLB Hall of Fame pitcher[15]

Keep Perspective

Accept that getting hurt sucks and you will feel bad at times, especially early in your recovery, when you're more disabled than recovering. You will be in pain. You may feel frustrated, angry, and depressed. You'll want to curl up in a ball and withdraw from life. These reactions are normal and, to some degree, healthy, as you have to allow yourself time to grieve your loss.

At the same time, if you allow yourself to stay in that funk for too long, you will surely slow your recovery by failing to follow your rehab program and take care of yourself in general. Thus, after a short time, you must get over your "pity party" and get your mind on your recovery; keep focused on the present ("What can I do now to get healthy?") and the future ("I will heal and get back better than ever!").

Another part of keeping perspective is that your injury might seem like a big deal at the moment, but when you look back on it in a few years, it will probably be just a blip in your athletic career and life. Also, think about the many professional and Olympic athletes who have suffered serious injuries but had the determination, patience, persistence, and perseverance to put in the time and energy necessary to get back in the game, with no guarantees it would happen.

Injury, in general, teaches you to appreciate every moment. I've had my share of injuries throughout my career. It's humbling. It gives you perspective. No matter how many times I've been hurt, I've learned from that injury and come back even more humble.

—Troy Polamalu, eight-time NFL All-Pro[16]

Stick with Your Rehab Program

A simple reality I learned in recovering from my own shoulder injury was that if you follow your rehab program, the chances are good that you will get better, and if you don't you won't. The problem is that rehab hurts (a lot) and is boring, tiring, and monotonous—in other words, it gets old fast. That's why so many injured athletes end up either shortening or skipping rehab sessions or not putting forth their best effort. The result: slowed or incomplete recovery.

There is also a subset of injured athletes who have the belief that more is better, so they do more sets and reps on more days than recommended by their rehab team. Unfortunately, this "more is better" mentality often results in overuse injuries and other complications, and a slowed rather than accelerated recovery. My recommendation here is straightforward: Do exactly what your rehab people tell you to do, no more and no less.

Become a Better Athlete

I have seen athletic careers saved by serious injuries. How is that possible, you might ask? Getting injured can teach you to be tough, endure hardship, and really find your motivation for your sport. Injuries can also enable you to focus on areas of your sport that have been weaknesses but you simply haven't had the time to work on them. Yes, a knee injury, for example, can prevent you from doing a lot. But it's also an opportunity to figure out ways you can improve as an athlete by working around your knee, for instance, strengthening your core and upper body, improving your flexibility, and increasing your stamina. The goal is for you to return to your sport a physically and mentally better athlete than you were before.

Do not let what you cannot do interfere with what you can do.

—John Wooden, collegiate basketball coaching legend[17]

Redirect Your Energies

One of the most difficult aspects of an injury is that you can't do what you normally do as an athlete and are often at a loss for how to expend the energy that builds up in you every day. Another downside is that you have lost something that has been a source of self-esteem, validation, meaning, satisfaction, and joy in your life.

Your best path is to find something toward which you can direct your energy so it can provide what your sport used to give you. It can be anything, for instance, learning to play a musical instrument, cooking, reading, school, and so forth. The important thing is to find something you can care about and gain some satisfaction and fulfillment from, and then throw yourself into it just the way you threw yourself into your sport. It will not only bolster how you feel about yourself, but also take your mind off the disappointment of your injury and difficulty of the recovery.

Stay Involved in Your Sport

Chances are much of your life revolves around your sport, and being injured can cause you to feel isolated and at a distance from the sport you love and the people you enjoy being with. This separation can also hurt your motivation because you aren't experiencing many of the good things you get from your sport.

It is important to look for ways to stay connected with your sport. For example, become an apprentice coach (this will help you learn more about technique and tactics) or help out at training and competitions. I realize this might be difficult because you may be "jonesing" to be out there, and you may not like seeing your teammates and competitors moving ahead of you. At the same time, the connection and seeing others having fun and getting results will further motivate you to rehab and get back to your sport.

Injuries cause a pain so deep. Not because you're out of shape and can't go out and play. You're missing a part of you. That's what's painful, that's what hurts.

—Jamila Wideman, former professional basketball player[18]

The Bottom Line

When you get seriously injured, it's a real bummer. But what is an even bigger bummer is not returning as fully or as quickly as possible to your sport. For you to return to the field, court, course, hill, or what have you, you need to do everything possible to facilitate your recovery. That, of course, means following your physical rehab program to the letter. But it also means developing and following a mental rehab program so that your body and mind are fully recovered and prepared for the rigors of your sport when you return to training.

Tip from the Top: Develop a Rehab Imagery Program

There is nothing more important to your mental recovery than mental imagery. As detailed in chapter 5, imagery is not just something that goes on in your head. It connects your mind and body, and, amazingly, activates muscles in the same way as when you are actually performing in your sport. Mental imagery, in a way, fools your body into thinking you are really skiing.

Imagery can significantly impact recovery from injury. Research has shown you can improve your skills in your sport without training by engaging in regular mental imagery. Hence, by doing imagery regularly, you can maintain or maybe even better your athletic skills. Seeing and feeling yourself continuing to train and compete (in your mind's eye) will keep your motivation up (because you'll be inspired to get back to your sport), your confidence high (because you'll regularly see and feel yourself performing well), and your mind focused (because you'll be exercising your mental muscles, and, as a result, they will stay in shape for your return to your sport). Importantly, imagery will make you feel like you're still progressing as an athlete.

No athlete is truly tested until they've stared an injury in the face and come out on the other side stronger than ever.

—Jerome Bettis, Super Bowl champion running back[19]

EXERCISE

USE VIDEO AND IMAGERY
WHILE REHABBING

1. During your recovery, three times a week, watch 10 minutes of video of yourself and top athletes in your sport.

2. Immediately, close your eyes and, for 10 seconds, imagine yourself performing the way you want when you return to your sport.

7

Prime Sport: The Payoff

We began the journey of *Train Your Mind* by introducing you to Prime Sport, which I define as "performing at a consistently high level in the most challenging conditions." This book is devoted to showing you how to ensure that you are mentally prepared to experience Prime Sport. Chapter 7 concludes our journey by demonstrating what might prevent you from getting where you want to go and how to reach your destination of Prime Sport.

SEVEN REASONS ATHLETES DON'T DO MENTAL TRAINING

Throughout the many years I've been working in the field of sport psychology, I have championed the benefits of mental training for sports to thousands of athletes. My profound belief in the value of mental training for athletic success comes from three places. First, it comes from my years of conducting and studying the extensive body of scientific research that overwhelmingly supports the significant impact of mental training on athletic performance.

Second, for the last three decades, I have been working directly with athletes at all levels of ability in many different sports. I have seen firsthand how the tools and ideas expressed in *Train Your Mind* have improved the performance of countless athletes and teams, and allowed them to experience exceptional performances and gratifying successes on the field of play.

Third, my belief in the value of mental training to achieve your athletic goals comes from a personal place, after having experienced its power myself as an athlete. Mental training was singularly responsible for a quantum leap in my psychology, performance, and results as an internationally ranked alpine ski racer in my youth. In fact, these personal experiences were the foundation for my passion for and career-long commitment to the psychology of sport.

Convincing athletes and coaches of the value of mental training doesn't seem like a hard sell considering that, when I ask athletes how important the mind is compared to the physical and technical sides of sports, the vast majority say it is as important, if not more so. Given that so many of the athletes I speak to or work with have big goals, it seems only natural that they would take my ideas to heart and incorporate them into their training regimens.

Yet, despite my best efforts, if I had to guess how many athletes actually make mental training an integral part of their preparations, I would put the number at less than 10 percent (and I'm probably being generous). The question I have been asking is why? I have concluded that there are seven reasons that explain athletes' lack of investment of time and energy into the mental side of their sport.

They Don't Care Enough about Their Sport

Talk, as they say, is cheap. It's easy to say that you have big goals in your sport. It's an entirely different thing to translate those goals into motivation and action. Thus, one reason why some athletes don't make mental training part of their efforts is that, despite their lip service about wanting to be the best athlete they can be, they just don't care enough to do the work necessary to develop themselves mentally. There's nothing inherently wrong with this lack of motivation; if you don't want to be the best athlete you can be, that is your choice. At the same time, when you don't accomplish the lofty goals you say you want to achieve, you shouldn't be surprised.

They Don't Believe Mental Training Works

As much as I like to think that I make a convincing case for the value of mental training in sports, there are plenty of athletes who just don't think it matters that much. Rather, they believe that if they work on the physical and technical aspects of their sports, it will be enough to reach their goals.

One of the big challenges of persuading athletes of the value of mental training is that, unlike the physical and technical aspects of sports, the benefits aren't tangible. If you want to see improvements in your strength, you can see how much weight you lifted before you began a weight-training program and then after. If you want to see your technical progress, you can watch old and new video of yourself performing. But you can't directly measure confidence, intensity, or focus, and you can't know whether improvements in those areas will translate into greater competitive success.

As a result, you can't be sure that mental training helps at all, and without clear proof, it's easy to be skeptical about whether it works. Buying into mental training is, to some degree, a leap of faith you have to make on your own if you want it to be part of your sports efforts.

There's No Program

Thanks to the Internet, there is a wealth of information about mental training available to anyone who wants to learn about it. But there is a big difference between having information about mental training and being able to apply it to your sport. Unlike, for example, physical conditioning, where you can go online and find thousands of strength programs to follow, you would be hard pressed to find similar structured programs for mental training. Without a clearly defined program, the simple reality is that it is difficult for an athlete to create a mental training program that will actually work.

It's Not Part of Their Usual Routine

Another reason is that mental training is simply not part of what most athletes usually do in their training, so they just forget. I find this often occurs before and during training. I will have, for instance, described the importance of a training routine and how to implement one; however, minutes later, athletes will still be hanging out and chatting it up with their friends, doing nothing to mentally prepare themselves for training. As with physical muscles and technical skills, until mental muscles are strengthened and mental tools well used, they will usually slip your mind unless you focus on them constantly.

It's Repetitive and Boring

Hopefully, you participate in sports because you have fun and love doing it. At the same time, the fact is that all aspects of sports are not always fun. Whether conditioning, taking care of equipment, or doing repeated drills, sports can get repetitive and monotonous. The same holds true for mental training. If you do too much of it or don't create some variety, you are going to get tired and bored. But another reality of sports is that continuing to do things in your sport, even when it's not fun—remember the grind—is essential for athletic success. And, although many aspects of your sport may be boring, what isn't boring is achieving your athletic goals.

They're Not Supported by Coaches and Parents

It's difficult for you to make a commitment to mental training if you aren't supported by your coaches and parents. Two reasons. First, you base your judgments on the value of different aspects of your sport partly on the messages you get from those around you. If your coaches and parents aren't sending you messages about the importance of the mental side of sports, you're unlikely to buy into it yourself.

It is up to coaches and parents to send messages that mental training is important. This can be done by talking about it and making it part of their team culture and family discussions, respectively.

Second, athletes these days don't have a lot of free time on their hands. Between physical conditioning, training, equipment maintenance, and video analysis, not to mention school, sleep, meals, and socializing, there just isn't much time in which to slot mental training.

It's the coaches' responsibility to carve out time in their athletes' daily schedules for such mental training as goal setting and mental imagery. Coaches must also help mental training become a habit in daily training efforts and on the day of a competition by including mental tools in their feedback and giving reminders to use those mental tools in training and competition preparations.

Mental Training Is Weird

I'll be honest, some of the things I ask athletes to do in training and before competitions can seem pretty weird. Examples include running around and jumping up and down to raise intensity, moving their bodies while doing mental imagery, and talking themselves into an aggressive mindset. And one thing I've learned over the years is that most young people don't want to stand out (in an odd sort of way anyhow) because being accepted by their peers is one of their most important needs.

Imagine this scenario: You're at the start of a training session, and your friends are goofing around and talking to one another. But I've asked you to not talk so you can focus, be physically active in your warm-up, and really move your body while doing mental imagery. Wouldn't you feel a little self-conscious? And might you be reluctant to do those things, even if you know it will help you perform better?

But here's my argument against that need to fit in. If you want to perform like everyone else, be like everyone else. The surest path to acceptance by your peers is to do what everyone is doing. And the surest path to mediocrity as an athlete is to do what everyone else is doing.

It has been my experience, both personally and professionally, that to be great at something, you have to be different than others. And, yes, that some-times means being weird or, at least, doing things others might perceive as weird. And it also means you won't necessarily be accepted by everyone. But do you think Stephen Curry, Serena Williams, Tom Brady, Roger Federer, or Aly Raisman are normal people? Do you think they worry about being accepted? In both cases, no way! All they care about is performing their best and winning. Be average (and normal) or be your best (and a little weird)? The choice is yours.

Physical strength will get you to the start line. But mental strength will get you to the finish line.

—Unknown[1]

THREE GOALS FOR ATHLETIC SUCCESS

Defining success in sports is a difficult task. When I ask most athletes and coaches how they define success, it is usually in terms of results, whether wins, rankings, or times. While, admittedly, results are the ultimate deter-minant of success, I have found that a preoccupation with them can both interfere with achieving those results and produce feelings of disappointment and frustration (or worse).

As discussed in chapter 2, one problem is that focusing on results can ac-tually prevent you from getting the results you want for two reasons. First, if you're focusing on results before a competition, you're not focusing on what you need to do to get those results. Second, focusing on results, specifically the possibility of bad results, is what causes you to get nervous before compe-titions, which will only hurt your performance.

Another problem with sports is that your efforts don't always lead directly to the results you want because you can't control everything in a competition. In other words, "stuff happens" in sports that can derail your best efforts.

To help demonstrate this point, let's compare success and failure in sports to success and failure in school. Let's say you have an exam coming up. If you study hard and are well prepared, assuming the test is fair, the chances of your doing well are high, say, more than 95 percent. Why? Because there are few external and uncontrollable variables that can prevent you from doing well. There is no bad weather or rough field conditions when it comes to taking tests.

Sports, however, are different. You can be completely ready to have a great competition, but things may not work out in your favor. For instance, you could experience bad weather, like fog or high wind, or make a costly mistake you can't recover from. As a result, the odds of doing well in a competition, if you are really prepared, are, I would say, about 80 percent.

Given the uncertainty of sports, basing how you feel about your performance (and yourself) solely on your results is a recipe for experiencing the very thing you want to avoid—failure and some pretty bad feelings. I prefer to define success in terms that are controllable. To that end, the following are three goals that, if you accomplish them, will not only give you considerable satisfaction in your athletic efforts, but also likely the results you want.

Before the Competition: Total Preparation

On the day of the competition, the only element you can control is yourself, which means your preparations. When I work with athletes, I tell them that when the competition starts, I want them to be able to say, "I'm totally prepared to achieve my goals today." Ultimately, that's all you can do.

Being totally prepared is the only chance you have to get the results you want. If you aren't completely prepared, you have zero chance, because many of your opponents, who are just as good as you or better, will be really prepared. If you are totally prepared, you don't, as indicated earlier, have a 100 percent chance of success, but your chances are pretty darned good.

If you aren't totally prepared to perform your best, I have no sympathy for you, since, as I just noted, you can control your preparations. If you're not completely ready to perform your best, you have no one to blame but yourself. On the other hand, a tough break during a competition, for example, a bad call from a ref, is worthy of some sympathy (although not too much because that's the unpredictable nature of sports).

Total preparation involves looking at everything within your control that can impact your performance and taking steps to maximize those areas. On the day of the competition, these areas include your sleep, nutrition, equipment, tactics, and warm-up. Just before the competition, they include a comprehensive precompetitive routine comprised of final equipment preparations (if your sport involves gear) and getting physically (e.g., warm-up, breathing, reaching your ideal intensity) and mentally (e.g., imagery, focus, mindset) ready, so that when the competition begins, you feel totally prepared and confident you can perform your best.

Success is where preparation and opportunity meet.

—Bobby Unser, two-time Indianapolis 500 winner[2]

During the Competition: Bring It!

I would argue that "solid" play isn't usually enough to get the results you want. If your outcome goals are at all high, your only chance of accomplishing real success and achieving those goals is to "bring it." You must push your limits, take risks, and compete with abandon.

This goal seems pretty obvious given that we all know that holding back usually doesn't work (more on this in the next goal). So, what prevents you from bringing it every time you compete? An inherent danger of bringing it is that the risks you take in the process may not pay off; bringing it may lead to a costly mistake. In other words, bringing it may result in failure. And, for most athletes, failure is the worst possible thing to experience and is to be avoided at all costs. Yet, by not bringing it, you have no chance of achieving success.

You didn't wake up today to be mediocre.

—Unknown[3]

After the Competition: No Regrets

Have you ever been at the start of a competition and just wanted a solid performance? Maybe you've had a string of poor performances and just want to get through one without any major mistakes. So, you perform tentatively and cautiously. When the competition is over, you're relieved at finally having not had any major fails.

But what is the result of this sort of attitude? Usually a pretty mediocre performance and a loss. What's your immediate emotional reaction? Regret. What's regret? Wishing you had done something differently. In other words, you wish you had gone for it (even risking mistakes) rather than perform so tentatively. You look back at the competition and wish you had charged more rather than held back.

Regret is a huge value for me both in my personal life (I want to look back on my life and have as few regrets as possible) and my professional work with athletes. I want you to look back on a competition, season, or career, whether you experienced success or failure, and be able to say, "I have no regrets because I left it all out there. I may not have achieved my greatest goals, but I did everything humanly possible to be the best I could be." You will certainly be disappointed in not fully achieving your goals; however, you will get over that feeling and likely feel great pride and inspiration in knowing that you did everything you could to accomplish your goals. Regret, by contrast, can gnaw at you forever.

In the end, we will only regret the chances we didn't take.

—Unknown[4]

You want to give yourself every opportunity to achieve your outcome goals. Yet, when you fail to achieve these three goals, you have about a zero chance that you'll get the results you want. Conversely, I can't guarantee success today or tomorrow, no matter what you do. But if you commit to and consistently strive toward these goals, I'm willing to bet that good things will happen in your sporting life and life in general.

DEVELOP A MENTAL TRAINING PROGRAM

Train Your Mind is filled with practical information and dozens upon dozens of mental exercises and tools you can use to strengthen your mental muscles and be better prepared mentally to perform your best in both training and competition. But this information might seem a bit overwhelming because it's one thing to have learned a lot about mental preparation, but it's an entirely different thing to be able to put all that you've learned into action. This is where I want to return to the notion that you should approach mental training the same way you approach your conditioning and sport training. Just as those two areas of performance are organized into comprehensive and structured training programs, now you are ready to take what you've learned in *Train Your Mind* and organize it into a comprehensive and structured mental training program. To that end, I have created a four-step process to help you identify what you need to work on mentally, set appropriate goals for those areas, and create a mental training schedule for developing those mental areas.

Identify Three Mental Areas

I will assume you have completed the Prime Sport Profiles at the beginning of chapters 1 through 5. Having completed the book and after gaining a deeper understanding of the range of topics described, I want you to retake the five profiles.

Having completed the Prime Sport profiles again, you should have a more nuanced understanding of the mental areas that impact your training and competitive performance. With that information, I want you to identify at least three mental areas you believe are most important for you to work on in the immediate future. It doesn't make sense to deal with all of them, as you'll become overloaded and won't give adequate attention to any of them. It's best to focus on a few, strengthen them, and then move on to the others.

The question is, if you have more than three areas that require work, which ones should you choose? The decision should be based on several concerns. First, you should look at which ones are most important for your long-term development. Just like working on the physical and technical aspects of your sport, you should focus on the factors that will help you in the long run. Second, some weaknesses are symptoms of other weaknesses. By dealing with one factor, another one can be relieved without having to work on it directly. For instance, you may not handle pressure well because you lack confidence. By building your confidence, you also improve your ability to handle pressure. Third, you need to balance your immediate training and competitive needs with your long-term development. You may have an important competition coming up for which you need to be ready. You may decide you need to improve your focus and intensity immediately, even though working on your motivation and confidence will be more important in the future.

Organize Your Exercises and Tools

Use the following list to reacquaint yourself with the many mental exercises and tools available to you and think about which ones you would like to use in your mental training program.

EXERCISE

MENTAL EXERCISES AND TOOLS

Motivation Exercises

- Set goals.
- Focus on your long-term goals.
- Train smart. Have a training program that includes variety and plenty of rest, and allows for balance in your life.
- Have a training partner or group of people who can push you.
- Use motivational cues—words, phrases, photographs.
- Identify your greatest competitor. Ask if you're working hard enough to beat him or her.
- Ask two daily questions: Morning: "What can I do today to become the best athlete I can be?" Evening: "Did I do everything possible today to become the best athlete I can be?"

Confidence Exercises

- Engage in preparation.
- Use your mental toolbox.
- Prepare for adversity.
- Seek support from others.
- Aim for success.
- Do positive self-talk.
- Use fire-up negative thinking.

Intensity Exercises

- Psych-up. Move your body, perform intense breathing, do high-energy self-talk and body language.
- Psych-down. Do calming self-talk, perform deep breathing, engage in muscle relaxation, move at a slow pace.
- Use mental imagery.
- Talk to friends.
- Listen to fire-up or chill-out music.
- Smile!

Focus Exercises

- Have clear goals and process.
- Identify and limit distractions.
- Use mental imagery.
- Practice your breathing.
- Establish routines.
- Write messages on equipment.
- Use the three Ps: positive, process, present.

Mindset Exercises

- Do self-talk.
- Practice your breathing.
- Use imagery.

Emotional Tools

- Frustration
  - Step away from the cause of frustration (get physical and emotional distance).

(continued)

(continued)

MENTAL EXERCISES AND TOOLS

- ◦ Breathe and relax your body.
- ◦ Get perspective. Be patient.
- ◦ Identify the cause of frustration.
- ◦ Look for a solution.
- Emotional mastery
  - ◦ Know your "hot buttons."
  - ◦ Create healthy alternative reactions.

Imagery Tools

- Create an off-sport imagery program.
  - ◦ Goals: Determine what you want to work on in your sessions.
  - ◦ Ladder: Identify a progression of training and competitive situations you will imagine.
  - ◦ Training-specific/competition-specific: Choose a venue, event, and either a training situation or a specific competition you'll be in this season.
  - ◦ Scenarios: Create narratives that will guide you through each session.
- Engage in imagery sessions.
  - ◦ Do imagery sessions three times per week.
  - ◦ Identify a specific time in your day (10 to 15 minutes).
  - ◦ Set alerts in your phone so you don't forget.
  - ◦ Find a quiet, comfortable place.
  - ◦ Follow imagery scenarios.

Routine Tools

- Create a routine that begins the night before.
- Create a final routine that begins when you arrive at the competition.
  - Key areas
  - Equipment
  - Physical
  - Mental
  - Location of routine
  - Specifics of routine
  - Order of routine

Breathing Tools

- Use different types of breathing.
  - Deep and slow
  - Aggressive
- Use breathing as a tool.
  - As part of training and competitive routines
  - During performances
  - To recover after performances

Trust Tools

- Have a physical, technical, and mental program you believe in.
- Achieve total preparation.
- Make a conscious commitment to trust.

Create a Mental Training Goal Plan

For you to get the most out of your mental training program, just like with your conditioning and sport training, you want to create a mental training goal plan that will provide you with a destination in your mental training efforts and a specific route for getting there. Your goal plan should include several key areas to help you get from where you are now to where you want to be in your mental preparation.

Setting

To begin the process of setting goals for your mental training, you want to identify where you are going to do your mental training. There are three settings in which you can use the mental exercises and tools. The first is away from your sport, where you can, for example, implement a structured and consistent mental imagery program or use a gym routine in your conditioning. The second is in your actual sport training, to complement your efforts to improve yourself technically, tactically, and in your overall performance, for instance, using keywords to focus better and commit to taking more risks. The third is on the day of the competition, where you might use breathing, game-day imagery, and your competitive routine.

Mental Area

For each of these three settings, decide which mental areas identified in the Prime Sport Profile you want to work on. For example, away from your sport, you might train your confidence muscle in your imagery program and retrain your self-talk to be more positive. In your sport training, you might work on letting go of your frustration when you can't get a new technical change right away or creating a more aggressive mindset in practice competitions. On the day of the competition, you might use psych-down exercises to reduce your intensity or focus on trusting yourself just before you compete.

Current Status

Before you begin your mental training program, it's helpful to take stock of where you are so that as you commit effort to your mental training you will be better able to judge your progress. For each mental area you have decided to work on, describe your current status. For example, if you are focusing on being more positive in your self-talk, describe how, where, and when you are negative and what causes the negativity. If you are going to work on consistently reaching your ideal intensity in training, describe your current level of intensity.

Goal

Now that you have a clear understanding of where you are in the mental areas you want to improve, you can establish a goal of where you want to be. Using the SMARTER criteria discussed in chapter 4, describe the goal you want to achieve in this mental area.

Mental Exercises and Tools

With your mental goals established, your final step in the goal-setting plan is to identify the mental exercises and tools you will use to accomplish them. Referring to the box of mental exercises and tools, select those that you want to use to develop the mental areas you have chosen.

Create a Mental Training Schedule

Like most athletes, I'm sure you are busy and don't have a lot of free time on your hands. Between school and/or work, sleep, the various aspects of your sport training, and your social life, you have a full plate. Yet, I am asking you to add mental training to your seemingly maxed-out schedule. As noted previously, the great thing about mental training is that it doesn't require a lot of time. About an hour a week away from your sport and including it in your normal conditioning and sport training efforts will do the trick. But the simple reality is that if you don't make mental part of your weekly schedule, you will probably forget to do it.

Whether you use an online or paper calendar to schedule your week, for your mental training program to work, you need to designate specific times during the week to make a commitment to doing your mental training. Take a look at your weekly schedule and see where you can dedicate time to it. Add your mental training to your calendar. For example, if you have dinner at 7:00 p.m. every evening and you know you are just hanging out the 30 minutes before, schedule your thrice-weekly, 15-minute imagery sessions at 6:30 p.m. on Mondays, Wednesdays, and Fridays. If you are incorporating mental training into your conditioning and sport training, add what specifically you will be working on mentally in those settings to your calendar so you can refer to it before you go to work out or train.

Putting your mental training in your calendar is just the first step in making it a regular and consistent part of your overall training regimen. The reality is, even if it's in your schedule, there's no guarantee you will remember to do it at its scheduled time. Thus, you should set notifications in your smartphone that will pop up at the designated time (I would also encourage you to set them to go off 15 minutes before) and either vibrate or sound a tone to alert you of your upcoming mental training session.

As you put your mental training program into action as part of your overall training schedule and stick to it consistently, in time, you will ingrain it to the point that it becomes automatic (you don't have to remind yourself when it's time to work out or go to training) and simply a necessary part of what you do to be the best athlete you can be.

Commit

Once you have the pieces of your mental training program in place, there is only one more thing you must do: Commit! This commitment involves treating your mental training program the same way you do your conditioning and sport training. It means making your mental training a priority and doing what is necessary to develop yourself mentally to the same degree you are developing yourself physically in your conditioning and technically and tactically in your sport training. At a practical level, it means following your mental training program precisely as you have scheduled it because you truly believe that it is necessary to achieve your athletic goals.

PRIME SPORT CHALLENGE

Ultimately, as with other aspects of your sport, you have to decide how important the mind is to achieving your goals. If you truly believe that it is essential to your athletic success, you must do what is necessary to weave mental training into the fabric of your training and competitive efforts. You want to get to the point where it is simply what you do to be the best athlete you can be, just like physical conditioning and technical training.

In *Train Your Mind*, my objective is to convince you that mental training is worth the investment of your time and energy. But perhaps you remain a bit skeptical. Let me now present you with my Prime Sport Challenge and start with a question. How much improvement would I need to guarantee you for you to commit to doing mental training consistently? Oftentimes, when

I ask this question to groups of athletes, someone will blurt out something like 25 percent. Let's consider that number. This means that, for instance, a miler who runs a five-minute mile would need to improve by 75 seconds to achieve that goal. Well, I think mental training can help you improve, but mental training can't enable you to make those kinds of big leaps in your performance. But what if I could promise you that you will improve by 1 percent? That doesn't sound like much, but would it be worth it? Returning to the example of the miler, a 1 percent improvement translates into being three seconds faster. Three seconds in the mile is an enormous improvement.

Now consider the time and effort you would have to put into your sport, in the gym and during training, to get your sport's equivalent of that three-second improvement. I'm guessing that you devote several hours or more each day to your conditioning and training, and other activities related to your sport. Why do you put forth that much time and effort? Because you know it is necessary to have the kind of success you want. I hope that reading *Train Your Mind* has convinced you that a commitment of time, effort, and energy to mental training is equally important.

Fortunately, mental training doesn't take nearly that much time. As we've discussed, perhaps an hour a week away from your sport doing mental imagery and using other mental tools will be sufficient, and then incorporating such mental training as routines, breathing, and mindset directly into your sport training. A small investment of time and energy will give you a big return, as you will be more mentally prepared to perform your best. That sounds like a good investment to me.

Making this commitment to mental training will be a big step in allowing yourself to achieve those three goals and live by a cardinal rule that is fundamental to athletic success: At the end of a competition, a season, or your life, you don't want to have to ask yourself, "I wonder what could have been?" That may be the saddest question you could ever ask, because there are no "redos" in life. You want to look back and, win or lose, be able to say, "I left it all out there." And, as I allude to earlier in this book, only by leaving it all out there do you have any chance of fulfilling your goals. In the end, I want you to be able to say, "I gave it everything I had," and experience two emotions, pride and satisfaction, in having given it your all. If you can achieve those three goals and live by this one rule, I believe you will experience Prime Sport and find success in your sport however you define it.

Notes

INTRODUCTION

1. "Mental Toughness Quotes," *Mental Toughness Trainer*, accessed March 8, 2017, http://www.mentaltoughnesstrainer.com/quotes/.

2. "200 Motivational Fitness Quotes," *Coach Calorie*, accessed March 8, 2017, http://www.coachcalorie.com/motivational-fitness-quotes/.

CHAPTER 1

1. "Thomas Jefferson Quotes," *BrainyQuote*, accessed November 8, 2016, https://www.brainyquote.com/quotes/quotes/t/thomasjeff120994.html.

2. "A Father Dedicated to Helping His Son," *ESPN*, accessed November 8, 2016, http://www.espn.com/nba/story/_/page/kyrieirving_120224/nba-father-laid-plan-kyrie-irving-followed-it.

3. "Sport Quotes," *UNT Center for Sport Psychology*, accessed November 8, 2016, https://sportpsych.unt.edu/resources/athletes/31.

4. "CBC Interview with Marnie McBean," *CBC News*, accessed November 8, 2016, http://www.cbc.ca/news/health/stress-mental-athletes-1.3712675.

5. "Letter to Olympic Medalists," *Players Tribune*, accessed November 8, 2016, http://www.theplayerstribune.com/brandon-slay-usa-wrestling-olympics-rio/?utm_medium=email&utm_campaign=August%209%20AM&utm_content=August%209%20AM+CID_61f19405de2a38879ca7f50a54b08f9c&utm_source=newsletter&utm_term=Letter%20to%20Olympic%20Medalists.

6. "Be Bold . . . Hit the Ball!" *Athletic Mindset*, accessed November 8, 2016, http://theathleticmindset.com/resources/inspirational-quotes/be-bold-hit-the-ball/.

7. "Athletics: Holly Bleasdale," *Sky Academy*, accessed November 8, 2016, http://www.skysports.com/scholarships/news/23850/9527081/athletics-holly-bleasdale-stands-by-long-term-approach-after-missing-2014-season.

8. "Ray A. Davis Quotes," *Goodreads*, accessed November 8, 2016, http://www.goodreads.com/quotes/tag/goals?page=4.

9. "50 Awesome Quotes on Risk-Taking," *Heart of Innovation*, accessed November 8, 2016, http://www.ideachampions.com/weblogs/archives/2010/06/security_is_mos.shtml.

10. "10 Memorable Muhammad Ali Quotes," *Men's Fitness*, accessed November 8, 2016, http://www.mensfitness.com/life/sports/10-memorable-quotes-muhammad-ali.

11. "Awesome Quotes on Risk-Taking," *Extreme Sports*, accessed November 8, 2016, http://extremeactivity.blogspot.ca/2012/02/awesome-quotes-on-risks-taking.html.

12. "50 Awesome Quotes on Risk-Taking."

CHAPTER 2

1. "Laird Hamilton Quotes," *AZ Quotes*, accessed November 9, 2016, http://www.azquotes.com/quote/519594.

2. "Top 10 Carl Jung Quotes," *Words of Wisdom*, accessed November 9, 2016, http://wordsofwisdom.com/top-10-carl-jung-quotes/until-you-make-the-unconscious-conscious.

3. "Subconscious Mind Quotes," *Quotes Gram*, accessed November 9, 2016, http://quotesgram.com/subconscious-mind-quotes/.

4. "Confession," *Someecards*, accessed November 9, 2016, http://www.someecards.com/usercards/viewcard/over-thinking-is-just-a-painful-reminder-that-you-care-entirely-too-much-even-when-you-shouldnt-88d27.

5. "Great Football Quotes," *QuoteAddicts*, accessed November 9, 2016, http://quoteaddicts.com/topic/great-football-quotes/.

6. "Think You Know Bode Miller?" *Team USA*, accessed November 9, 2016, http://www.teamusa.org/News/2015/October/12/Think-You-Know-Bode-Miller-38-Facts-You-Might-Not-Know.

7. "Quotes on Excellence and Perfection," *Quotes Gram*, accessed November 9, 2016, http://quotesgram.com/quotes-on-excellence-and-perfection/.

8. "Done > Perfect," *Happy by Design*, accessed November 9, 2016, https://happybydesignparenting.com/tag/creative-living/.

9. "Arianna Huffington Quotes," *Comforting Quotes*, accessed November 9, 2016, http://comfortingquotes.com/arianna-huffington-quotes/.

10. "Try Your Best!" *Marcie's Daily Motivational*, accessed November 9, 2016, https://marciesdailymotivational.com/2016/04/07/try-your-best-its-all-you-can-do/.

11. "We All Want Control, but We Need to Know What We Can Control," *Life without Anorexia*, accessed November 9, 2016, http://www.lifewithoutanorexia .com/2016/03/we-all-want-control-but-we-need-to-know.html.

12. "Mike Ditka Quotes," *AZ Quotes*, accessed November 9, 2016, http://www .azquotes.com/quote/79380?ref=fear-of-failure.

13. "Denis Waitley Quotes," *AZ Quotes*, accessed November 9, 2016, http://www .azquotes.com/quote/533838?ref=fear-of-failure.

14. "Tom Landry Quotes," *AZ Quotes*, accessed November 9, 2016, http://www .brainyquote.com/quotes/quotes/t/tomlandry154664.html.

15. "George Halas Quotes," *BrainyQuote*, accessed November 9, 2016, http://www .brainyquote.com/quotes/quotes/g/georgehala160094.html.

16. "John Cena Quotes," *AZ Quotes*, accessed November 9, 2016, http://www .azquotes.com/quote/621022.

17. "Peter Ralston Quotes," *Motivational Quotes About*, accessed November 9, 2016, http://www.motivationalquotesabout.com/quotes/your-perception-of-the -world-around-you-is.aspx.

18. "Helen Keller Quotes," *BrainyQuote*, accessed November 9, 2016, https://www .brainyquote.com/quotes/quotes/h/helenkelle164579.html.

19. "Lou Brock Quotes," *BrainyQuote*, accessed November 9, 2016, http://www .brainyquote.com/quotes/quotes/l/loubrock131377.html.

20. "Quotes from Johan Cruyff," *Dutchsa*, accessed November 9, 2016, http:// www.dutchsa.com.au/discussion/topics/551947/messages.

21. "Jack Canfield Quotes," *Quotes Gram*, accessed November 9, 2016, http:// quotesgram.com/img/fear-quotes-business/9064270/.

22. "Recent Highlights: Sports Quotes," *Board of Wisdom*, accessed November 9, 2016, http://boardofwisdom.com/togo/?viewid=1011&listname=Sports&start=511#. WEXu0XeZNE5.

23. "Hope Solo Quotes," *AZ Quotes*, accessed November 9, 2016, http://www .azquotes.com/quote/601732.

24. "Michael Jordan Quotes," *AZ Quotes*, accessed November 9, 2016, http://www .azquotes.com/quote/150620.

25. "The Great Mistake," *Quotes Codex*, accessed November 9, 2016, http://www .quotescodex.com/the-great-mistake-is-to-anticipate-outcome-engagement-you-ought -not-to-be-thinking-whether-it-ends-in-victory-defeat-let-nature-take-its-course -bruce-lee-182182/.

26. "Tommy Lasorda Quotes," *BrainyQuote*, accessed November 9, 2016, https:// www.brainyquote.com/quotes/quotes/t/tommylasor158240.html.

27. "Ronda Rousey on Performing under Pressure," *MMA Quotes*, accessed November 9, 2016, http://mmaquotes.blogspot.com/2013/08/ronda-rousey-on-performing-under.html.

28. "Negativity Quotes," *Quote HD*, accessed November 9, 2016, http://www.quotehd.com/quotes/words/negativity.

29. "Chikku George Thomas," *Board of Wisdom*, accessed November 9, 2016, http://boardofwisdom.com/togo/Quotes/ShowQuote?msgid=325274#.WDNqR_krLDc.

30. "I Will Fight for It," *Avid Quotes*, accessed November 9, 2016, http://www.avidquotes.com/67901/i-will-fight-for-it-i-will-not-give-up-i-will-reach-my-goal-absolutely-nothing-will-stop-me/.

CHAPTER 3

1. "100 Most Inspirational Sports Quotes of All Time," *Keep Inspiring Me*, accessed November 10, 2016, http://www.keepinspiring.me/100-most-inspirational-sports-quotes-of-all-time/.

2. "Derek Jeter Quote," *Marketing Your Art the Right Way*, accessed November 10, 2016, http://marketingtrw.com/blog/there-may-be-people-that-have-more-talent-than-you-but-theres-no-excuse-for-anyone-to-work-harder-than-you-do-derek-jeter/.

3. "Success Quotes," *Daily Inspirational Quotes*, accessed November 10, 2016, http://www.dailyinspirationalquotes.in/2014/09/23/persistence-can-change-failure-into-extraordinary-achievement-matt-biondi-success-quotes/.

4. "Mafia Baby Meme," *Meme Generator*, accessed November 10, 2016, https://memegenerator.net/instance/65207936.

5. "Lifehack Quotes," *Lifehacks*, accessed November 10, 2016, http://quotes.lifehack.org/quote/emmitt-smith/for-me-winning-isnt-something-that-happens/.

6. "Practice Motivational Quotes," *QuoteAddicts*, accessed November 10, 2016, http://quoteaddicts.com/topic/practice-motivational-quotes/.

7. "Michael Phelps Quotes," *BrainyQuote*, accessed November 10, 2016, https://www.brainyquote.com/quotes/quotes/m/michaelphe425412.html.

8. "Consistency Quotes," *BrainyQuote*, accessed November 10, 2016, http://www.brainyquote.com/quotes/keywords/consistency.html.

9. "The Surprisingly Simple Key to Triathlon Success," *Ironman*, accessed November 10, 2016, http://www.ironman.com/#axzz4S67m2t00.

10. "Five Tips for Being Consistently Consistent," *Life with No Limits*, accessed November 10, 2016, https://lifewithnolimitscoaching.com/2013/12/02/5-tips-for-being-consistently-consistent/.

11. "Motivational Sports Quotes," *Like Success*, accessed November 10, 2016, http://likesuccess.com/topics/20464/motivational-sports-2/.

12. "Comfort Zone," *Daily Quotes*, accessed November 10, 2016, http://thedaily quotes.com/tag/comfort-zone/.

13. "Extreme Sports Quote of the Week: Laird Hamilton," *Wild Child Sports*, accessed November 10, 2016, http://wildchildsports.com/extreme-sports-quote-week -laird-hamilton/.

14. "Leave Your Comfort Zone Quotes," *Quotes Gram*, accessed November 10, 2016, https://quotesgram.com/leave-your-comfort-zone-quotes/.

15. "Practice Hard Quotes," *Quotes Gram*, accessed November 10, 2016, http:// quotesgram.com/practice-hard-quotes/.

16. "Motivational Quotes with Pictures," *MMA Quotes*, accessed November 10, 2016, http://mmaquotes.blogspot.com/2014/05/first-you-will-practice-mindfully -and.html.

17. "501 Awesome Basketball Quotes," *Basketball for Coaches*, accessed November 10, 2016, http://www.basketballforcoaches.com/basketball-quotes/.

18. "Don't Stop When You're Tired," *Quotes Cloud*, accessed November 10, 2016, http://quotescloud.com/dont-stop-when-youre-tired-stop-when-youre-done/.

CHAPTER 4

1. "Motivational Quotes for Athletes by Athletes," *Lifestyle Updated*, accessed November 11, 2016, https://www.lifestyleupdated.com/motivational-quotes-for-ath letes-by-athletes/.

2. "100 Most Inspirational Sports Quotes of All Time," *Keep Inspiring Me*, accessed November 11, 2016, http://www.keepinspiring.me/100-most-inspirational-sports -quotes-of-all-time/.

3. "Famous Olympic Quotes," *Huffington Post*, accessed November 11, 2016, http://www.huffingtonpost.ca/2014/02/07/famous-olympic-quotes_n_4745472.html.

4. "15 Motivational Quotes," *Entrepreneur Quotes*, accessed November 11, 2016, https://www.entrepreneur.com/slideshow/244486.

5. "Goals Quotes," *BrainyQuote*, accessed November 11, 2016, http://www .brainyquote.com/quotes/keywords/goals.html.

6. "Mario Andretti Quotes," *BrainyQuote*, accessed November 11, 2016, http:// www.brainyquote.com/quotes/quotes/m/marioandre130613.html.

7. "Commitment Means Staying Loyal," *Master Jonathan Field*, accessed November 11, 2016, https://masterjonathanfield.com/2013/09/04/commitment-means -staying-loyal/.

8. "Unknown Quote," *Board of Wisdom*, accessed November 11, 2016, http:// boardofwisdom.com/togo/Quotes/ShowQuote?msgid=178561#.WCpgGvkrLDc.

9. "Samuel Johnson Quotes," *BrainyQuote*, accessed November 11, 2016, https://www.brainyquote.com/quotes/quotes/s/samueljohn122529.html.

10. "The Masters: 10 Inspirational Golf Quotes for Entrepreneurs," *Entrepreneur*, accessed November 11, 2016, http://www.lifehack.org/articles/communication/22-quotes-about-self-confidence.html.

11. "Carl Lewis Quote," *Very Best Quotes*, accessed November 11, 2016, http://www.verybestquotes.com/if-you-dont-have-confidence-olympic-motivational-sports-quote-with-picture/inspirational-olympic-quotes-if-you-dont-have-confidence-youll-always-find-a-way-not-to-win/.

12. "Self-Confidence Quote," *Lifehack*, accessed November 11, 2016, http://www.lifehack.org/articles/communication/the-quickest-way-acquire-self-confidence-exactly.html.

13. "Nicholas Cage Quote," *AZ Quotes*, accessed November 11, 2016, http://www.azquotes.com/quote/1178912.

14. "Ruth Fishel Quote," *Like Success*, accessed November 11, 2016, http://likesuccess.com/1001403.

15. "Zig Ziglar Quote," *Simple Reminders*, accessed November 11, 2016, http://www.lifehack.org/articles/communication/22-quotes-about-self-confidence.html.

16. "Quotes on Motivational Sports," *QuoteAddicts*, accessed November 11, 2016, http://quoteaddicts.com/tags/motivational-sports/2.

17. "Sports Quotes," *Board of Wisdom*, accessed November 11, 2016, http://boardofwisdom.com/togo/?start=831&viewid=1004&listname=sports#.WB3_nvorLD4.

18. "George Karl Quote," *Quotter*, accessed November 11, 2016, http://www.quotter.net/i-m-tired-of-excuses-i-think-it-s-playing-with-your-heart-playing-with-intensity-and-playi-quote-by-george-karl_1846781.

19. "Sports Quotes," *Like Success*, accessed November 11, 2016, http://likesuccess.com/topics/105/sports.

20. "Simone Biles: Six Secrets to Success," *Olympic Athletes Hub*, accessed November 11, 2016, https://hub.olympic.org/news/simone-biles-six-secrets-to-success/.

21. "Bruce Lee Quote," *Positively Positive*, accessed November 11, 2016, http://www.positivelypositive.com/quotes/the-successful-warrior-is-the-average-man-with-laser-like-focus/.

22. "Simone Biles: Six Secrets to Success."

23. "Venus Williams Quotes," *AZ Quotes*, accessed November 11, 2016, http://www.azquotes.com/author/15732-Venus_Williams.

24. "Five Daily Practices That Can Transform Your Life," *Huffington Post*, accessed November 11, 2016, http://www.huffingtonpost.com/ashley-navarro/awareness_1_b_8199570.html.

25. "Michael Phelps Quote: Six Secrets to Success," *AZ Quotes*, accessed November 11, 2016, http://www.azquotes.com/quote/553292.

26. "12 Powerful Growth Mindset Quotes to Empower You," *Fearless Motivation*, accessed November 11, 2016, http://www.fearlessmotivation.com/2016/07/05/12 -powerful-growth-mindset-quotes-empower/.

27. "12 Powerful Growth Mindset Quotes to Empower You."

28. "Anything Is Possible Quote," *BrainyQuote*, accessed November 11, 2016, http://www.brainyquote.com/quotes/keywords/anything_is_possible.html.

CHAPTER 5

1. "Aimee Mullins Quote," *AZ Quotes*, accessed November 12, 2016, http://www .azquotes.com/quote/537456.

2. "Quotes about Being Emotionless," *Quotes Gram*, accessed November 12, 2016, http://quotesgram.com/quotes-about-being-emotionless/.

3. "Frustration Quotes," *Profile Picture Quotes*, accessed November 12, 2016, http://profilepicturequotes.com/frustration-quotes/.

4. "Eleanor Roosevelt Quote," *Quotes.net*, accessed November 12, 2016, http:// www.quotes.net/quote/1940.

5. "Napoleon Hill Quotes," *BrainyQuote*, accessed November 12, 2016, https:// www.brainyquote.com/quotes/quotes/n/napoleonhi152875.html.

6. "Gabby Douglas Quote," *Quotes.net*, accessed November 12, 2016, http://www .quotes.net/quote/64306.

7. "Emotional Quotes Softball," *Quotes Gram*, accessed November 12, 2016, http://quotesgram.com/emotional-quotes-softball/.

8. "Ms. KG Quote," *Board of Wisdom*, accessed November 12, 2016, http://board ofwisdom.com/togo/Quotes/ShowQuote/?msgid=378095#.WDXN_OYrLD4.

9. "Motivational Quotes with Pictures," *MMA Quotes*, accessed November 12, 2016, http://mmaquotes.blogspot.com/2013/05/georges-st-pierre-gsp-quotes.html.

10. "Mastery Quotes," *BrainyQuote*, accessed November 12, 2016, https://www .brainyquote.com/quotes/keywords/mastery.html.

11. "Running Quotes from Olympic Runners," *Verywell*, accessed November 12, 2016, https://www.verywell.com/running-quotes-from-olympic-runners-2911763.

12. "Allyson Felix Quotes," *Quotes Gram*, accessed November 12, 2016, http:// quotesgram.com/quote/allyson-felix-quotes/408051.

13. "Georges St-Pierre on Visualization," *MMA Quotes*, accessed November 12, 2016, http://mmaquotes.blogspot.com/2013/06/georges-st-pierre-on-visualization .html.

14. M. Bailey, "Sports Visualization: How to Imagine Your Way to Success," *Telegraph*, accessed November 12, 2016, http://www.telegraph.co.uk/men/active/10568898/Sports-visualisation-how-to-imagine-your-way-to-success.html.

15. R. Maese, "For Olympians, Seeing in Their Minds Is Believing It Can Happen," *Washington Post*, accessed November 12, 2016, https://www.washingtonpost.com/sports/olympics/for-olympians-seeing-in-their-minds-is-believing-it-can-happen/2016/07/28/6966709c-532e-11e6-bbf5-957ad17b4385_story.html.

16. Maese, "For Olympians, Seeing in Their Minds Is Believing It Can Happen."

17. "Visualizing Quotes," *Relatably*, accessed November 12, 2016, http://www.relatably.com/q/visualizing-quotes.

18. "Quotes on Outcome," *Quote Addicts*, accessed November 12, 2016, http://quoteaddicts.com/tags/outcome/.

19. "Visualizing Quotes," *Relatably*, accessed November 12, 2016, http://www.relatably.com/q/visualizing-quotes.

20. "Being Prepared Quotes," *Hippo Quotes*, accessed November 12, 2016, http://www.hippoquotes.com/being-prepared-quotes.

21. "Babe Ruth Quotes," *AZ Quotes*, accessed November 12, 2016, http://www.azquotes.com/quote/255392.

22. "The Best Sports Quotes," *Board of Wisdom*, accessed November 12, 2016, http://boardofwisdom.com/togo/?viewid=1005&listname=Sports&start=21#.WCpcEfkrLDc.

23. M. Bishara, "Super Bowl 50: Quarterbacks Seek Mental Strength Edge in Cutthroat NFL," *CNN Sports*, accessed November 12, 2016, http://edition.cnn.com/2016/02/04/sport/russell-wilson-cam-newton-mental-strength-coach-super-bowl-50/.

24. "Quotes on Preparation," *Quotes Gram*, accessed November 12, 2016, http://quotesgram.com/movie-quotes-on-preparation/.

25. "Hope Solo Quotes," *BrainyQuote*, accessed November 12, 2016, http://www.brainyquote.com/quotes/quotes/h/hopesolo567387.html.

26. "Djokovic Makes Quick Work of Raonic in Indian Wells Final," *Grandstand*, accessed January 4, 2017, http://tenngrand.com/2016/03/21/djokovic-makes-quick-work-raonic-indian-wells-final/.

27. "Arthur Ashe Quotes," *Quotter*, accessed November 12, 2016, http://www.quotter.net/i-don-t-care-who-you-are-you-re-going-to-choke-in-certain-matches-you-get-to-a-point-where-quote-by-arthur-ashe_148365.

28. "Breath Quotes," *Daily Quotes*, accessed November 12, 2016, http://thedailyquotes.com/tag/breath/page/2/.

29. "Muhammad Ali Quotes," *Fresh Quotes*, accessed November 12, 2016, http://www.thefreshquotes.com/famous-muhammad-ali-quotes/.

30. "Trust Quotes," *Search Quotes*, accessed November 12, 2016, http://www.search quotes.com/quotation/Trust_because_you_arewilling_to_accept_the_risk,not_be cause_its_safe_orcertain./475998/.

31. "Trust Quotes," *Search Quotes*, accessed November 12, 2016, http://www .searchquotes.com/search/trust/#ixzz4Q6aGt0kj.

CHAPTER 6

1. "The Brain-Training Secrets of Olympic Athletes," *Huffington Post*, accessed November 13, 2016, http://www.huffingtonpost.com/2014/02/11/mind-hacks-from -olympic-a_n_4747755.html.

2. "Sports Quotes," *UNT Center for Performance Excellence*, accessed November 13, 2016, https://sportpsych.unt.edu/resources/athletes/31.

3. "Heat's Ray Allen Says Don't Hate the Player, Hate the Team," *CBS Sports*, accessed November 13, 2016, http://www.cbssports.com/nba/eye-on-basketball/ 20607624/ray-allen-says-dont-hate-the-player-hate-the-team.

4. "Stephen Curry Quotes," *AZ Quotes*, accessed November 13, 2016, http://www .azquotes.com/quote/1458553.

5. "A. J. Kitt Quotes," *Think Exist*, accessed November 13, 2016, http://thinkexist .com/quotation/you_have_no_control_over_what_the_other_guy_does/222277.html.

6. "100 Most Inspirational Sports Quotes of All Time," *Keep Inspiring Me*, accessed November 13, 2016, http://www.keepinspiring.me/100-most-inspirational -sports-quotes-of-all-time/#ixzz4CchN2Fho.

7. "Nolan Ryan Quotes," *BrainyQuote*, accessed November 13, 2016, http://www .brainyquote.com/quotes/quotes/n/nolanryan393133.html.

8. "Michael Jordan Quotes," *BrainyQuote*, accessed November 13, 2016, http:// www.brainyquote.com/quotes/quotes/m/michaeljor129399.html.

9. "15 Famous Quotes on Creativity," *Twisted Sifter*, accessed November 13, 2016, http://twistedsifter.com/2012/03/15-famous-quotes-on-creativity/.

10. "Johnny Bench Quote on Slumps," *Like Success*, accessed November 13, 2016, http://likesuccess.com/87599.

11. "Slumps Quotes," *Like Success*, accessed November 13, 2016, http://likesuccess .com/topics/25562/slumps.

12. "Yogi Berra Quotes," *BrainyQuote*, accessed November 13, 2016, https://www .brainyquote.com/quotes/quotes/y/yogiberra145940.html.

13. "100 Most Inspirational Sports Quotes of All Time," *Keep Inspiring Me*, accessed November 13, 2016, http://www.keepinspiring.me/100-most-inspirational -sports-quotes-of-all-time/#ixzz4CchqRNtZ.

14. "Cartier Martin Quote on Slumps," *Like Success*, accessed November 13, 2016, http://likesuccess.com/1389211.

15. "Randy Johnson Quotes," *BrainyQuote*, accessed November 13, 2016, https://www.brainyquote.com/quotes/quotes/r/randyjohns480495.html.

16. "Injuries Quotes – Page 2," *BrainyQuote*, accessed November 13, 2016, http://www.brainyquote.com/quotes/keywords/injuries_2.html.

17. "John Wooden Quotes," *BrainyQuote*, accessed November 13, 2016, https://www.brainyquote.com/quotes/quotes/j/johnwooden105700.html.

18. "The Best Sports Quotes," *Board of Wisdom*, accessed November 13, 2016, http://boardofwisdom.com/togo/?viewid=1005&listname=Sports&start=861#.WCuQnPkrLDc.

19. "14 Best Comebacks of Players from Injury," *Buzzle*, accessed November 13, 2016, http://www.buzzle.com/articles/best-comebacks-of-players-from-injury.html.

CHAPTER 7

1. "NYC Running Mama: The Mental Side of Running," *Women's Running*, accessed November 14, 2016, http://womensrunning.competitor.com/2015/03/nyc-running-mama/nyc-running-mama-the-mental-side-of-running_36966#Rvs9jSzDJX7aUYca.97.

2. "Opportunity Quotes Sports," *Relatably*, accessed November 14, 2016, http://www.relatably.com/q/opportunity-quotes-sports.

3. "Unkown Quote," *QuoteSaga*, accessed November 14, 2016, https://www.quotesaga.com/quote/3966/.

4. "26 Famous Inspirational Sports Quotes in Pictures," *Fearless Motivation*, accessed November 14, 2016, http://www.fearlessmotivation.com/2015/07/09/inspirational-sports-quotes/.

About the Author

Jim Taylor has been a consultant for the U.S. and Japanese ski teams, the United States Tennis Association, and USA Triathlon, and has worked with professional and world-class athletes in tennis, skiing, cycling, triathlon, track and field, swimming, football, golf, baseball, car racing, and many other sports. He has been invited to lecture by the Olympic committees of Spain, France, Poland, and the United States, and has consulted with the athletic departments at Stanford University and the University of California, Berkeley.

Dr. Taylor speaks regularly to elementary and secondary schools, parent and education associations, and youth-sports programs throughout the country.

Dr. Taylor received his bachelor's degree from Middlebury College and earned his master's degree and Ph.D. in psychology from the University of Colorado. He is a former associate professor in the School of Psychology at Nova University in Ft. Lauderdale, Florida, and a former clinical associate professor in the sport and performance psychology graduate program at the University of Denver. He is an adjunct faculty member at the University of San Francisco.

He has published more than 800 articles in scholarly and popular publications, and given more than 1,000 workshops and presentations throughout North and South America, Europe, and the Middle East.

Dr. Taylor is the author of 14 books, including *Positive Pushing: How to Raise a Successful and Happy Child* (2003), the four-book *Prime Sport* series

(2002), *Your Children Are Listening: Nine Messages They Need to Hear from You* (2011), *The Triathlete's Guide to Mental Training* (2005), *Dance Psychology for Artistic and Performance Excellence* (2015), *Raising Generation Tech: Prepare Your Children for a Media-Fueled World* (2013), *Your Children Are Under Attack: How Popular Culture Is Destroying Your Kids' Values, and How You Can Protect Them* (2005), and *I Couldn't Disagree More: Insight, Inspiration, and Irreverence from an Idea Guy* (2014). Dr. Taylor's books have been translated into 10 languages.

He is also the lead editor of three textbooks, *Applying Sport Psychology: Four Perspectives* (2005), *Developing a Consulting Practice in Sport and Performance Psychology* (2014), and *Assessment in Applied Sport Psychology* (2017).

Dr. Taylor blogs on sports and other topics on his website (drjimtaylor .com), as well as on Huffingtonpost.com, Psychologytoday.com, and Skiracing .com. His posts are aggregated by dozens of websites worldwide and have been read by millions of people.

Dr. Taylor has appeared on NBC's *Today Show*, Fox News Channel's *Fox & Friends*, ABC's *World News This Weekend*, UPN's *Life & Style*, and the major television network affiliates in the United States. He has participated in many radio shows. He has been a columnist for the *Denver Post* and been interviewed for articles in the *New York Times*, the *Los Angeles Times*, the *Times of London*, the *Chicago Tribune*, *U.S. News & World Report*, the *Christian Science Monitor*, the *London Telegraph*, the *Miami Herald*, the *Ft. Lauderdale Sun-Sentinel*, the *Baltimore Sun*, the *Denver Post*, *Skiing*, *Outside*, and many other newspapers and magazines.

A former alpine ski racer who competed internationally, Dr. Taylor is also a second-degree black belt and certified instructor in karate, a marathon runner, and an Ironman triathlete.

He lives north of San Francisco with his wife and two daughters.